Lake Superior Profiles

GREAT LAKES BOOKS

A COMPLETE LISTING OF THE BOOKS IN THIS SERIES CAN BE FOUND ONLINE AT WSUPRESS.WAYNE.EDU

Lake Superior Profiles

People on the Big Lake

John Gagnon

W WAYNE STATE UNIVERSITY PRESS DETROIT

16 15 14 13 12 5 4 3 2 1

Library of Congress Cataloging-in-Publication Data

Gagnon, John, 1946–
Lake Superior profiles : people on the big lake / John Gagnon.
p. cm.—(Great lakes books series)
ISBN 978-0-8143-3628-1 (pbk. : alk. paper)—ISBN 978-0-8143-3629-8 (e-book)
1. Superior, Lake, Region—Biography. 2. Superior, Lake, Region—Social life and customs. 3. Interviews—Superior, Lake, Region. I. Title.
F552.G34 2012
977.4'9—dc23

2011027515

Designed by TG Design
Typeset by Alpha Design & Composition of Pittsfield NH
Composed in Sabon

Photos by author unless otherwise noted.

For Marilyn

This map shows the locations of the stories in this book. (Drawing by Sandy Slater.)

Contents

Preface

I grew up on the Keweenaw Peninsula in the late 1950s and early 1960s. The Keweenaw pokes a gnarled finger northeast into Lake Superior, which locals call "the big lake." We kids visited a camp at Little Traverse Bay, on the south shore of the Keweenaw, where we smoked driftwood—the size of crayons, with dry, punky hearts that burned like tobacco—and thought we were big shots. We scurried across the dry beach sand (hot enough to cook a hot dog) to the hard and cool wet sand (where the waves erased our footprints in an instant). We took saunas and ran naked through the trees and down to the beach and into the cold water that took our breath away. We rowed around the bay in a three-person skiff just to see how far out we could see bottom on a calm, clear day. It is hard to judge the depth of water. Twenty feet? Forty feet? It was deep. We'd peer over the side, shielding our eyes from the glare of the sun. In all that water, on all those days, we never saw a fish. In the dark of night we made dancing bonfires. At night we slept like babies.

We took the lake's measure by throwing or skipping rocks. We knew from school that we lived on the largest freshwater lake in the world, but that meant nothing. We were just kids with no sense of perspective. We thought it was a big deal to do belly floppers in the city pool in Milwaukee. It took living in Detroit to make me appreciate a slow pace, a quiet winter forest, and a vast lake. In the city, I learned to tune out the noise. Back in Upper Michigan, I had to listen hard to tune back in to the birdsong and breezes—and the people with a link to the water. I knew a man who lay on the shore ice with a soup ladle taped to a broomstick, digging for agates; an ice fisherman who sounded the depths with a piece of sucker and a hook and said, "Everybody's different but basically they're all the same"; and a crusty old mariner who told me, "Don't believe anything you hear and only half of what you see."

This book recounts the stories of some of these folks. "They're ordinary people," I told a recreational sailor from Thunder Bay.

"I don't know any ordinary people," he said.

Waino Asunmaa is eighty-four and lives in Calumet, Michigan. He quit school after the eighth grade to go to work with his father, Ansel Asunmaa. Ansel, a big strapping fisherman, drowned off Betsy Location, on the south side of the Keweenaw, near the town of Gay, when Waino was fourteen.

Ordinarily, Waino would have been out on the lake with his dad, but he had stayed behind that day preparing to boil and clean the nets when his father had lifted them and brought them in. "He wasn't showing up," Waino recalls, "so I went to the neighbor's. I told 'im, 'Geez, my dad's been out there a long time. There's gotta be something wrong.' So we went out there, and the boat was there, but my dad wasn't in it."

He and his father lived in a shack at Betsy, on property owned by somebody else. When Waino's father disappeared, the owner kicked Waino out. "Get out of Betsy!" So Waino dismantled his dad's shack, hauled the lumber to Pumphouse Location a few miles southwest, built a net house, slept in his boat, and continued fishing. A family took him in. "They didn't want me living inside the boat, under that teepee for keeping the rain away."

He fished for three years. Then he lied about his age and went into the service in World War II. When he returned, he worked as a miner and fished part-time, then ten years later got back into fishing "in a bigger way," going after herring, which brought a penny a pound, and chubs, which brought 2 cents a pound.

One time Waino was fishing near Stannard Rock, south of Keweenaw Point, where there was a lighthouse, and his helper remarked that there weren't any life preservers.

"Sure there's life jackets," Waino told him. "Go up in the bow there. Bring one of them chains." Waino meant lengths of ore boat chains, with links as big around as his fist, that he used for anchors. "You said there's no goddarn life jackets? This is the best we've got. It'll save you from suffering."

My old aunt says, "Never trust someone who laughs at nothing." Waino laughs at everything—even what he calls "that fourteen"—by which he means his age when his father disappeared.

There are many tales on Lake Superior of fishermen who sailed off and never returned. There is a myth that the lake never gives up its dead. Through the years, some people have attributed this to the gods. The real reason: the water is so very cold that the bodies don't bloat up and float. There are certainly many down there, for Superior has seen more than three hundred shipwrecks. Perhaps thousands of men have lost their lives.

Elmer Haltunen, another old fisherman, remembers a few of them. Elmer, who lives in Copper City, Michigan, once rescued a man who went overboard.

Elmer, like Waino, quit school to go to work. His first job was when he was eleven, loading rocks onto a stone boat—10 cents a day.

Those were more dangerous times. No GPS. No weather buoys gauging wind and waves out in the lake. "Many times I should have died," Elmer says. Born in 1914, he started working for fishermen before he shaved and then made a living on the lake for twenty-five years. "Them were the days," he remembers. "I thought they'd never end. We worked like mules."

Before he fished, he used to take time off from grade school in the fall to gather milt and eggs from spawning lake trout for a hatchery program. "Now you have to be a biologist to do that," he says. "I did that when I was twelve."

Elmer tells me he has "mystic powers" to heal.

"They work?"

"Oh, yah, they work."

But he recalls a man on the Keweenaw with more down-to-earth ways. He drank his own urine, believing it to be medicinal. "Oh, oh," Elmer says. "Don't ask him for a highball."

People like Waino and Elmer intrigue me, but some of this lake business is lost on me. One day an old Finn named Paddy Jaaskelainen, now gone, from Mohawk, Michigan, takes me to a lighthouse he owns at Bete Grise, twenty miles northeast of Gay. The lighthouse overlooks a shoreline Paddy calls "singing sand beach." Walk through the soft sand, or listen to the wind wafting over the sand, Paddy instructs, and you'll hear music. I try it, but nothing doing. I chalk it up to clay feet and a tin ear.

Paddy says Lake Superior eases his mind, spirits, and ailments, and he loves the lake. Many people do. Some are in this book, which is not in the least exhaustive. I didn't hit every big town on the lake. I write about three fish; there are scores. I write about six scientists; there are many of them, too. I did not begin this project with a grand plan. I met people casually. A ferryboat captain steered me to an ore boat captain. A forester steered me to a botanist. A leaflet steered me to the saga of the voyageurs. I don't remember all the steers, but all these people kindly spoke to me. Different though they are, they share a character: steadfast and true. These stories, then, are about a moody lake and people who are religious about their work.

As for the lake, a man I know says of Superior, "It eats you and bites you, yet it can be calm and collected. It reminds me of people."

As for the people in this book, they remind me of the story of the old Finnish woman who told a long-lost visitor that her husband had died, and she summed up his life this way: "He's a work, he's a sweat, he's a drink beer, he's a go."

Acknowledgments

I've had a lot of help with my writing, and not just with this book. My friend Paul Lehmberg taught me about rewriting; no matter how strong or weak a story, he can make it better. My friend Timo Koskinen has an encouraging nature and a good eye for wooden prose. As for this undertaking, the fellows in our writers' group—Wally, Steve, Tom, and Mark—scoundrels all, patiently read and reread my stuff. Donna Hiltunen helped me. I'm thankful that Kathryn Wildfong saw the possibilities.

Prologue

Shining Big-Sea-Water

Lake Superior is not as old as the hills. The hills around the lake date back 1 billion years, while Lake Superior dates back just 9,500 years—to the last thrust of a 2-million-year-old ice age, when glaciers advanced and retreated across much of North America. When the ice moved south from Canada for the last time, it gouged out a basin which, when the glaciers melted, left behind a lake that stretched from Canada to the lower Midwest, from the Dakotas to New York. Today's promontories were little islands. This behemoth body of water drained and left behind today's Great Lakes. Lake Superior, now the biggest, is actually today at its very smallest.

French explorers called Lake Superior and the other Great Lakes *mers douces,* or sweet seas. These five lakes contain one-fifth of the world's freshwater. Lake Superior, 350 miles long and up to 160 miles wide, covers nearly 32,000 square miles. All of the other Great Lakes, topped off with three more Lake Eries, could fit into Superior. The lake is bigger than ten states, is as big as Austria, and could accommodate the Bahamas six times over.

The surface of Superior is 600 feet above sea level. The deepest point is 1,333 feet. The bottom of the lake is 700 feet below sea level and 418 feet below the level of Death Valley.

Two hundred rivers and streams dump into the lake, which has a small watershed for so large a body of water. The biggest inlet is the Nipigon River at the lake's northernmost point; the only outlet is the St. Mary's River at the lake's easternmost point. On average, a drop of water entering the lake takes two hundred years to find its way out.

The salient geographical features of the lake are Isle Royale in the north, the Keweenaw Peninsula in the south, the Apostle Islands in the west, and Whitefish Point in the east.

Because of Lake Superior, the westernmost of the Great Lakes, the United States is the only country in the world with a major seaport (Duluth)

This map, produced by Vincenzo Coronellis, a Franciscan monk and cartographer, dates to the 1680s.

E TRACY,

ou

AC DE CONDE'.

le Lac des Hurons.

Riu. de

Apisintas

Le Pik

Bagouach

Messinaigan ou Escriture

Teste de Loutre

R. Michipicoton

Ance de Michipicoton

I. Montreal.

Riu. Batchian

Quelques

Lac, on trou

Les Grandes Isles.

Les Grands Sables.

Les I. Parisien.

Ance a la Pe

Sauteurs, S

Pointe au Pin

Destroit

quand

R. Manistic

R. Minatoulin

P. aux Iroquois

R. Pouchitamy

Mission de S.te Marie du Saut

Vill. des Hurons

le Takouamina

Pointe de

I. Missilimaki

Destroit

Outao

twenty-three hundred miles inland. Six hundred thousand people live in the Lake Superior basin; the major cities are Duluth, Thunder Bay, Marquette, Munising, Sault Ste. Marie, Canada, and Sault Ste. Marie, Michigan. The American Soo, as it is called, is the oldest city in Michigan and the third-oldest in the United States.

Indians called Lake Superior Kitchi-gummi, a name of many spellings. Longfellow called it Gitche Gumee and "Shining Big-Sea-Water." It is believed the Anishinabe arrived on the north shore of the lake between 1200 and 1500. Europeans came to the area in the early 1600s. Early French explorers called these waters *lac superieur,* uppermost lake. These pioneers were enticed by furs, lodes of iron and copper, expansive forests, and a fishery deemed inexhaustible. One of these fish, the lake trout, was decimated by overfishing and sea lamprey, an invasive, life-sucking predator that proved to be the spawn of Satan.

A more heavenly aspect is its bracing chill air; a day on the lake makes one logy. When I was a lad, there used to be a sign in the Keweenaw Peninsula: "You are now breathing the purest, most vitalizing air on earth." It's said the college fellows used to nail skunks to the sign. I don't know if that's true, but it's a good yarn. The lake makes for many. As Longfellow wrote in *Song of Hiawatha*, "You shall hear a tale of wonder."

I

Paddle, Pipe, and Portage

Grand Portage, Minnesota

Natives called Lake Superior "the water too far to see across." White explorers braved this water in birch-bark canoes, paddling while singing songs to bolster their spirits and pace themselves. They were called *voyageurs,* or travelers. Indians described them as "men with hairy faces who have no women." In their heyday in the late 1700s and early 1800s, these hard-bitten men supplied beaver pelts, called "soft gold," to make top hats, capes, and muffs for the fancy crowd in Europe. It's been said the voyageurs were "mighty men taming mighty country." Some, called "Montreal men," took trade goods from eastern Canada to Grand Portage, midway along the north shore of Superior. Others, known as "north men," laden with furs, navigated the rivers and lakes from the Canadian interior, which was called *le pays d'en haut,* or upper country, to Grand Portage, a French name for *great carrying place.* It refers to a portage from Lake Superior up to the Pigeon River, which flows from the north but has rapids and waterfalls above the mouth, necessitating the voyageurs' nine-mile trek overland. It was at Grand Portage that the two groups of canoers traded cargo and returned to where they had come from—one to the city, one to the bush—but not before indulging in a fleeting but grand time.

The spirit of this rendezvous enlivens people yet. Each August, three hundred or so people travel to a campground at Minnesota's Grand Portage National Monument, fifty miles west of Thunder Bay, where they participate in a four-day reenactment of the days of the voyageurs, creating personas, dressing in costume, and telling stories of the past.

On the first evening of the gathering, in the waning light, Rodney Brown, a wandering minstrel from Thunder Bay, sings of the past. He has dedicated an album to the voyageurs. Save for a yellow do-rag and cloth belt, Brown wears modern street clothes. In front of him, in a little meadow, perhaps a hundred people sit on the grass in the cool, still evening. Some men smoke little clay pipes; a few women knit. Behind Brown, there is a copse of tall white spruce. Black flies are pesky.

"Our hearts long for drink and song," he sings.

One song is about William McGillivrary, for whom Fort William is named. For a time, McGillivrary ran the Northwest Company's fur trade out of the north shore. McGillivrary had two wives: a white and a Cree. Brown's favorite lyrics in his voyageur songs are about the Cree wife. They include her tombstone epitaph—"Mother of the country, daughter of the land"—to which he adds, "We leave you poor, with beggar hands." Those words, Brown says, recall a bad time for the natives, who faced starvation when the fur industry dried up.

Gone, then, were the voyageurs—and the clerks, traders, and managers who were called "company men"—gone were all except the mixed breeds who were, and are, called the métis. These people opened up the region, this north shore of Lake Superior and beyond, all the country northwest of Lake Huron's Georgian Bay—an area, Brown says, that the voyageurs called "the big lonely."

The first European to view these expansive waters was probably Etienne Brulé, who came to what was called New France in 1610, at age sixteen. He traveled up the St. Lawrence River to Quebec, which had been founded by Samuel de Champlain in 1608. Champlain took the young Brulé under his wing and sent him to live among the Huron people, whom Champlain had befriended, to learn their way of life and how to survive in his new world. Brulé is variously described as a scout, pathfinder, and the very first *coureur de bois,* or woods runner.

Champlain reached Georgian Bay in 1615, his farthest foray west. It is believed that Brulé pushed on from there, traveled up the St. Mary's River, and reached what is now Sault Ste. Marie between 1620 and 1622. Brulé was ahead of the crowd. Jean Nicolet didn't discover Lake Michigan until 1634. Claude Allouez didn't reach the west end of Lake Superior until 1666. The backdrop of this time in the New World was the continual squabbling and warring between the French and British, both with their Indian allies. When the British captured Quebec in 1629, Brulé switched his allegiance from the French to the British. One historical sketch says of Brulé and this ill-fated move, "Despite his notable accomplishments, his death was unheroic and gruesome; for changing his loyalty from the French to the British, he was killed, quartered, boiled, and eaten by his blood brothers, the Bear Tribe of the Huron Indians."

Those who followed Brulé were mostly French, and they became the voyageurs. They pushed west, following the sun and the watercourses. To admirers, these men were brave and daring; to the English they were "corrupt, and debased as savages." Whatever their character, they had tough hides as they sought furs and the Northwest Passage. Along the way, the French built more than a hundred forts and made what one observer calls "a long-stretched supply route."

The voyageurs took a lesson from the natives and navigated these waters by canoe. The birch-bark canoe was to the opening of the Great Lakes region as the horse was to the opening of the West. These "birch-rind canoes" were made by the Algonquin people of the Ottawa River valley and southern Ontario. Lightweight, they were like sailing on "a dried leaf." It was said, "They can sail them before the wind, but not else." One chronicler of the period likened them to "a wretched fragile water lily."

The French used bigger canoes for large rivers and Lake Superior, and smaller ones to negotiate the many rapids and portages in central and western Canada. A bigger one, the *canot de maître,* or master canoe, was thirty-four to forty feet long and had a crew of eight to fourteen. A smaller one, the *canot du nord,* or north canoe, was about twenty-five feet long and had a crew of four to six. The men who hired on to paddle these vessels were a colorful and stouthearted bunch. One contemporary, Daniel Harmon, wrote in 1819:

> The Canadian Voyageurs possess lively and fickle dispositions, and they are rarely subject to depression of spirits, of long continuance, even when in circumstances the most adverse. Although what they consider good eating and drinking constitutes their chief good, yet, when necessity compels them to it, they submit to great privation and hardship, not only without complaining, but even with cheerfulness and gaiety. They are very talkative, and extremely thoughtless, and make many resolutions, which are almost as soon broken as formed. They never think of providing for future wants. . . . They are not brave; but when they apprehend little danger, they will often, as they say, "play the man." They are very deceitful, are exceedingly smooth and polite, and are even gross flatterers to the face of a person, whom they will basely slander, behind his back. . . . A secret they cannot keep. They rarely feel gratitude, though they are often generous. They are obedient, but not faithful servants. By flattering their vanity, of which they have not a little, they may be persuaded to undertake the most difficult enterprises.

Their odyssey was indeed formidable—grueling days, and thank the Lord for nightfall. Their journeys were mainly between May and October when the waterways were free of ice. It was common for "brigades" of up to twenty canoes to venture forth together. The men worked fourteen to eighteen hours a day, covering sixty to eighty miles. On portages, they had to carry seventy- to ninety-pound *pièces,* or bundles, of supplies. They endured injury, death, and nature's unfriendliness, including, according to one account, "clouds of black flies and mosquitoes against which the best repellent was a mix of bear grease and skunk urine."

According to writer Eric Morse, "The voyageur's daily routine was a killing one." Up at two or three o'clock to the shout of *Leve, leve, nos gens!*—Up, up, we men!—they traveled twelve miles before breakfast, which was cooked overnight but not provided until eight o'clock. Lunch was limited to dried meat eaten on the run. "Fairly regularly," Morse writes, "a stop was made for a few minutes each hour to allow the men to smoke a pipe." This event was so important that distances came to be measured in pipes; three pipes might be fifteen to twenty miles, "depending on wind and current." Such a break from routine and labor, Morse writes, was "a motivating and enticing thought." Dinner, at eight or ten o'clock in the evening, typically was dried meat mixed with flour and water, creating a potage that the voyageurs called *rubbaboo.* After one last pipe, the voyageurs slept on the ground—"on turf, moss, or beach," Morse says—with their heads under an overturned canoe and a tarp stretching from the canoe to protect them from "the rain and dew." Johann Kohl, a chronicler of the period, describes these inconveniences as "extremely unpoetical." He reports a common lamentation among the voyageurs: *Au misère!*

Their food had little variety, though it differed by region. At the outset of the journey in Quebec or Montreal, the voyageurs ate maize, dried peas, beans, and cured pork; at Sault Ste. Marie, there was wild rice, maple syrup, fish, venison, and corn; in central and western Canada, buffalo and pemmican. The corn was soaked in a mixture of wood ashes and water and boiled to a thick hominy that was sometimes spiced with bacon fat or bear grease. Not until they reached Grand Portage did the men eat sumptuously; then, according to Kohl, there were delicacies such as beaver tail, buffalo hump, bear paw, and moose nose.

In 1824, Edward Talbot wrote about the voyageurs and their lot: "How the men who are employed in this difficult navigation exist, without ruining their constitutions, is a mystery which I am utterly unable to explain." Perhaps to their advantage, these men were believers in God. They prayed for safety and to be remembered. Some, of course, succumbed along the way.

Where they were buried, crosses were set in place. Upon encountering one, it is said, the voyageurs tipped their heads and said a prayer.

Washington Irving wrote of the voyageurs in 1836, "They are dexterous boatmen, vigorous and adroit with the oar and paddle, and will row from morning unto night without a murmur. The steersman often sings an old traditional French song . . . in which they all join, keeping time with their oars; if at any time they flag in spirits or relax in exertion, it is but necessary to strike up a song of the kind to put them all in fresh spirits and activity."

Our voices keep tune and our oars keep time . . .
Row, brothers, row, the stream runs fast,
The rapids are near and the daylight's past.

Voyageurs who sang and paddled and smoked their way from Montreal to Grand Portage were called "pork eaters," after the French appetite for that meat. They also were called *engagés,* laborers or hired hands. These men returned to Montreal. The north men who lived in the Canadian wilderness were called *hivernants,* or winterers. A pork eater became a north man only after a winter in the backcountry and a rite of passage, described this way: "The newcomer was sprinkled with water from the first north-flowing stream, and made to promise never to kiss another man's wife without his permission. This ended with the drinking of rum and a boistering barrage of back-slappings."

Whether pork eater or north man, there were three kinds of laborers in each canoe: the *avant,* or bowman, in front, acted as guide; the *gouvernail,* or steersman, in the stern, directed the craft; and the *milieu,* or the paddlers, were stationed in the middle. As well, there were the express men, they of the highest stature, who carried important people or messages at twice the pace of a supply canoe.

The cargo capacity of the lake canoes was up to eight thousand pounds, half that for the smaller canoes going into the interior. Each voyageur's supplies were limited to thirty to forty pounds—basically, tobacco, a blanket, and clothing, including a good set of clothes to play the dandy in Grand Portage. It is said that God turns a blind eye to all soldiers for an hour before battle. Perhaps he turned a blind eye to all voyageurs at the rendezvous at Grand

Portage, where, after eight weeks of toil and isolation and more than two thousand miles of wilderness, the men took to rum and women. Their women were called "temporary wives" or "fair Partners."

Alexander Ross, one man who was a part of this commerce, wrote:

> I have now been 42 years in this country, for 24 of them, I was a canoe man; I required but little sleep, but sometimes got less than I needed. No portage was too long for me, all portages were alike. My end of the canoe never touched the ground 'til I saw the end of the portage trail. Fifty songs a day were like nothing to me. I could carry, paddle, walk, and sing with any man I ever saw. During that period, I saved the lives of 10 Bourgeois [members of the upper class], and was always their favorite, because when others stopped to carry at a bad step, and lost time, I pushed on—over rapids, over cascades, over chutes; all were the same to me. No water or weather ever stopped my paddle or my song. I had 12 wives in the country; and was once possessed of 50 horses, and 6 running dogs, trimmed in the finest style. I was then like a Bourgeois, rich and happy; no Bourgeois had better dressed wives than I; no Indian Chief finer horses; no white man better-harnessed or swifter dogs. I beat all Indians at the race, and no white man ever passed me in the chase. I wanted for nothing; I spent all my earnings in the enjoyment of pleasure. 200 livres, twice told, have passed through my hands; although now I have not a spare shirt to my back, nor a coin with which to purchase one. Yet, were I young again, I should glory in commencing the same career again, I would willingly spend another half-century in the same fields of enjoyment. There is no life so happy as a voyageur's life; none so independent; no place where a man enjoys so much freedom as in Indian country. Huzza! Huzza! *pour le pays sauvage* [for the savage country].

Ross wrote this remembrance in 1850. He was the last of a breed. In 1802, the rendezvous was relocated from Grand Portage to Fort William, at what is now Thunder Bay. The 1820s sounded the death knell for the entire operation. The beaver simply ran out; and anyway, silk hats had replaced beaver hats as the fashion in Europe. So the fur trade ended—yet it still tugs at the imaginations of the reenactors, who are quite serious about their masquerade.

The 2007 reenactment is made up of 133 encampments—a setting of white canvas tents and lean-tos. To the north are green hills that spill down to

Grand Portage Bay, half a mile long, with an island, a few acres in size, a quarter mile offshore. Soft, halfhearted waves lap at the narrow, boulder-strewn shoreline. A bulky young man stands facing the water and plays bagpipes. His audience is a few seagulls and a little dark-haired girl who sits on a big rock. Wood smoke from many campfires scents the cool evening air. All about are the artifacts of the fur trade: a birch-bark canoe, wooden kegs, flintlock rifles, fire-blackened pots and kettles, a wooden yoke for carrying pails, and colorful wool blankets. Piles of firewood are there for the taking. People mill about, all in period dress, the men in white shirts with no buttons, breechcloths, moccasins, and leather leggings, and the women in long dresses. A good many men sport dashing beards, mustaches, and sideburns. There is all manner of head cover: chukes (from the French *toque,* for hat), berets, do-rags, squat stovepipe beaver hats (the point of this whole business, after all), and cocked hats, or tricornes, which one man describes as "the most useless hat ever invented in the world. When you walk through the woods, it's like having a cowboy hat with treble hooks. It catches on everything."

Karl Koster has organized this annual reenactment since 1998. "He's in deep," a friend says of his involvement. On this night he wears a faded red shirt, black neck scarf, burgundy sash, moccasins, and a white do-rag. He also carries a walkie-talkie, one of the few deviations from the traditional at this gathering (although I do run into a woman who hides a rubber spatula). Koster keeps events on schedule, makes sure all campfires are out by one thirty in the morning, and makes himself useful.

Trade goods that the Montreal men carried included firearms, ammunition, metal tools, cloth, beads, twine, salt, and liquor. Koster says the furs (70 percent were beaver) that the north men brought to Grand Portage were gathered by Indians with nets, spears, snares, and clubs through holes in the ice. In contrast, he says, "In the Rocky Mountains, there were a handful of guys with traps." He adds, "The Lake Superior fur trade, in all aspects, really blows away that Rocky Mountain fur trade. There was so much more—from here to the Pacific, here to the Arctic."

Grand Portage, Koster explains, is "a small, little spot on the map, but for a lot of people here, this was the center of the world." He describes the area as "a chunk of land" between two watercourses—on one side Lake Superior and on to the Atlantic Ocean; on the other side the Pigeon River and on to the Pacific Ocean. "So if you think about it," Koster says, "that's what this portage does—gives you the route to go from the Atlantic Ocean to the Pacific Ocean. It's the center of the continent. This is where you go east and west, right here."

The Great Lakes fur trade opened up not only the Lake Superior region but also the Canadian west and northwest. Looking for the Northwest Passage,

Sir Alex McKenzie, head of the Northwest Company, journeyed west out of Grand Portage, took a right turn, and reached the Arctic Ocean in 1789. Four years later, he stuck to a westward route and reached the Bella Coola River, which dumps into the Pacific Ocean, eleven years before Lewis and Clark made it to that country.

Grand Portage, then, was a stepping-off point for a huge enterprise that Koster loves to talk about. Just outside of his canvas lean-to, a deer hindquarter and a buffalo roast, impaled with a spit, hang over an open fire. Visitors sit on bales of hay or canvas bundles of the same size. The bundles, wrapped with rope, represent the packs that the voyageurs carried over portages and sat on when they paddled their canoes, which had no seats. One is a cooler covered up to look like a bundle.

Koster, who is in his late forties, admits, "I'm too old and too fat to be a voyageur." He works for the National Park Service from May to October and is a freelance historian and consultant specializing in the fur trade. There are more than forty reenactments about the fur trade a year in Minnesota and Wisconsin alone. Grand Portage is one of the bigger and more popular ones. "Grand Portage was the exact site where a real rendezvous took place," Koster says. "That's what makes this one so special." He says the reenactment of the Grand Portage rendezvous began at least as far back as the 1970s. "It took over everything and became a profession," he says. "It's a strange life—dressing funny and doing old stuff." He adds, "The kids just absolutely love it."

Koster smokes a small, traditional pipe, made of kaolin, that he bought from a man who specializes in making them. On this day, Koster wears blue-and-white-striped stockings, a "finger-woven" wool garter, linen knee britches (the 1790s were "a trouser period," he says), a linen shirt (the color of the tents: unbleached white), a black silk scarf, a plaited straw hat right out of vaudeville ("The style dates from 1790"). Many reenactors wear head cover common to the period. "It's a sign of respect," Koster says. He is a student and a fan of this era. "I go home at night, relax, grab a beer, and read a fur trade journal. It's an everyday thing in my life and I never get tired of it because I don't know everything yet." He doesn't romanticize the history or the people. "The more I research the voyageurs, they didn't have much of a choice. These guys needed a job."

Recalling these people, the reenactors slip into the past so thoroughly that they talk of it as though it were the present. The coureur de bois? "They're earlier than us," Koster says.

I ask Koster what attracts him to this avocation.

"Like-minded people," he says. "Camping with guys who like to talk about the same things you like to talk about."

KARL KOSTER: *I go home at night, relax, grab a beer, and read a fur trade journal.*

Along with period costumes, there are period trades—silversmith, tanner, soap maker, tinsmith, hunter, and cobbler—and among these practitioners of the past there is some swapping going on. "There's an argument," Koster says, "about how much gear we can take to do our trading."

John Powers, who is in his sixties, is a forestry consultant from Duluth, Minnesota. He adopts the persona of a man he identifies as LaFrenierie. The Frenchman and his compatriots began their journey in Montreal with a visit to the Church of Saint Anne-de-Bellevue, where, Powers says, "They asked for protection to bring them safely home." They ended their journey at Grand Portage which, Powers says, was decidedly unholy—"a place that's wild, away from church and social stuff." He describes these men as "full of piss and vinegar and drunk—they just got paid, so you can imagine what this place was like." They swelled the population of Grand Portage from fifty stalwart souls braving the winter to fifteen hundred enjoying the summer. "They were adventurers for whom the civilized life back east was too confining," Powers says. Most were just contract laborers—the muscle behind the fur trade.

The lineage connecting LaFrenierie and Powers is a fanciful bloodline stretching back to the voyageur rendezvous, an event of legend and lore, and now make-believe. Powers camps in a tent and dons period garb—red head scarf, polka-dot scarf, light-colored pants and shirt, moccasins, and a *ceinture flesch,* a woven sash with an arrowhead pattern—and practices period activities. He uses a wooden water cup and a wooden spoon, cooks over an open fire, eats off rocks or birch bark instead of plates, and loves it all. "I slipped down the slippery slope into the hobby," he says of this reenactment. He is a tall, lean man who canoes and hunts and sews his own shirts.

Tim Peterson, who is in his late fifties, of Two Harbors, Minnesota, has been participating in the rendezvous for ten years. A graduate of the College of Saint Scholastica, he works for the Army Corps of Engineers in wetlands management. He has granny glasses, a white beard, and a light brown mustache. We sit on the grass and converse. It rained lightly last night, but the day is warm and sunny, and the ground is dry. Peterson says, "It was nice last night—listening to the rain on the tarp." He smokes a pipe; it's not kaolin, like most; the bowl is cherry, and the stem is dogwood. He is alone on this day; sometimes he comes with his wife and daughter. "You know what's nice about these?" he says of reenactments. "It's safe. You don't worry about the kids."

He wears buckskin leggings and a breechcloth. "You don't want the branches tearing up your legs." He also wears elk moccasins. Hanging from his waist is a small wooden cup for eating and drinking. He calls it a "noggin."

"How do you spell that?" I ask.

John Powers: *I slipped down the slippery slope into the hobby.*

Tim Peterson:
You know what's nice about these? You don't worry about the kids.

"Wrong," he says, and then adds, "I had beer out of this last night. You use it for everything. I got this and my bone spoon and that's all I need."

He also has what he calls a "patch knife." It's used to cut the cloth patch for a black powder gun. It has a handle that he made of deer antler.

Blue beads dangle from his neck. He wears a silver earring with a turquoise feather. I remark on it.

"I got it at a rendezvous someplace," he says.

"What kind of stone?"

"I really couldn't tell you. Blue?"

He sports a black beret. His persona is Scottish. Most of the voyageurs were French Canadian, he says, but after them, the Scots played a significant role.

Kids are all about, playing. "Aren't they great?" he exclaims. The rendezvous, he adds, "teaches them confidence. They know they can survive. If you're at one of these, you're usually self-sufficient." The children, he says, have an appreciation for food, fire, and shelter. "Drop them in the woods someplace, they'll do just fine."

He has four children, aged fifteen to thirty. He says his youngest daughter trails friends like a caboose does a train. "They have a ball at these things."

"Why do you go?" I ask him.

"History is a lot of it. Relaxation. I don't know. People play golf. I just like this. That's a question you can't answer."

He carries a buckskin pouch. Inside is a brass box filled with flint, steel, and char cloth, which is partly burnt cotton that's like charcoal—"It catches fire real quick." Strike the flint and steel, the spark lands on the char cloth and you can blow on it and coax a flame out of it. He's been on seven- and nine-day canoe trips in the Boundary Waters. "Nobody used a match that whole trip," he says.

He also carries a medicine bag, filled with "luck charms, beads, feathers, fur, part of a piece of eight, plus things I'm not going to tell you."

He's a trapper of beaver, fox, coyote, fisher, and martin. But, he says, "I'm not big-time." One of the rendezvous events is a trapping demonstration later in the morning. Peterson says he'll go. "You can always learn something new. That helps you out."

He also dries venison. "I cheat. I use the oven." And he gathers wild rice. "I know where the rice is and go when it's ripe. Actually, it makes good Christmas presents if you get a little extra."

He pauses and lights his pipe with his flint and steel and char cloth. He does it easily. He says of the voyageurs, "Those guys knew what they were doing."

I wander to the lakeshore where a man is putting on a trapping and hunting demonstration.

"Who are you?" I ask.

"My name is John Hayes."

"What do you do?"

"In the twentieth century, I'm an attorney. But right now I'm essentially a gouvernail in this setting right here. Doing hunting and gathering, mostly. Meat hunting and wild ricing, supporting my family."

John Hayes is in his early forties and lean, with dark hair in a long ponytail. He's been enthralled with voyageurs since he was a shaver. At age nine, he made his first leather pouch. At twelve, he made his first moccasins (he's made two hundred pairs since). At fourteen, he made his first buckskin shirt.

"Why do you do it?" I ask.

"I daresay it's trying to dig into history. To get it right. And always trying to improve your persona, your camp, your accoutrements, your approach, your mind-set. Do what they would have done with the stuff that they had. They were hard workers. They knew how to use their back."

He slips into the present tense. "You have to be able to paddle most of the day. When you get to a portage, you unload the canoe, carry the packs across, carry the canoe, put the packs back in, and you're ready to go again. And you do that day in and day out."

The people who revere this life will travel far for "a good camp," Hayes says. He has been to six states. He especially likes the Grand Portage reenactment. "I would rank this up there with some of the best camps."

The historical reenactments have become a blend of restriction and imagination. Some things are frowned upon at voyageur camps. "Your western mountain man—buckskins with beads and fringe—those things are heavily discouraged. The prairie dress and prairie bonnet—they're strongly discouraged." On the other hand, he says, "Take a persona and run with it." Name. Parentage. Religion. Background. "It never quits. No. Never does. You got to look at it like a backwards funnel. You start coming in the nozzle, backwards, and it just opens up and gets wider and wider."

Under a tarp, before an audience of eight, Hayes puts on a short course in woodlore and a way of thinking. Voyageurs, he says, had few needs and a use for everything. "The practicality of the eighteenth-century mind is a kind of a minimalism."

Much of the trade of that time revolved around animals. Beaver, of course, "for the true felted hat." Deer hides for tradesmen's britches. Tough red squirrel hide for gloves. Soft groundhog hide or moose maple ("that little rubbery tree") for sewing. Deer for meat. Salted buffalo, sent east (it lasted a

John Hayes:
The practicality of the eighteenth-century mind is a kind of a minimalism.

year in a springhouse). Corned bear hams and bacon. ("They didn't have pigs back then around the country. They had them on the East Coast and on the farms, but in the borderland, in the rough areas, in the frontier, bear took the place of pig.") Deer tallow rendered into grease both for cooking and to oil a gun barrel.

Hayes demonstrates the fashioning of a rabbit deadfall made out of a few notched and shaven sticks. He makes a turkey call, rubbing a small slab of slate with a birch dowel. "That's a hen calling," he says. "'Come here, boy, come here. Come here, you handsome devil.' I can almost purr with this. It's a feeding call. A call of contentment." Use hot lead, a ladle, and a can of water to make lead shot for grouse, swans, and muskrats and round ball for deer and buffalo. Fashion antlers and bones for implements. For warmth in the winter, line moccasins with pieces of blanket, leaves, cattail down, or hair from deer, elk, and caribou, which is hollow. "Hollow hair is an incredibly good insulator."

"What's the name of the game here?" Hayes asks his small audience. "What's the common thread you see happening here?" He answers himself: "Self-sustaining. Self-sufficient. Resourceful. Reliant."

He instructs about hunting deer with stealth. "Don't stomp, stomp, stomp" through the bush, he says. "Go in there . . . gently. Try to move into the wind. Keep that wind in favor." Some hunters, he says, are so concerned with odors that they won't eat meat for three days prior to hunting and will cleanse themselves in the sauna immediately beforehand. In mimicking the past, he doesn't go that far, but he nonetheless cautions about a deer's sense of smell. "A smell out of place is a smell out of place." A deer near a farm will be accustomed to the smell of oil, he says. On the other hand, "Don't rub yourself with pine needles and duff and then go into an oak forest." "Resourcefulness," he repeats. "You're always thinking ahead. . . . The first rule of thumb is not to get in a pickle. And the second, I guess, is if you're in a pickle, you're going to have to get yourself out.

"These people," he continues, "weren't so gadget-burdened as some people nowdays. You don't need a whole bunch of stuff." One spoon, one knife, one cup, and so on, he says. "Abe Lincoln said, 'Most people are as *happy* as they want to be.' Most people are as *satisfied* as they want to be, as far as I'm concerned."

Hayes practices some period skills and methods. For instance, he uses one muzzleloader for hunting, whether the game is squirrel or deer. "The only time I use a modern gun is if I'm out duck hunting late-season divers, and they're coming, screaming in, about sixty miles an hour. It's nice to have a couple of shots there for that big bluebill or whistler."

Hayes has built a home in the style of the late eighteenth century, with both French and Dutch aspects. By living the way he does, caught up in a bygone time, he hopes to impart to his children "an appreciation of what we have nowdays." He wants them to keep alive skills from the past. He wants to teach them "to be able to do without, to put up with some discomfort once in awhile" and "to appreciate a warm fire when you get home, a hot bowl of soup."

"Were you born in the wrong century?" I ask.

"No, I was probably born in the right century, but if I could go back right now, I'd take a huge notebook, and I'd be looking for the answers that people have nowdays for questions."

Which are many. "We can pick up guns and knives and cooking utensils," he says. "We can see how they were used and where their wear marks are. But the soft culture—the way people spoke or what they taught—isn't always clear."

For Berit Allison, this is especially true. I sit on the grass in the sweet evening air with her. She is a small, dark-haired woman with silver bracelets and silver earrings. Allison, from Long Lake, Minnesota, became a reenactor about fifteen years ago. She has a degree in Native American studies and has two names—Crow Woman in Dakota, Little Horse Woman in Lakota. She has worked as a sign language interpreter, in special education, and as a teacher of English as a second language.

Her rendezvous persona is a métis woman whose father and grandfather were French traders and whose mother and grandmother were Dakota. "Having grown up in my mother's village, I've met, many years ago, a Scottish trader and have gone to live with him. When a trader married a native, they called it a marriage *à la façon de pays*—a marriage in the fashion of the country. When they would have children, if the child was a boy, he would frequently, at a certain age, go back to Montreal and perhaps even to Europe, to be educated . . . in hopes that he would come back here and work as a clerk for the fur company, and this kept the cycle going. Whereas girl children, daughters, would stay here in the wilderness and the frontier with their mothers—in the hopes of marrying a trader and continuing the fur trade cycle that way."

Allison says that native women were key to the fur trade. "They made moccasins. They made snowshoes for the men, without which they couldn't have left the posts in the winter because of the deep snow. They helped them with the process of learning the construction of the birch-bark canoes, which are actually sewn. Frequently, because the European men were not familiar with this area and procuring food in the wintertime, the native women would snowshoe out of the posts and snare rabbits and squirrels and bring them back and often kept the traders from starving over the winter." Allison says the women's role was unheralded. "Men of the time wrote in excess about themselves and about the men around them, and there was no detail too small to record. They'll go on and on and on about their voyageurs, and they'll say, 'And he had this native woman with him,' and that would be it. It's very difficult to find good, rich detail about these women."

They were stalwart. "Early on, some of the traders tried bringing European women over, and they were called 'the fragile exotics' because, transplanted from their homes in Europe and plopped down here, it was just such an incredible culture shock. They weren't prepared for the harsh climate, the incredible demand for physical labor. The European men couldn't believe how strong the native women were. They were pulling sleds that the dogs couldn't get through the snow, they were hauling wood and fur bales alongside the men—they'd never seen women work this hard and be that physically strong. And they soon saw that the European women just were not going to make it here, and so for awhile, there was an actual ban at the fur posts: 'Don't even try to bring European women here. It's terrible. It's a terrible mistake. We use the native and métis women.'"

Besides providers, Allison says, the native women and métis were "liaisons": "They helped the traders to understand and learn their native languages, to understand the cultural differences. They were really bridges, cultural bridges, between the fur traders and the native people."

The differences between the two cultures were at times dramatic—natives loyal, traders opportunistic. "If a trader came in and married a native woman, then he was family, and I think the traders didn't often fully understand the meaning of that. When that man, that trader, became a relative, you should be able to count on him. Relatives support you. They keep promises to you. If you're having trouble with your enemies, your relatives will come and help you." In that context, she talks about Pierre La Verendrye, an early French trader. "He traded with the Cree and the Ojibwe, and then traded with the Dakota. Well, when the Dakota traded with him, he became a family member, and then when he traded again with the Cree, the enemies of the Dakota, it was seen as a terrible betrayal—'Why would our brother, our relative, give weapons to our enemies, who are immediately using them against us?' So then they retaliated and murdered La Verendrye's men, including his son, and made a very strong statement. Because when they murdered them, they cut off their heads and put them around a fire and wrapped each head in a beaver pelt, as if to say, 'Here's the beaver pelt you want so badly. You have to have your hats. You need these beaver pelts. Well, here they are, wrapped around the heads of your dead.' . . . A pretty grim message, but you know, to them it had to be made. 'How can you betray us like this? You are our family, and yet you're arming our enemies.' So I think that cultural difference was hard to grasp."

Allison shows off a line of red paint along the part in her hair as well as a short horizontal line on each temple. "The red I have is a trade item called vermilion, and it was a powder. This intense pigment that was traded all the way from China. Unfortunately, during the time, the recipe for vermilion started with a hundred parts mercury and twenty parts sulfur, so I'm fairly certain it was not good to be wearing it on your skin every day. Before trade with Europeans, the native people would wear red ochre to color themselves, but once they saw this vermilion, the brilliant red, as opposed to the rusty red of the red ochre, people just couldn't get enough of it. It was such a fantastic color, and red was a color of power and life and joy. Among Dakota people, it's said that a man each morning would paint the part of his woman's hair red as an outward sign of his regard for her." Often, Allison adds, the women sported red decoration on their cheeks, forehead, chin, ears, and jaw. "It was really just cosmetic. It looked good . . . and then also, practically, it's great protection from the sun."

While Allison and I visit, her husband, a paramedic whose persona is a Scottish craftsman, brings her a cup of syllabub, an eighteenth-century beverage. "It's a mixture of port and brandy and brown sugar, and then you put cream and layer it on. If you were a fine person of social standing, you'd have this in a lovely glass and you could see the cream swirl down into the drink, and it's this beautiful garnet color. You want to taste it? It's spectacular. It's funny how, because of this passion, we seek out eighteenth-century recipes for food and beverages, and when someone has something new, it's all exciting."

She and her husband attend reenactments in Wisconsin, Minnesota, Iowa, and Illinois, including a couple in the winter. There is an air of camaraderie in all of them. "Absolutely. Some of the people have become our dearest friends." They come from all directions and distances. Sometimes, she says, "we only get to see each other a few times a year"—only at rendezvous—"and then it's a great, huge, special occasion."

What's the point of all the detail?

"As we started out, we were really, really loose. We really had no idea what we were doing. It was like, oh, people dress up and you wear buckskin. As you learn more, you really want everything you're doing, or wearing, or talking about, to be right. And as you come to a place like this, it's almost a tribute to those who have gone before us."

A friend brings food. He's cooked up a dish called haggis, which is a Gaelic word meaning "to hack up"— organs, in this case. "It's a traditional meal of Scotland," Allison explains. "It's cooked in the stomach of a sheep. It's made of hearts and liver and lung and kidneys. I think that's it. All chopped up with onion and, traditionally, oats, and lots of nice spices." Instead of oats, her friend uses wild rice to translate the traditional Scottish meal to the Great Lakes, where oats aren't available but wild rice is plentiful. "Put it all in the stomach of a sheep, tie it closed, and boil it for about three hours."

"Why do you do all this?" I ask Allison.

"I don't know," she responds. "It's just a passion."

She likes to teach what she calls "the public" that visits a rendezvous. She likes the good company of fellow reenactors, whom she describes as kindly and generous. She simply admires them. "The people here are the most knowledgeable group of people I've ever encountered." She treasures the evenings when they all sit around flickering campfires and talk about history. Most of all, she loves to teach schoolchildren about the history of the fur trade, especially the role of the native women and métis. "If we can see how very strong and powerful women can be, not in a feminazi sort of way, but to see that, 250 years ago, 300 years ago, women were making the difference between life and death for men who were new to this place—if that can be presented to a native girl and have her take some extra pride in who she is, and who her forbears were, it's just splendid."

"The folks are as good as the people," my old aunt says. That was not the case in history at Grand Portage. The fur trade occurred during a time of class distinction. The company men ("That means you shave and put on a suit," one reenactor says) were mostly Scottish or English, and they lived inside the stockade. Voyageurs, along with farmers, woodsmen, tradesmen, and *habitants* ("all washed-up voyageurs") lived outside of the stockade with the natives and métis. "A trader wouldn't touch any manual labor," one reenactor tells me, and the voyageurs' attitude was, "He pays us—we don't like him."

The fort, then, would be off limits to Tim Timmerman, were he displaced to 1800 and his voyageur persona, but these days he's allowed to hold forth in a small room in the Great Hall. Timmerman is from Waukon, Iowa, and he introduces himself as a knot tier. "I do all the different sailing knots," he says. "My persona in the rendezvous—my story goes—I served on a French frigate, a man-o'-war. Actually, a sailmaker is what I was, and I decided that was enough and I wanted to become a craftsman on the shore. So I decided to come inland, and I ended up in a canoe, and this is how I became a voyageur."

Berit Allison:
The people here are the most knowledgeable group of people I've ever encountered.

Timmerman, who is in his midforties, has dark hair that is starting to whiten. He has been going to reenactments for eighteen years. He describes the early days as "the infancy stage" of what he now calls "the rendezvous circuit," which attracts acolytes like him from afar. "As you grow into the hobby, you start learning all the niches and the tricks of the trade—what's period-correct and what's not period-correct. It's a history thing."

He likes to read fur trade journals and figure out what these people did, how they did it, and why they did it. "Who would run around in clothes like this and drive nine hours to be along Lake Superior? I talked to a public person and she was amazed we did this. All my friends do it. It's a normal thing to me."

He's a man of diverse talent. Blacksmith. Silversmith. A sewer of ditty bags. "Knot tying came in probably eight years ago," he says. "I was always fascinated with knots and ships, the older vessels, and knot tying goes hand in hand with being a sailor, and that's one of my personas." He ties many knots—a Turk's head, which he says is also known as a Gordian knot, monkey fists, and sheepshanks—"the whole works." Even a noose. "Nooses are a common sailor knot. They used it for all kinds of applications, because it's a jam knot. It never comes out. Once you lock it on to something, it's tight." Historically, he says, some knot tying was suspect. "Knot tying was considered a black art, because you could trick people with knots. They called it knot sorcery. In the late 1600s, they had a law that if you tricked somebody with a knot, they could have you incarcerated. People were scared because they didn't understand it. It's like a Turk's head. A Turk's head is a blind knot. There's no beginning and no end."

"What were they used for?"

"Decoration. You could tie big balls with them."

"Were they weapons?"

"Yeah. The one hanging down at the camp, we tied it tight enough that you could thump somebody pretty good."

"You must be handy," I tell him.

"I'm a dyslexic, and dyslexics are very good with their hands."

He claims he can tie knots backward.

Timmerman has another period pursuit—hunting with a flintlock rifle. (Matchlock muskets are too early, and caplocks too late.) He's made his own flintlock. "You learn something new from everybody that you encounter. You stop learning, you're dead." He likes to know how things are done. "Modern people don't know," he says. "They've never seen a weapon being built, a chair being built, or a fire started with flint and steel. People are just, like, amazed. They're stunned. It's like magic."

Tim Timmerman: *It's a history thing.*

"Why do you do it?" I ask.

"I don't know," he says. "The epitaph on my tombstone is going to say, 'He did everything one time, and he did it well.'"

He brags that his children are "historically sound," and he chuckles as he recounts that they sometimes correct their history teachers.

His voyageur persona is not his only one. He also does an eighteenth-century naval surgeon.

I ask him about venereal disease. He says that he knows from researching his naval surgeon persona that VD was rampant in ports of call. "They used mercury to cure it. It was one of the compounds they used to cure a lot of things. There's a very old eighteenth-century saying that goes, 'A night with Venus leads to a lifetime with mercury.' I don't know about the voyageurs so much. There's a lot of maladies in the fur trade. Broken bones to starvation to typhoid. So they fixed you with anything they could. They'd bathe you in rum, for God's sake."

He likes to tease people by acting out his persona. "People say, 'You're dressed funny.' 'No, I'm not dressed funny. You, my friend, are the one. I do not recognize your clothes.'"

That's the point of it all, he says. "We're trying to impress on people: How did we get to this point? It's like the lacrosse tournament out here today. Lacrosse is a very violent game. It prevented wars, because the tribes would get together and that's what the war would be—on the field. They called it 'the little brother of war.' It wasn't a full-blown war, but it was a war between tribes to prove who was who." It's important stuff, he says. "There's a lot of things that brought us to this point in history. If none of that had ever happened, we probably would never have made it this far."

In 1995, Timmerman took a canoe trip from Minneapolis to Prairie du Chien, Wisconsin, in period dress and a birch-bark canoe. Paddling the canoe was tricky. It was somewhat leaky. Somewhat frail. Somewhat tippy. "You don't want to do handstands or somersaults."

He has canoed on Lake Superior, too. The voyageurs weren't foolhardy, he says. "The misconception that people have is that they paddled across Lake Superior. They came along the shore. I mean, the lake, she could change her mind any day, any second of the day. Eat you right up." Earlier on this day, he was part of a group that went by canoe to Grand Portage Island, the little piece of land offshore from the campground, and back. "The wind"—another reenactor calls it "old woman wind"—"changed probably four times," Timmerman says.

To the northeast of Grand Portage Island is Hat Point, one arm of Grand Portage Bay. Timmerman says there's a cedar called the witch's tree at the end of the point. "It's about five hundred years old. It's a very beautiful tree. It only stands probably eight feet tall, but it's gnarled up, and it's growing right out of a rock. That's why they call it the witch's tree, because it's so gnarled and old." The voyageurs, he says, put their tobacco offerings at the base of the tree at the start of their return trip to Montreal—"for luck and for safe passage on Lake Superior, because it's a mean place out there."

I part ways with Timmerman and make my way back to the campground, to Karl Koster's lean-to, where there's a group of men sitting around talking. I ask Koster about the witch's tree. There's no documentation of the voyageurs putting tobacco down there, Koster says. "Maybe. Doubtfully." Another man in the group allows that some voyageurs adopted some Indian ways. But, putting tobacco down? "That would be appalling to a lot of them. These guys were devout Catholics. That's a whole other God."

I wander to the stockade. In a room perhaps twelve feet by thirty feet, a man with a drawknife fashions a canoe paddle out of a slab of white cedar. Two big canoes hang overhead. He explains their traditional construction: the bark shell comes before the frame. The birch bark is sewn together, the joints sealed with pine tree gum. Then the interior ribbing, also white cedar, is steamed and bent and sewn to the bark. All the lashing is done with spruce roots, which don't shrink as they dry.

Outside of the Great Hall, the bagpipe player puts on a show again, this time for a bigger audience. He is Jeremy Kingsbury of Milwaukee, and he studied American Indian culture and the Ojibwe language at Bemidji State University. He wears gillie brogues, hose and garter, a kilt, shirt, vest, and silk scarf.

"What are you wearing under the kilt?" I ask.

"Shoes," he says.

He's been playing the bagpipes since he was ten. "I'm pleased with my progress, but I definitely have a lot of advancement to go." He describes the sound of bagpipes as "honey milk."

Kingsbury gives me a paper handout with a Cree's description of the looks, sound, and playing of a bagpipe. "One white man, dressed like a woman, in a skirt of funny color. He had whiskers growing from his belt and fancy leggings. He carried a black swan which had many legs with ribbons tied to them. The swan's body he put under his arm upside down, then he put its head in his mouth and bit it. At the same time he pinched its neck with his fingers and squeezed the body under his arm until it made a terrible noise."

I return to the campground. Karl Koster has organized a little cooking contest. Start with flour, salt, and water and "do anything you want to it." Mark Baker of Grantsburg, Wisconsin, is cooking braised rabbit, spiced with

Jeremy Kingsbury: *I definitely have a lot of advancement to go.*

balsamic vinegar sauce and stuffed with sausage. He's also folding pepperoni, mushrooms, onion, and Italian sausage into flatbread, which he'll deep-fry and cover with a red sauce. "This is a joke," he says, "to woo the judges. It's definitely not authentic to the time period." He's got a third concoction going—a beverage of rum, water, sugar, fruit, spices, cloves, nutmeg, and cinnamon—called shrub.

"Let it sit," he says.

"How long?"

"Depends on how thirsty you are." He'll leave it overnight.

While he works on his concoctions, he jests, "I'm ready to get back to civilization and switch the lights on."

John Powers, the Duluth forester, wins the cooking contest with a simple bread and thimbleberry concoction. He wins a small, flat chunk of lead painted yellow to look like a gold coin.

Neil Grunke, a thirty-seven-year-old natural-gas technician from Deer River, Minnesota, has been reenacting for ten years. His persona is Simone Benoit LeBoeuf. "I am a voyageur for the Northwest Company." He wears a Cross of Lorraine on his chest and on his head rag.

"Are you religious?" I ask.

"Oh, but of course," he replies.

He also wears a silver pin of two kissing otters. "A typical trade good."

A hunter, Grunke tans deer hides, and he has brain-tanned them. "I'm told every animal has enough brains to tan their own hide," he says.

He explains why he is not worried about not knowing where his two young children are. "This creates an atmosphere for my children that they can't find anywhere else outside of a rendezvous. Trust everyone. Speak to strangers. They can be left alone and I know they're safe." The rendezvous is an education, he says. "They're learning cultures and history even though they don't realize they are."

Wayne Krefting is a puppeteer from Minneapolis. At the rendezvous, he entertains children with a puppet he fashioned from a small bear head and cape. He wears a cocked hat, a vest, and a scarf. Krefting's persona is a clerk, and he carries a handsome wood writing box filled with quills, ink, and paperwork for inventory, debits, credits, and such. Krefting is still learning the accounting methods of the time. His handwriting on the papers is striking. "I'm still practicing," he says. "It's still too, too thick."

He has studied the economy of this historical period, a task he describes as "slippery" due to the fact that there were three or four currencies in use in this part of the country at that time. The beaver trade was "huge"—with

Neil Grunke: *It's all about accoutrements and a persona.*

WAYNE KREFTING: *My handwriting is still too, too thick.*

"millions of dollars changing hands." The "big money" was made in the 1780s and 1790s. By 1820, the trade was "on the edge, on the margin."

The common workingman, like the voyageur, made an annual wage that would equal $3,000 or $4,000 in today's money, Krefting says. Clerks made three times that, and guides made six times that. Besides pay, the Northwest Company also gave each laborer a blanket, moccasins, a shirt, trousers, and a ration of rum and tobacco. The price of a blanket in that day ranged from $4 in Montreal to $14 in Fond du Lac, Minnesota. A beaver pelt sold for about $3.50.

Just before I leave the reenactment to rejoin the real world, I wander to the stockade again and sit down on a hewed timber next to a little boy and watch a group of preteens play two-ball. The little boy is eleven. He has black hair and tawny skin. He fingers a shiny tin candleholder.

"Did you make that?" I ask.

He nods but says nothing.

"How long did it take you?"

"Hours."

"Can I see it?"

He hands it to me. It has a platelike base and finger handle. The part that holds the candle is soldered to the base. It's nicely done.

"You should be proud," I say.

"It's my first one," he says.

2

A Work Farm

Grand Marais, Minnesota

It's five thirty in the morning, and I make my way from the main street of Grand Marais, Minnesota, down a sloping driveway to a pier behind the Dockside Fish Market. An invisible dog barks at me. About a hundred feet from the road, a fisherman named Harley Toftey, and his helper, Marty, wait for me by a fish boat with no name. We get on board, throw off the lines, ease off the pier, and head slowly toward the open water. Just offshore, a small breakwater, running parallel to the land, protects small craft. A quarter mile beyond that, two long breakwaters, both with lights, embrace this harbor on the north shore of Lake Superior. It is late October, mildly windy and decidedly cold, with a bright sickle moon. The starlight is brilliant, like that seen from a mountaintop.

Harley is fishing for herring. He has six five-hundred-foot nets to pick; the farthest is perhaps two miles from shore. They're set in about sixteen feet of water. Normally he fishes farther out (three to eight miles) and deeper (up to four hundred feet), but that's when the fish are more scattered and the catch is more lean. Now it is near spawning time, and the herring are congregating and moving close to shore, and the catch is concentrated and fruitful—"more of a volume deal," Harley says. "They're not spawning yet," he adds. "They come in to take a look." They are ripe with eggs, which Harley's wife, Shele, processes into herring caviar, plebeian fare compared to beluga caviar but highly favored in Europe, especially Sweden, Denmark, and Finland. This relatively pricey product drives this autumn fishing operation, although the herring itself is sold, too.

Past the big breakwaters, Harley moves strong and fast to his first set. He has GPS and knows exactly where he's going in the dark. "You don't monkey around looking for nets," he says. "You can drive right to 'em." Behind us, a few town lights glow; ahead is darkness.

Harley's boat is twenty-seven feet long, with a ten-foot beam. Made of aluminum, the vessel has an open deck except for a four-by-four-foot, three-sided, glassed-in pilothouse, where two is a crowd. Harley, with the help of an Alaskan boat builder, constructed this boat ten years ago. It cost $15,000. It is powered by twin 115-horsepower motors; one is for necessity, and the other is for safety. "You don't want to have just one out on this lake here," he says. Midway along the boat, the deck—Harley calls it "a wet deck"—is just eighteen inches off the water, and a mildly rough sea breaks across it and drains out of the scuppers. On this day the waves are choppy but small.

There is a reason Harley is out on the lake at this hour. Besides having to stock the market for the day, he says, "You can beat the wind when you come out early. The sun comes up—a lot of the time the wind comes with it." The weather has to be "pretty bad" for him not to go out. The swells are harder on the nets than on him. They "jerk the net around" and cause wear and tear, which he mends in the winter when the harbor is iced in and the lake inaccessible.

Harley is a tall, broad-shouldered, solid man, with thick dark hair that is beginning to gray, a dark mustache, and a few days' worth of whiskers. Marty calls him "the grand mariner of Grand Marais." Marty says of himself, "It ain't all bad being a nobody." The pair works the nets together. At each set, Harley powers down and turns on two spotlights on the roof of the pilothouse that cast a small halo around the boat, showing fish bellies as white as the moon and scaly sides and backs that flash like crystal daggers.

Each net drapes over the bow of the boat, across a plywood table, which is soon smeared with blood and scales. Harley and Marty disentangle the fish and throw them in plastic tubs. Two tubs are filled with ice and lake water for fish that are still alive and in really good shape. "I pick out the ones I'm going to fillet," Harley explains. "They got nice color when they're fresh."

These gill nets have small mesh—a couple of inches square—to capture small fish. The herring range from eight to twelve inches long and weigh half a pound to a pound. Occasionally, Harley catches a lake trout. "You can keep 'em, but you can't target 'em," he says. Typically, they are too big to get caught in the herring net, but some get tied up by their teeth.

Harley and Marty are clad in colorful rubber—dark boots, overall slicks (Marty's are green, Harley's yellow), yellow arm sleeves, and orange gloves. They look like rainbows. They also wear hooded sweatshirts. The wind is biting and the cold raw. Marty says to me, "Aren't you gonna ask why anyone is dumb enough to do this?"

Orange buoys, twice the size of basketballs, mark the ends of the nets; smaller floats in between ensure that the net doesn't sag. Below the surface, lead weights and cork floats support the monofilament mesh so that it stands up like a tennis net.

After lifting the first net, instead of going to his next set, Harley detours to where another fisherman, Dick Eckel, who is in his seventies, tends his nets. He's been out on the lake since three o'clock in the morning—"Out here in the middle of the night," Harley says. "We're only a quarter crazy, he's half crazy."

"How's it going?" Harley hollers to Dick.

"Lousy," comes the reply.

No current, Dick reports. They talk about current, which can complicate matters, the way gardeners talk about the frost.

Harley returns to business and heads to his next net. I ask him how he knows where the fish are. "Just years of trial and error. You don't get 'em every day. They swim around." He has been skunked, but not often. "You never know from one net to the next." No matter how good the catch, he says, "We're never happy."

In the spring and summer, when the operation is smaller, Harley goes out alone. "Me and the dog. You probably heard him barking." He didn't take the dog on this trip because I'm along and it's cramped quarters. "He's one mad dog," Harley says.

Summer fishing yields just enough fillets and smoked fish to stock his market. He has a mechanized net lifter for deep, bottom fishing when he gets a lot of ciscoes, which he calls "deep-water" or "bottom" herring. They're commonly called chubs. "There's quite a bit more oil in them," he says. "Any fish that feeds on the bottom has a higher oil level. They're really good smoked." Also, the colder the water, the slower the growth rate and the smaller the fish. Shallow-water herring, then, run two to a pound; deep-water herring run three and four to a pound.

As Harley and Marty labor, the eastern sky turns from black to indigo, then to purple and green, then a sliver of orange and blue appears. One lone seagull rides on the waves. As the sky lightens, the stars disappear until there is only one, low in the western sky. In the gathering light, to the north and west, scalloped hills hunker above the water. "Off-land winds aren't bad," Harley says. "These hills break it." Unless the weather is severe, he goes out every day. "It ain't right to not pick 'em," he says of his nets.

On this day, sometimes his nets have a fish every foot. Other times there are three or four or five feet between them. Most of the fish have a light-colored girdle mark behind the gills where they are caught in the mesh.

After lifting another net, Harley heads to where Tommy Eckel, Dick's brother, is working. Tommy is in his eighties, and Harley says of the old man's labors, "You think he'd be smarter than that."

When Harley eases off his engines, Tommy hollers. "The current is running like a river."

"Your brother says it's slack," Harley says.

"That's a true fisherman's lie."

"That's for darn sure."

We're out on the lake for three and a half hours. Returning to harbor, Harley goes full speed and the vessel plows through the bumpy water assuredly. At the big breakwater, Harley slows, creeps past the small breakwater, and moments later eases up against the pier, where the Eckel brothers are already tied up. The three fishermen weigh their respective catches—a thousand pounds, in all. In the summer, Harley might catch three hundred pounds by himself. These fish are now headed for the processing shed.

"Okay, we survived it," Harley says of this day's venture. He pauses and adds, "I'm just going to keep working out here 'till I drop. They ain't made a fisherman's retirement home yet."

There are three principals involved in this autumn Grand Marais fishing operation. Harley "feeds the store." Shele is the straw boss of the caviar operation, "a forty-day deal." Dick Eckel oversees the handling and packing of the herring—what Harley calls "the flesh."

HARLEY TOFTEY: *I'm just going to keep working out here 'till I drop.*

Harley and Shele own the processing shed, which is forty feet long and twenty-four feet wide. On one end, there is a small table on which Harley adroitly fillets the fresh-caught herring that is headed for the market. Along one wall of the shed, there is a table four feet wide and twenty-eight feet long, on which four men empty tubs of fish and pile them up, eighteen inches high. The men wield stout knives that have six-inch-long blades, are as wide as a butcher knife, and have blunt, round tips. The men perform seven or eight quick and sure movements. Grab a fish. Sever the head in one motion. Slice it along the back instead of the belly (these are called backsplits). Make a little scrape where the entrails affix to the stomach wall. Pick out eggs and toss them in a pail if it's a female. (Marty can spot the females before he opens them up. "You can tell from a block away if you've seen enough of them.") Scrape the blood and guts, in two easy motions, into a barrel. Toss the backsplits into a rubber tub. If they were to gut a fish at the belly, it would hold its form; opening it along the back means it is hinged at the soft belly and folds open and flat, like a butterfly steak.

On the other side of the processing shed, a fifth worker uses what looks like a short canoe paddle to slosh the herring around in a twenty-five-gallon hopper filled with water. The fish go from the hopper to a small conveyor and boom, eight inches wide and eight feet long, along which they are sprayed with water. The conveyor dumps the fish into a rubber tub that sits on a scale—fifty pounds of fish per tub. These tubs are shifted into the middle of the shed and stacked up five feet high, waiting for the other men to finish their cutting and begin to press the fish, flesh side down, in salt. The men layer the salted fish in rubber barrels that hold four hundred pounds.

It's a gory and gaudy operation. A stink. Blood and guts. Orange eggs. Milky bellies. Light brown flesh. White and black beady eyes. Black tails, which are left intact. Silver scales. The men are decked out in colorful rubber and repeatedly hose themselves down.

The Minnesota herring season ends in late October; the Canadian season ends in late December. Besides the Grand Marais catch, other fish come in by truck—from Knife River, Minnesota, northeast of Duluth, to Black Bay, Ontario, northeast of Thunder Bay. The Grand Marais facility is the only processing operation on this stretch of the north shore. On this chilly, drab day, they will process 8,569 pounds of herring (about 6,400 fish, each handled twice). They also will collect 640 pounds of roe. All in all, "a big day for Minnesota stuff," Marty says. In November and December, when the Canadian herring comes in full tilt, they'll handle three times that, and it'll take nine or ten people to cut the backsplits and three people to wash and weigh them. Harley says the Canadian fish run a little bigger and are more plentiful. "Better herring grounds up there," he guesses.

Marty, who is part Indian ("I've got a feather in me"), works for the U.S. Forest Service. While on vacation, he fishes for Harley and cuts backsplits for the Eckels for the extra money. He and the rest of the cutters average between $20 and $25 an hour during this short but fruitful season. They get paid by the pound before the fish are gutted, what he calls "in the round." He has no clue where these fish end up. "Texas. Carolina. Someplace far away." Actually, the backsplits and roe go to Interlaken Fishery International, in Spirit Lake, Iowa, for I don't know how much a pound—for Shele is not talking, and I don't blame her; I'm just nosy. Both products are shipped by refrigerated truck. So far this season, they have processed thirty-one thousand pounds of fish. By the end of December, they'll have processed close to five hundred thousand pounds of backsplits and fifty-four thousand pounds of caviar. Marty doesn't savor the fare. "Never tried it," he says of the salted backsplits.

Outside of the processing shed, the harbor is thick with white sailboats and other pleasure craft. Seagulls cry and squat all over—hundreds on the small breakwater and scores on the roofs of buildings, which are whitewashed with droppings. They wait for what Dick Eckel calls "the garbage route"—a pickup truck chock-full of trash barrels filled with guts and heads, minus some heads that will go to a local kid who uses them to trap mink. The guts and heads are hauled to a farm four miles north of Grand Marais. The gulls will follow the truck. "They know," Marty says. Gulls and eagles feast on everything but the juice, a leftover that triples the yield of the farmer's hay field.

Back inside the processing shed, a group of fifth-graders is on a tour. Several kids are holding their noses. One says, "I've seen my dad cut fish, but not fish all over." Marty gives a herring to a few kids who want one. "Put it in your pocket and forget about it for awhile," he tells them. The men, who take short smoke and coffee breaks every hour, keep working while they have this audience. Not long after the students leave, the men start salting and packing the backsplits. When that's done, one by tedious one, Marty says, "We clean the joint one more time." He's bushed. "You get tired standing here," he says.

Earlier that day, Harley and I retreated to his living quarters overlooking the bay and talked about fishing. Harley, who is in his early fifties, was born and raised in Grand Marais. As a lad, he was venturesome. A year out of high school saw him fishing in Alaska, where he was part of a small contingent of Minnesota fishermen—about fifteen boats among a fleet of two thousand.

Harley spent twenty years fishing for herring, salmon, cod, and halibut in Alaska, returning to Grand Marais each winter. His Alaskan commercial fishing license cost him $100,000. Over those two decades, he had four different salmon boats, all thirty-two feet long, the maximum length allowed by the state. His last and most expensive boat cost $130,000. He broke even on both boat and license when, in 1998, he and Shele decided to start their Grand Marais business and they "sold out of Alaska." It was the end of a lucrative operation. During the good years, Harley grossed between $200,000 or $250,000 just during the short six-week salmon season, netting a profit of $100,000.

"Do you make that kind of money here?" I ask him about Grand Marais.

"Oh, God, no. Not even close. If it wasn't for our retail store—me providing for the retail store—there's no way you could do it."

Harley says that the backsplits become gefilte fish: "It's a Jewish product. It's like a fish sausage. They bless it a little bit and charge a little more."

While we talk, Harley's friend Dick Powell comes in to visit and sits down. Harley explains to him what we're up to and says, "You'll get bored to death here with this."

Dick says Harley is just trying to get rid of him so he can tell yarns. "He may hear about this later is the problem—like at drinks," Dick says. Actually, he adds, exaggeration is not in Harley's nature.

I ask Harley about Lake Superior storms.

"It gets pretty rough," he says. "Oh, yah. I've seen some awful storms in November, December, in the wintertime. Forty-foot waves, I suppose, if you get a real big northeaster running down the whole length of the lake here."

"Are you ever out in that kind of weather?"

"Oh, God, no. You know, it's taken ore boats down. So, no, you don't want any part of that. The way we fish around here, we can get in here real quick if you have to."

Harley says the superabundant fall fishing season contrasts with the rest of the year when the fish roam around more. "They follow the feed," he says. "The plankton just goes with the current, so the fish are right behind them."

"Is there a heavy current?" I ask.

"It's no rhyme or reason to it. It's just crazy, but it can get real strong. Yah. It runs like a river. It'll run five miles an hour." Harley says there's no telling which way the current is going to run, and it might run differently in different areas. "It'll put you out of business sometimes," he says. He explains that a heavy current sometimes drags the nets into a wishbone or worse, they end up running with the current instead of across the current. In either case, he says, "you're missing a lot of fish."

Dick interrupts us. "You're missing some very fertile ground to plow here," he tells me. "He's made rescues out here. He'll be more modest than you want him to be."

Harley: "Oh, no. I haven't really done any rescues."

Dick: "Well, you rescued me."

Harley: "Yah, I guess so."

Dick: "I was doing my father-in-law's ashes out there. The prop fell off the boat, and my ancient, ninety-year-old stepfather and I were marooned out there. Harley had to come out and rescue us."

A few years ago, Dick says, Harley "braved the seas" to try to rescue two kayakers who got caught beyond the big breakwaters in ten-foot seas and overturned. "He would never tell you that," Dick says of Harley who, when pressed, recalls the incident: "It was about this time of year. The water was real cold. Somebody spotted them out there. They tipped their kayak over. They were hollering out there, waving their arms and stuff. So then I went out."

He found only one man.

Dick coaxes the story along. "He was so big and heavy and waterlogged, with all that freeboard, couldn't get him in the boat."

"I got him up alongside," Harley says. Even though he's hefty, he couldn't heave the man on board. "So I took a rope and tied him up high there and just brung him into shore."

Dick adds, "He ended up down to Duluth, where he died."

"Hypothermia," Harley says. "He was in just a little bit too long."

The body of the second man was found two days later.

Dick says of Harley, who apparently is not seduced by attention, "He's probably one of my best friends up here, and I'll be in enough trouble for this, but he's a very modest man. He will tell you exactly what you ask him."

Harley says, "You can't get in trouble that way. You don't want to offer any extra."

"I'd like to get the extra," I say.

"Take him down to the tavern," Dick says.

Harley is less reserved when talking about the fishery on the Minnesota north shore. He can't fish for herring during the November spawn or lake trout at any time because the state is essentially managing lake trout and salmon as "a sport fishery." The herring fit into this scenario as food for both, so fishing during the spawning season is curtailed. Harley says there are only twenty commercial licenses on the entire Minnesota north shore. "That's a lot of water out there," he says, adding about the fishery: "The commercial fishermen aren't hurting it any. It's overregulated. No new people want into it. It's pretty hard to make a living at it." But he and Shele manage.

"Do you have a good life?" I ask.

"It's kind of a work farm," he says, "but we like it."

The next morning, I join Shele and a crew of four in the shed where they process the roe collected the day before. Everybody wears the uniform of the day in this operation—rubber gear like the fishermen, plus hairnets. Processing herring eggs is largely a cleaning operation. Herring eggs are the size of birdshot, and they are in a transparent membrane the size of a forefinger. One worker puts them into a tumbler with tongs that circle like a drive shaft and break down the sacs. It takes ten minutes. Then the eggs and the now stringy pieces of membrane are dumped onto a vibrator that functions like a flat sieve. The eggs drop through, while the filaments of membrane get caught in the mesh. It is truly a bloody mess. After twenty minutes on the vibrator, pails of eggs go to Shele, who pours them in buckets and washes them over and over and over again. The dirty water she pours off starts out red and three washings later ends up clear.

When Shele finishes washing eggs, they are salmon pink. She spills them onto three-foot-square shallow trays lined with fine plastic mesh. She has drained out most of the water, so the eggs have more body—like cooked grits. Three workers use small rubber spatulas to work their way through the eggs, row by eighth-inch row. They look for stray scales, blood clots—"anything that ain't eggs," a woman named Tess says. "The wonderful thing about this is the color," she continues. "It makes it easy to see the stuff that don't belong." Tess moved from the Twin Cities to Grand Marais just two years ago. "I love it up here," she says. "I ain't going home." Unlike Marty, the backsplitter, she knows her product. Herring has been a big part of her family's diet for three generations. "The best fish in the world is up here, the lake is so clean."

When the pickers are finished with a bunch of eggs, they bundle them in the mesh that lines the trays and hang them up to drain overnight. The next day they will be salted (how much salt, Shele isn't saying), and packaged in 1-kilogram (2.2-pound) plastic containers. "Once they're salted, they're good," Shele says. "They really are delicious, I think." She likes them with crackers and red onions or fried with scrambled eggs or "just on your finger." She explains, "It's not like that black caviar at all. It doesn't taste anything like it." Her product sells for about $25 a pound in her market.

Washing the eggs, hosing down the floor, cleaning pails—"They're very, very clean," a worker says of the Tofteys' operation. Shele, like the men in the backsplit shed, goes through a lot of water. "You can imagine what our water bill is like," she says. At this time of year, it's $1,500 a month. That goes with a $500 electricity bill.

Shele has been processing herring roe for three years. "It was all learning," she says of the outset. "It's taken us three years to get it down pat." The crew finishes this day's cleaning operation by eleven o'clock. In November, when the Canadian fish come in, the crew of five will blossom to more than twelve people just to do the picking, and it's a labor that will stretch to the end of the year. Shele says, "It's a lot of work. Nonstop. Nonstop. I look forward to New Year's Eve. We close."

Shele is a small woman but flinty, given to laughter and gesture. She says she has been casting nets and trawling since she was fourteen. "I always knew I wanted to be a fisherperson." She was born in 1957 in Astoria, Oregon, and started fishing for salmon and sturgeon in the Columbia River in 1971, helping out on a fishing boat owned by the family of her childhood sweetheart. She and her boyfriend parted waves, but Shele found a new love, Alaska, in 1982, when she started pursuing halibut and black cod, and later salmon and three kinds of crab. At the time, Alaska had a halibut "derby"—one or two days set aside for halibut fishing. Typically, boats trailed twenty miles of "long lines," and it wasn't unusual to catch one hundred thousand pounds of halibut in those frenzied hours, which were preceded by long days of preparation, mostly baiting twenty to thirty thousand hooks with saltwater herring, octopus, or squid. At the start of the derby, it was "set your gear, set your gear, set your gear," Shele says. Then turn around and haul in the lines, which were the diameter of an extension cord and anchored to the bottom, three hundred to six hundred feet deep. The derbies ran for either twenty-four or forty-eight hours. "You're up the whole time. There's no sleep for almost two or three days."

There were derbies two or three times a year. The one- or two-day window of opportunity was set in stone, and the boats went out for those derbies, come rain or come shine. "It can be flat calm, or it can be storming, blowing eighty. You're going to fish because that's the date. That's why they called it a derby—it's fast and furious and you get in there and get it over with." A lot of lives were lost. "Stuff happened," is Shele's way of putting it. Now, quotas are set, and boats can take their time to fill them. "You can pick and choose when to go out. It's such a safer fishery now."

In those earlier years, a person on the deck crew got paid by the "share"—that is, a percentage of the value of the catch. Shele started out as a "half-share" hand—"because I was a girl." If another crew member made $10,000 on a halibut derby, she earned $5,000. She says there was no rookie hazing. The initiation was just seasickness from reeling boats in rough seas. She managed to get full-share status eventually. "I was ambitious, and I wanted to be there. You have to make that extra effort. They can see you're trying hard. You're baiting hooks fast. You're doing things fast, so I made it a competition—try to keep up with the guys or do better than them."

Shele spent one season fishing for king crab in the Bering Sea. The crews numbered five to seven. The deck duty involved maneuvering crab pots that weighed seven hundred to nine hundred pounds. Crabbing, she says, "is a dangerous catch." After her first run, "I could scoot a nine-hundred-pound crab pot by myself." And this is no amazon talking. At the time, she was the only woman crab fisher in an Alaskan crab fleet of perhaps eighty boats. She says about her crabbing days, "Endurance and caution is always on your mind. Everybody is kind of looking out for each other on those boats." Crew members carried knives to disentangle themselves if they got caught in ropes and went overboard.

Shele never went overboard but she has lost some friends. "Oh, yeah." She pauses a moment, then says the victims include that first boyfriend of long ago. "The boat just disappeared. It was full of crab pots—possibly overloaded. Bad weather. Not a Mayday. Nothing. It was just gone. The crew and everybody."

How do you keep your footing in rough seas, with decks awash? I ask.

"You get used to it," she says. "You get sea legs. You're alright when you're out on the boats. You're fine. So then, when you get onshore, and you take a shower, you just about fall over. Swear to God. Yes."

"Flat and steady were disorienting?"

"In water like that—taking a shower. You just get totally disoriented."

Shele is superstitious. "For fishing, I am." To avoid bad luck, she makes sure that her coffee cup is hung the right way (upside down "so the water doesn't fill it up"). Duffel bags are okay, but no suitcases ("Oh, yeah, that's big-time"). "Never whistle on a boat." "Never turn the boat around to pick your hat up." Gone are the days, though, when a woman couldn't set foot on a boat without cursing it by her very presence. "If you prove yourself, you fit right in," Shele says. The crabbing crew was made up of young people "with good, strong power" and older people with "experience"—both of them, it turned out, fair-minded.

The longest shift she ever pulled was four days sandwiched around one two-hour nap. "Forty-eight hours is doable. Seventy-two hours is hard. You're tired. You're numby. You're not working efficiently, but you've gotta keep going." Shele says the long shifts sometimes made her wonder, "What the hell am I doing out here? This is torture."

The trip to shore, though, was halcyon. "The one thing that I really remember is when you're done with the fishery—coming in, running in—on those beautiful calm days, you'd sit on top of the bait shed or somewhere, just sitting on the top of the boat, and thinking, 'I wonder what everybody else in the world is doing today.' Because it was just so beautiful out, so magnificent out, just peaceful. You felt—oh, I don't' know—just lucky to be where you're at. Especially to be alive."

She doesn't vaunt herself or her courage. "I don't think people realize that that's your job—that's what you do." She says it's no different than being an ironworker or coal miner. "You go to work. You do your job."

After unloading, sometimes they turned around and went right back out. "Hopefully, you get a day in town." Take a walk. Socialize. See how everybody was doing. Hit the bars. "I've always been a vodka drinker."

She met Harley in Egigig, Alaska, in 1990. In the river, the boats could "go dry." Shele explains that the boats would be tied up together to hold each other up on the mudflats when twenty-foot tides went out. One day Harley tied up to Shele's boat. "He flirted," Shele recalls, and it worked. She "jumped ship" and went to work on Harley's boat. They finished the season and then she went back to Oregon, and he to Grand Marais. They visited. She moved to Grand Marais in 1991, and they married and opened the market in 1998.

"You're a go-getter," I tell Shele.

"I have to be. There's no choice. Otherwise the fish rot."

"What drives you?"

"I don't know. Unfortunately, it's the only thing I know how to do. I mean, I'd rather be out fishing on the boat every day, but we've got to keep going and working. Do what you do."

Midmorning, I walk to the shed where the men are processing the herring. "How was the lake?" I ask Marty.

"Flat calm," he says. "We like it flat calm." Cold, though. "Frost every morning this time of year."

He reports that they finished salting the herring about eight o'clock the night before.

"You put in a twelve-hour day," I remark.

"Fourteen," he says, "but who's counting?"

That means he earned about $300. "We work for it a little bit," Marty says.

They filled twenty seventy-five-gallon barrels with salted fish. Marty uses a forklift to load pallets of them onto a refrigerated semitrailer. Later, Harley puts forty-two containers of caviar into a blast freezer, which is set at twenty degrees below zero ("You don't want to get locked in there," he says). The eggs need to be frozen "quickly."

Harley is one of only three fishermen working out of Grand Marais. The other two, the old Eckel brothers, fish for herring only in the fall. Dick Eckel was born in Grand Marais in 1931 and grew up fishing for trout and herring. He has been fishing since he was a young boy. I visit with him in the processing shed.

I tell him that I've heard that lake trout from different reefs look different. "Definitely," Dick affirms. They have a different look and size—"just like they don't want to associate with each other." Years ago, he says, some old-timers claimed there were twenty-five subspecies of lake trout in Lake Superior alone.

Dick started fishing on his own out of Grand Marais in 1955, when he was twenty-four. He fished for an uncle out of Washington Harbor on the west end of Isle Royale for twenty-one years. He also fished for salmon in Alaska for fifteen years. He had a 32-foot aluminum boat there and it was close quarters. "We lived on that boat—snarling at each other after two weeks." He made $147,000 one year. Then he built a $150,000 crab boat, 103 feet long, and fished for crab in Alaskan waters for nine years. He grossed $200,000 in a month. These days, back in his home waters, he is one of the few fishermen permitted by the Minnesota Department of Natural Resources (DNR) to target lake trout in September and October, for purposes of the DNR's assessment of the fishery. Add to that the fall herring season. He sums up his current career: "I putz around and play a little bit."

As overseer for the Interlaken operation, Dick says that the backsplits are a sideshow. The roe is the main feature. "They wouldn't be buying these fish if they didn't have the eggs in them," he says.

I ask him whether there are as many fish now as when he was young.

Not even a shadow of the past's plenty, he says. When he was young, there were three hundred fishermen on Minnesota's north shore alone, between Duluth and Grand Portage. "You could throw floats from one boat to the other, they were so close." At that time, he adds, the biggest herring fishery in all of the Great Lakes was on Minnesota's north shore, where Norwegian fishermen settled. The way of life was "Live off the land. Fish. Shoot a moose or a deer. Grow some potatoes," he says. "Now we wait for the tourists"—Harley calls them "leaf watchers"—"to come and spend their money."

Grand Marais is French for big marsh. Indians call Grand Marais Kitchibitobig, which means a double body of water—that is, lake and marsh. With a population of two thousand, it is a tourist town, but there is a blue-collar aspect. Carl, one of the roe pickers, describes Grand Marais as a "fishing town, forestry town, hunting town, guiding town—however you can eat and make a buck." He himself is a fishing guide, too. "You become part of the lake up here," he says.

I go to the market, upstairs from the roe shed, at road level. Inside, there is a picture of a man at a helm, with the inscription: "The Old Salt Gathering Place—where sailors of yesteryear recount their adventures and tell tall tales." On the wall by the counter there is an old ship's clock mounted inside a brass porthole frame. Hanging on the wall above the entry is a thirty-one-pound lake trout that Shele's father caught off Grand Marais while visiting in 1998.

The store is a model of cleanliness, a miracle of supply. Crab, squid, shrimp, and scallops. Tuna loins that look like thick, boneless steaks. Many fresh and smoked fish, including herring, halibut, lake trout, steelhead, sockeye salmon, Coho salmon, chinook salmon, whitefish, and walleye. Prices vary—$5 a pound for fresh herring, $12 a pound for walleye, $19 a pound for Copper River sockeye salmon out of Prince William Sound. (These are bloodred. "They're beautiful," Shele says. "The premium of the premium.") Her steelhead and Atlantic salmon are farm raised.

"Do farm fish taste different than wild fish?" I ask.

"Most people wouldn't know the difference, but in any fish you can tell. You know by the price, for starters."

Most of her fish is from Alaska and the East and West coasts, and it reaches Grand Marais from "out of the cities" (a common term for Minneapolis–St. Paul), two hundred miles to the southwest, from which she gets two or three deliveries a week. Herring come from her own waters. Walleye come from Canadian inland lakes. Whitefish come from "across the lake," Bayfield, Wisconsin. Shele's own favorite fish is sturgeon from the Columbia River.

Shele also sells caviar, cheese, fish spreads—and all kinds of condiments, such as pepper jelly and a horseradish spiced with cucumber, chives, and lingonberry.

Shele and Harley were partners with Dick when they opened the fish market. The couple wanted kids and realized they needed a more stable business and family life. The kind of business was never in doubt—"something pertaining to fish, and what we knew how to do," Shele says. That first year of retail business, Harley was still in Alaska, so she and Dick set nets, picked nets, and ran the store by themselves for half of the summer. "She's good out on the boat," Dick says of Shele.

At the outset, their place was cramped. In 2002, they expanded. The old space is now a small office and kitchen. The new space accommodates two large display cases, a counter, shelves, a small deli, a gift shop, and tables and chairs to seat eighteen. In 2004, Harley and Shele bought out Dick. Shele says that the market is vital—that she and Harley couldn't make a living just fishing.

Besides walk-in customers, she sells herring to restaurants in town. Restaurants are good business but, she says, "It doesn't support us in the winter. That's why we close." From December through March, Harley manages snowmobile trails, and Shele works as a waitress and bartender.

I sit with Shele in her small office. Her day has gone from busy to frenetic. "I'm so far behind I'll never get caught up," she says about her paperwork. On a shelf above where I am sitting, there's a fifth of Canadian whisky, which Harley favors. Shele says his nickname is Captain Windsor. After a half hour of phone calls and paying bills, she says abruptly, "I gotta cook."

It's noon, and she prepares several orders of fried, skinless, herring fillets and serves them with french fries and a tartar sauce that she makes herself. She is prepared to serve several fish, but orders are usually for herring and walleye. Normally, she has on hand halibut cheeks, which are bigger than a silver dollar, but the halibut season is over and she's out. "The halibut cheeks are just the best," she says. "They're so tender."

"How big are they?"

"Oh, they can be little guys . . . or they can be huge. They can get two or three in a pound."

Eyes?

"No. Just cheeks. Halibut cheeks. Walleye cheeks. Salmon cheeks. They're a delicacy. Great." They go for $15 a pound fresh, $17 a pound smoked.

Shele throws out very little. "Each fish has its own shelf life. You can tell by what it looks like, how fresh." They run out of herring before it goes bad. Lake trout and salmon are more "delicate." Generally, Shele says, "Four days is still really good. Five days is okay. But you don't want to go past that. It gets fishy." The old fish go from the shelf to the smoker. Smoked fish are good for ten to fourteen days. Shele smokes four days out of ten, three hundred pounds at a time.

After the lunch business is over, Shele tends to sales. An old man comes in and buys two small herring fillets for a buck and a half. A woman buys four big fresh lake trout fillets and two big smoked lake trout. She is from Iowa, and Shele tells her that she ships the roe there. "That's funny—landlocked Iowa," the woman says. Her bill is over a $120. When she leaves, Shele says, "I like these kinds of customers."

In between customers, she opens up boxes of plastic forks and lettuce and fish. She picks fish for display, wraps fish for orders, breaks cardboard

SHELE TOFTEY: *I gotta keep moving. It takes a whole person.*

boxes down and saves them, unpacks four- to five-pound fillets of Atlantic salmon—"Beauties." She washes each fish and fine-tunes the fillets by trimming off fat. She repeatedly washes her hands, and she eats on the run.

"You go like crazy," I tell her.

"Oh, I know. I gotta keep moving. It takes a whole person."

She's been busier. In July and August, she says, "I really don't get a break."

The key to success? "Good employees. Otherwise, I wouldn't be able to keep going."

Shele says Grand Marais is a place she has come to love. "Next to Alaska, this is the best thing. It's like living near the ocean."

3
STURGEON
A River on the Keweenaw Peninsula

> If you ever had a chance to look into the eyes of a sturgeon, there are unfathomable depths there that take you back millennia; they take you back ages and ages ago. And having looked into the eyes of a sturgeon, you can fully understand that these animals swam practically unchanged from the way they are today when dinosaurs walked the earth.
>
> Christopher Letts, *Sturgeon: Ancient Survivors of the Deep*

Not long before he died, Jacques Cousteau went to the bottom of Lake Superior at its deepest. What might he have seen? "Probably a whole lot of not much," says biologist Nancy Auer. The reason? The big lake is nutrient poor and fairly sterile. What nutrients enter the lake, Nancy says, are dispersed and quickly diluted. "We wouldn't expect to come up with huge numbers of fish."

But there are small numbers of a particularly big fish: lake sturgeon, which Nancy has studied since 1987. She does this as a researcher at Michigan Technological University. She calls her work "poking around." Science suits her, for she has a deliberate manner appropriate for inquiry. She has a tranquil nature, but she is a person of drive and accomplishment. Besides her sturgeon work, for instance, she edited and cowrote the book on identifying fishes in their larval stage. It's 744 pages long and includes every species of fish in the Great Lakes—an enterprise, one colleague says, for which Nancy doesn't get enough recognition. For her part, she feels "lucky"—even "blessed"—to have the opportunity to study both larval fish and sturgeon—one diminutive, one big and bulky.

I accompany Nancy on a foray to a local river in search of lake sturgeon. She doesn't want to name the watercourse because she fears poaching. The river, a hundred feet wide, runs wine dark. It is 120 miles long and we are 45 miles upstream. Nancy, as sure-footed as she is soft-spoken, directs her students, who do the netting. The students remind each other to net the fish nose first. "Touch the tail and they take off like a torpedo," one says. Over the course of three hours, they net eight fish, which range in size from twenty-four to sixty-eight pounds, from fourteen to twenty inches in girth, and from fifty to sixty-five inches long. Nancy and another biologist measure and weigh the fish, collect a blood sample, clip a fin for genetic analysis, and put two tags on, one electronic. Then they collect milt and eggs. Of the eight fish caught, one has a round lamprey scar the size of a nickel. Another has a long white scar on its head—probably from a propeller cut. "They repair very well," Nancy says. One thing she doesn't want to do: an autopsy. "We try not to kill," she says, because these fish may be big and old, but they are in "a tenuous state."

One hundred years ago, lake sturgeon were bountiful. According to one account, Indians claimed that when lake sturgeon spawned in the spring on Upper Michigan's Ontonagon River, "You could almost walk across the river on their backs." Natives called these sturgeon "the buffalo of the water," and they ate them, made soup from the cartilaginous backbone, savored the brains and belly as delicacies, and fashioned arrowheads from the tailbone.

Pioneer traveler Johann Kohl wrote a book in 1860 called *Kitchi-gami: Wanderings around Lake Superior. Kitchi-gami* is Ojibwe for big water. Kohl, a colorful and congenial writer, marveled at how rich Lake Superior is in "peculiar varieties of fish." He singled out the sturgeon, which afforded the Ojibwe both sustenance and legend. French explorers reported that the Ojibwe (Kohl spells the name Ojibbeways) called the sturgeon the *poisson blanc,* white fish, because of its savory white flesh; they also called it "devilish." The Ojibwe, Kohl writes, had a mythical hero, Menaboujou, who was a demigod, a great brave and chief, the discoverer of how to make sugar, the kinsman of the animals, and the inventor of the canoe. The belief among the Ojibwe was that a sturgeon ate Menaboujou, canoe and all, and so the fish frequently represented "the evil principle" in native lore. Thus, the fish represented at the same time both manna and malevolence.

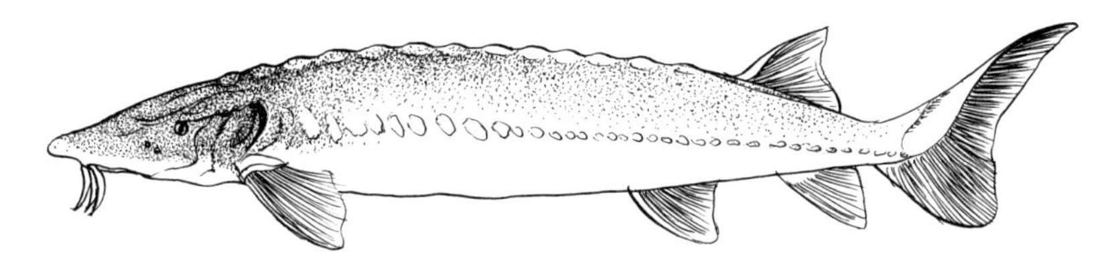

LAKE STURGEON. (Drawing by Sandy Slater.)

The Ojibwe both fished and hunted for food and therefore were called by the French *gens du lac* and *gens du terre,* people of the lake and people of the land. Kohl writes that among Indians he heard "magic" songs for hunting "the animals of the chase" but no songs to invoke success in fishing for "the finny brood." Nevertheless, the sturgeon "may be called the daily bread of the fisherman on this lake; for it is, in the first place, the most abundant, and may be caught the whole year through; and then it is the most wholesome sort of fish, and has a very agreeable taste. The meat is snow-white, and, when carefully boiled, rather flaky, though never dry. You can eat it for breakfast, dinner, and supper, without growing surfeited—especially when cooked by Indian women, for they manage to serve it up deliciously . . . and if it should happen to be watery, or over-boiled, the severe head of the house is sure to give the squaw a hint."

Kohl's main objective in writing about the sturgeon was to describe what he called "the human art and guile" by which the Indians caught the fish. They used hook, net, and spears that were up to forty feet long. "They handle them so cleverly that their prey, Lake Sturgeon, which they fetch up from such a depth, rarely escapes them. Of course this is only possible in such transparent waters as that of Lake Superior."

If Indians relied on sturgeon for subsistence, early settlers and commercial fishermen considered lake sturgeon a scrap fish with little food or commercial value; they used, as one contemporary said, "neither skin nor scale." At the time, sturgeon were not even worth throwing back; fishermen routinely buried them onshore, used them for fertilizer, or dried and burned them as firewood. Lake sturgeon eggs were fed to hogs.

In time, though, lake sturgeon came to have much utilitarian value. The skin was tanned to make an ornamental leather or bookbinding. The air bladder, which made a good gelatin for pottery and for waterproofing, was also dried to make isinglass to clarify jellies, beer, and wine. The oil was a lubricant, and the gristly skeleton made good glue. These days, it also is prized as a game fish because of its strength, size, and speed. The sturgeon's premier association, though, is with its unfertilized black eggs. Treated with salt, they make caviar, which has been called "black gold."

Lake sturgeon became a source for caviar in the mid-1800s; by 1860, they were smoked and sold as a substitute for halibut; by 1880 they constituted a major fishery; by 1890 they were in serious decline; and by 1920 they were considered virtually extinct. A telling statistic: the combined Canadian and American catch in the Great Lakes shrunk from nearly 6 million pounds between 1885 and 1889 to 44,000 pounds between 1985 and 1989. A fish that has survived for ages nearly succumbed in one hundred years.

Sturgeon are a thing of beauty to Nancy, but they are a curious sight. They have a big snout, no teeth, four fleshy barbels the size of wood matchsticks for a mustache, and a mouth that hangs down from the underside of the head. Nancy calls the mouth "protrusible"; extended, it looks like a truncated vacuum hose. From a head-on perspective, these fish look like a triangle—a wide flat bottom that angles up to a pointy back. Their white bottom contrasts with their sides and back, which vary from tawny to gray to black. "You wonder where they come from, there is such a difference," Nancy says. The barbels allow them to identify organic matter—"tell food from rocks, essentially." These bottom feeders eat small fish, clams, snails, organic debris, worms, insects, lamprey, salmon roe—"almost anything that comes along," says one biologist.

Anatomically, sturgeon are an oddity. They don't have flesh covering a skeleton; rather, they have bone covering flesh. A rope of cartilage, called a notochord, serves as a backbone. Bony plates—Nancy calls them "scutes"—line the back, both lateral lines, the bottom sides, and the head. The scutes are said to be "as dangerous as a bag full of razors" when the fish is young and most vulnerable. "They're going to discourage most anything from eating it or touching it," Nancy says. Sturgeon, she explains, "are built pretty good" for their start in life. As the fish mature, the scutes remain, but they become blunt—but no matter, because by then the sturgeon are too large for other fish to eat. Another distinctive feature of the sturgeon is its tail fin; the upper lobe is much bigger than the lower lobe. This characteristic is a mark of antiquity—sturgeon are at the same evolutionary level as sharks and "are some of the earliest fishes," Nancy says.

The oldest sturgeon fossils date back 60 million to 100 million years, to the last days of the dinosaurs. The oldest lake sturgeon fossil is estimated to be about 2 million years old, but lake sturgeon were around for a long time before that.

Depending on who's doing the categorizing and the counting, today there are about thirty species of sturgeon worldwide, all in the Northern Hemisphere. Nine of the species are endemic to North America. The white sturgeon of the Pacific Northwest is the continent's largest sturgeon resource, second only to the famed beluga sturgeon native to Asia's Black and Caspian seas and their watersheds. The white sturgeon's cousin, the lake sturgeon, is native to Hudson Bay, the St. Lawrence River, the Great Lakes, and the Mississippi River. Lake sturgeon are small fry compared to the white sturgeon and the beluga sturgeon, which can reach two thousand pounds. Lake sturgeon reach two hundred pounds, are from three to six feet long, and live seventy-five to a hundred years. The largest lake sturgeon ever caught—in

1943 in Lake Michigan—weighed 310 pounds and measured just shy of eight feet. Lake sturgeon are also called freshwater sturgeon, rock sturgeon, bony sturgeon, and smoothback sturgeon. They are an eyeful when you can spot one—they are elusive.

On the south shore of Lake Superior, only two rivers, one in Upper Michigan and one in northern Wisconsin, have sturgeon populations. Overall, commercial fishing, pollution, habitat degradation, and the construction of dams have greatly reduced sturgeon numbers. Today their populations are said to be only "remnants" of what they once were.

Other than the actions of humans, the sturgeon's Achilles' heel is its life history. In contrast to modern fish—which mature quickly, are relatively short-lived, and produce massive numbers of offspring to perpetuate the species—sturgeon produce few offspring and bank on a long life, rather than reproduction, to maintain the species. Slowpokes in this regard, sturgeon take longer than any other species of North American freshwater fish to reach sexual maturation. Males spawn at eleven to twenty-two years, females at eleven to thirty-four years. Even after attaining maturity, they are not prolific reproducers, spawning only once every four to seven years, rather than annually. Their natural mortality rate after the first few years is extremely low, for—given their size and the makeup of their body, which is a redoubt—few things, including old age, can kill them. Nevertheless, they are easy prey during their spawning season, when they congregate in large numbers in rivers. Once a sturgeon population declines, it's been said, the fish will take so long to recover that "the decline seems permanent in terms of human life spans."

Sturgeon eggs are smaller than green peas and number in the hundreds of thousands in one fish. But the numbers deceive, for sturgeon offspring are few. The reason, says Nancy, is a "10 percent" rule in ecology—for example, four thousand eggs yield four hundred larvae, which yield forty juveniles, which yield four adults. After all the mortality, Nancy says, "One fish barely replaces itself."

The fertilized eggs are broadcast on the river bottom and fall between boulders and cobbles. Sticky, they adhere to the substrate, where they incubate for two weeks, absorb their yoke sacs, and then drift downstream in the dark of night, for they are light phobic. It takes a month and a half for them to travel the forty-five miles down the local river. At that stage in their lives, Nancy points out, they are 1.3 inches long and look like adult fish. And they are rare. Finding them is like searching for hen's teeth; it took Nancy a decade of netting to capture enough larvae to get data to present to her colleagues. She calls the larvae "these little guys" and says that once they hit the lake, they wander into obscurity. For, from that point on, and for the next twenty-five years it takes them to mature and spawn, information about their whereabouts and ways is sketchy. "There's a gap in our knowledge," Nancy explains.

Most of what is known about this species relates to adult sturgeon because they make themselves available for study when they spawn. "Everybody's been looking at what keys spawning," Nancy says. "It's always in the spring, and it's always after ice-out." On the river where she works, these fish take eight to ten days to reach spawning grounds—a destination that one biologist calls "the magical location." There are always fewer females, and more than one male attends a spawning female—a circumstance that another biologist calls "a very high 'buck to doe' ratio." The resulting genetic mix keeps the populations healthy, Nancy says.

Nancy has tagged more than a thousand adult sturgeon over the course of her labors. The adults, she says, have "a diverse array" of meanderings. Some have gone 150 miles east, some 160 miles west. They have reached Misery Bay, Keweenaw Bay, Munising Bay, Bete Grise, and the waters off Marquette, Michigan, and Ashland, Wisconsin. "They are drawn to bays and discharge areas," Nancy points out. When it comes to food, she adds, "They're a big search machine out there."

Scientists believe that lake sturgeon return to natal areas to spawn; Nancy says, "Fidelity to such streams is high." Some sturgeon may spawn on the wave-washed shores of the Great Lakes, but documentation of that behavior, Nancy says, "is historic and incomplete."

Michigan's DNR has collected milt and eggs for rearing stock at its Wild Rose Hatchery. The state agency has been planting this hatchery stock in the Ontonagon River, on the bottom of the Keweenaw. In 2007, the agency switched to streamside rearing there. The public catches sturgeon in the twelve-inch range. Restocking programs require the patience of a forester waiting for a tree to grow: given the sturgeon's mating habits, it takes twenty to thirty years before researchers know whether a stocking works. Nevertheless, the fish's ultimate survival might hinge on such efforts, biologists say. Another option is to transplant the fish, but that prospect might be unworkable. Nancy notes that there is a definite "genetic signal" in each population of sturgeon; there are differences between the fish in the two river systems with self-sustaining populations in Michigan and Wisconsin. Research shows that there are different movement patterns between native lake sturgeon spawned in a river and those raised in a hatchery. Another hitch: hatchery fish tend to be bigger than natives, Nancy says, and there's a worry that they will outcompete natural fish for space.

NANCY AUER: *We know so little. There's a gap in our knowledge.*
(Photo courtesy of Michigan Technological University.)

The sturgeon's own vulnerable life history "complicates" but doesn't "negate" recovery efforts, Nancy says. She outlines several important steps for that endeavor: identifying populations, their size, and their range; ensuring access up rivers to spawning grounds; protecting spawning grounds; and removing dams and weirs—or, short of that, building passages that will allow fish to migrate upstream.

One plus is that sturgeon appear to be adaptable and durable. Lake sturgeon from central Wisconsin's Lake Winnebago have taken five to eight years to get as far as Lake Huron and Lake Erie. To do that, those fish had to pass over or through seventeen locks and fourteen dams on the Fox River just to reach Lake Michigan. Nancy's work might give them an easier time of it. Recovery efforts will be a complicated affair involving the federal governments of the United States and Canada, eight states and two provinces that border the Great Lakes, twelve American Indian tribes, many Canada First Nations, and an array of private interests.

Nancy concludes that lots of work needs to be done with this fish of long past but uncertain future. "We know so little." But she is encouraged: "With time and effort, the lake sturgeon can be restored to greater prominence in the Great Lakes ecosystem and possibly sustain some aboriginal, sport, and commercial fisheries."

For they are delectable fare. Sturgeon, asserts one writer, is so good eating because it has a layer of flesh, then a layer of fat, and then another layer of flesh. It is like that throughout and makes a good meal.

That reminds me of an old cowboy I met in Colorado who barbecued the beef for a small-town summer festival. He said he used the front quarters instead of hindquarters. Why? For the same reason that the sturgeon is good—the front quarter of beef has a layer of meat, then a layer of fat, then a layer of meat. It is also like that throughout and makes for a good barbecue. The hindquarter, on the other hand, is marbled with fat instead of layered.

"Why," I asked the cowboy, "is the front quarter different from the hindquarter?"

"I don't know," he answered. "That's just the way the critter puts it on."

4
The Fable and the Fate of *la Truite de Lac*
Marquette, Michigan

Lake Superior, like other northern waters, is so cold that a unique species of fish has evolved: the fur-bearing trout. The fish has a normal head and fins; the rest of its body is covered with hair as white as that of a snowshoe rabbit in winter. According to one account, "The creature is sometimes referred to as the Beaver Trout, or (incorrectly) as the Sabled Salmon."

The name aside, a number of theories try to explain the emergence of this curious species. Some say the creature evolved its thick fur coat to protect it from extreme cold water. Others suggest that the fish first appeared in Colorado when a Kentucky hair-tonic salesman, on his way to a logging camp with an inordinate number of bald-headed lumberjacks, accidentally dropped two bottles of his potion into the Arkansas River. The bottles broke, and thus was born the "pelted piscatorial prize." The appearance of the fur-bearing trout has been affirmed by many witnesses, including Rocky Mountain characters named Narrow-Gauge Ed, Agate Creek Andy, Harrison Hickoryhead—and Texas Creek Tess, a Coloradoan described as a "one-time impresario of the naughty can-can at the Owl Ear Bar." Another eyewitness was Willy Axletree, who asserted that the hair-tonic story is a bald-faced prevarication. The fur-bearing trout came about, he said, when the trout started cavorting with silver foxes on moonlit nights in the Colorado high country.

Wherever and however they appeared, proof of their existence hangs on a wall in the Royal Scottish Museum in Edinburgh. There, plain as day, hangs a stuffed fur-bearing lake trout. A wood plaque points out that the fish was caught in Lake Superior near Sault Ste. Marie, year unknown. It is uncertain how the trout migrated from Colorado to Upper Michigan. That they did, though, stretches the imagination of the skeptics who scoff at the notion of a fur-bearing trout. Others avow that their existence is as certain as the fact that Paul Bunyan scooped out Lake Superior for drinking water for Babe the Blue Ox.

Lake trout, of whatever ilk, are the largest of trout. They are also the least colorful, ranging from light green to gray and dark green to black. They are dotted with white spots, and the belly matches the color of the spots. They grow slowly but are long-lived. Typically, they reach seventeen to twenty-seven inches in length but are known to exceed four feet. They routinely weigh in at three to nine pounds but are known to exceed one hundred pounds. The biggest one caught by a sport fisherman in Lake Superior weighed just shy of sixty-five pounds. The lake trout prefers cold water—forty to fifty-two degrees—and its range extends throughout Alaska, Canada, and the Great Lakes region. This natural niche is described by biologists as "cold, clean, infertile waters."

There are roughly ninety species of fish in Lake Superior (including bays and nearshore water); forty-four are native. Besides the lake trout, other major natives include the burbot (freshwater cod), herring, walleye, northern pike (the "water wolf"), bass, yellow perch, muskellunge, whitefish, lake sturgeon, and both the longnose and white sucker.

The lake trout are at the top of the food chain. In 1800, they lived in all the Great Lakes, usually associated with the lakes' many reefs. Some of these fish adapted to a specific reef's water depth and temperature cycles, and they differed from the more general population in looks and sometimes even in behavior. According to an exhibit at a visitor's center near Ashland, Wisconsin, "Fishermen could often tell which reef a fish came from by just looking at it." There are many names for lake trout: redfin, moss trout, salmon trout, yellowfin, Beaver Island trout, Mackinaw trout, forktail trout, grey trout, lake char, laker, land-locked salmon, mackinaw, mountain trout, lean trout, fat trout, and humper trout (also called paperbelly). French Canadians called this fish *le truite de lac* (lake trout) and *truite grise* (gray trout).

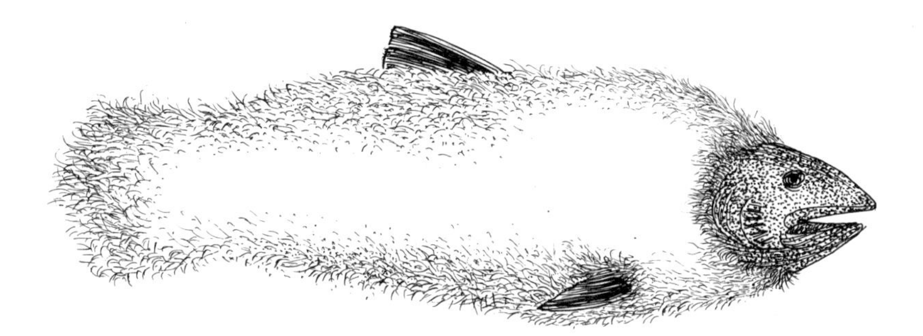

THE FUR-BEARING TROUT. (Drawing by Sandy Slater.)

Fishermen coming to Lake Superior thought there were enough lake trout to last to the end of the world. Starting in the late 1800s, there was heavy fishing pressure on herring, whitefish, and especially lake trout, which sustained both a good sport fishery and a commercial fishery. In 1920, there were 1,350 fishermen on Lake Superior. In the 1940s, the commercial trout harvest totaled 20 million pounds. The fishery bottomed out in the 1950s. The culprits were overfishing and sea lamprey—two woes that virtually wiped out lake trout in all the Great Lakes except Superior, where they were merely decimated.

Biologists have called sea lamprey "the vampire of the Great Lakes." Indians called lake trout, a voracious feeder, "the tyrant of the lakes." When the twain first met, vampire vanquished tyrant. A saltwater parasite, sea lamprey reached Lake Superior in 1938, six years after the Welland Ship Canal opened. They targeted lake trout because they swam atop the food chain, were big, and had no armor of flinty scales to deter this predation; thus, they constituted a sumptuous "blood meal."

Sea lamprey (there are small, native lamprey in the lake) are part of a tale of exotics in Superior that goes full circle. Lamprey attacked the most abundant fish, lake trout. When trout numbers declined, smelt, another exotic, became the most populous fish in Superior. Then yet another exotic, salmon, was introduced to Lake Superior in the early 1960s, to the glee of sport fishermen. With lake trout teetering, salmon initially thrived, partly on all the smelt. But as salmon flourished, they became the prey of the resurgent lake trout, which benefited from a lamprey-control program and fishing restrictions. "There isn't a lot of forage fish in Lake Superior," says one biologist, "so a small salmon is a dandy meal for a lake trout." The salmon population, then, was cut way back. While sport fishermen may lament that turn of events, it helped restore the lake trout fishery—so much so that today Lake Superior is the only one of the Great Lakes with a self-sustaining lake trout population.

Two biologists I have talked to regarding this reestablishment are Phil Schneeberger and James Peck. Phil is a tall, lanky, congenial fellow with a passion for fish. Jim is a retired fishery biologist whom one admirer calls "the godfather" of lake trout researchers on Lake Superior. Jim is uncomfortable with that plaudit; there are a lot of good men doing good work, he says.

Phil has always been interested in the outdoors, and a mentor interested him particularly in water and marine life. Early in his career, he was on a team of scientists that traveled to Gambia to assess the effects of building a dam on the Gambia River on the fishery, public health, economics, and wildlife. Phil was in the aquatic group. He and his colleagues studied fish from the estuary

PHIL SCHNEEBERGER: *Fish are amazing. They do all kinds of stuff.*

to the headwaters. He saw so many different and fascinating kinds of fish that he was in awe. "Oh, it was absolutely fantastic," he recalls. One species was called the electric catfish. "It looks like a typical catfish with the whiskers and everything. But the body, it looks completely puffy, and because of the insulation it has developed around itself, it creates an electric field between, like, its head and tail. And it uses it offensively and defensively. There are quite a few, actually, electric fish over there. A lot of 'em use it as radar because the water is so murky that they can't see, so they send out these electric waves and have it bounce back." He says that they use the capability both to stun prey and to ward off predators.

"How much electricity is there?" I ask.

"Well, we only caught one. So I thought to myself, well, this is my one chance to see what this thing will do. I grabbed it and you could feel the vibration. We took it out of the net, put it in a bucket, brought it back to camp, and processed it as we did all the fish. And then I was taking a series of pictures of fish against a uniform background. This fish has been out of the water for probably an hour in the African heat, well over one hundred degrees, and I'm lining it up, you know, situating it against this uniform background so that it made a good picture, and it hit me again."

The shock bowled him over. "It was great. I feel like that thing was smiling—'One last jolt!'"

I get to pondering that and later I ask another fishery biologist: "What do you suppose they called the electric catfish before they discovered electricity?"

He answers: "Probably 'the fish that knocks you on your ass.'"

This man is James Peck, now retired from the Michigan DNR. He has seen fishery research on and around Lake Superior go from a Spartan, toehold effort in the 1960s to a sophisticated, concerted program today. When he started in this business, Jim and his small crew had boats no larger than twenty feet long and no sophisticated technology such as radar, GPS, or good sonar. Now there are sufficient manpower, thirty- to fifty-foot boats outfitted well and suitable for the open lake, and computer programs for analyzing data.

DNR biologists routinely set gill nets to catch lake trout and collect such data as size, sex, age, and location. One task is to gut the fish, take the entrails to the lab, cut open the stomachs, and then record the contents. Sometimes the stomachs are empty, Jim says. The reasons vary: the fish has been in the net long enough to digest all the contents, it has regurgitated everything because of all the stress and struggle, or it has endured an enforced fast ("There isn't a lot of food in Lake Superior").

One measure of the lean pickings is what Jim calls "terrestrial input"—insects and bats and birds, which constitute part of the fish's diet in the spring and early summer.

"Birds?" I ask.

"Yah. Lake trout feed on birds. A lot of birds die crossing Lake Superior when they migrate in the spring of the year, and they make up a measurable portion—a small measurable portion—but these birds show up enough that you can actually get a measure on them in terms of frequency or weight."

"What's the most unusual thing you've found in a fish?" I ask.

"Corncobs. No jewels or money or anything like that."

I have read about other biologists who have found tin cans and ham bones, a watch and chain, rags and raw potatoes, and an open jackknife.

I tell Jim that I once caught a frisky fourteen-inch pike that had a wire leader hanging out of his mouth and a hook protruding from its belly. The hook was glazed over and there was no wound.

"Well," Jim says, "he encapsulated that foreign body. It's pretty amazing stuff—they can do that."

Phil Schneeberger, who has studied walleye in Green Bay for thirteen years, agrees. "Fish are amazing," he says. "That's one of the joys of studying them and working with them. They do all kinds of stuff."

There are two kinds of trout native to Lake Superior: brook trout, called coasters, and lake trout, of which there are three subspecies: lean trout, fat trout (or siscowets), and humper trout. "I don't know if you could see the difference," Phil says. "It takes a practiced eye." All three are distinguished mainly by fat content and habitat. The deeper the water, the more fatty the fish. Lean trout, the least fatty of the bunch, generally stick to waters shallower than 230 feet. Siscowets, the fattest (up to 50 percent of their weight is fat), are generally found at depths of 200 to 600 feet; however, there is some overlap. Humper trout, so named because of their habitat (they prefer a lake bottom with reefs, called humps), are few in number and live on isolated, offshore humps by Grand Marais, Isle Royale, and Caribou Island. Humper trout have more fat than lean trout but less fat than siscowets. "The lean trout are what most people think of as lake trout," Phil says.

Siscowets thrive in Lake Superior and are the most dominant of lake trout, comprising 70 percent of Lake Superior's predator species. They are long-lived but slow growing. Take a lean lake trout and a siscowet of the same weight, and the siscowet will be older. They are known to live forty years or more; some leans attain that age, too, but not commonly.

Siscowets range farther than lean trout. At one time it was thought they confined themselves strictly to the depths. Fish surveys, however, have shown

Jim Peck *is called the "godfather" of lake trout researchers on Lake Superior.*

that, while adapted to the cold and the deep, "they are everywhere," Jim says. Lean trout, on the other hand, generally don't wander into siscowet water. In shallower water, then, sixty feet and less, the lean trout outnumber the fat trout; one hundred feet and deeper is mainly siscowet water. But the lay of the lake bottom comes into play. Because Superior is more like a bowl than a plate, "There isn't a lot of water one hundred feet and shallower," Jim explains. "It's mostly one hundred feet and deeper. So most of Lake Superior is siscowet water. That's why they're so abundant."

In the 1980s, Jim says, siscowet demanded almost the same price as lean trout on the fish market. But its insulation is its spoiler. Pesticides lodge in fat, and siscowets, therefore, carry a load of them. When testing revealed the contaminant load, "It kind of killed the siscowet market," Jim says. The fishery was shut down.

The siscowet diet is one-third fish, one-third crustaceans, and one-third terrestrial insects and birds. Their fish diet is mainly burbot, ciscoes, chubs, sculpins, herring, and smelt.

"Can a siscowet see at six hundred feet?" I ask Jim.

"Well, one of the characteristics of a siscowet is that they have a bigger eye than a lean trout."

"Is that fact or folklore?"

"I suspect that siscowet have greater visual acuity at depths greater than lean lake trout—just because it evolved to live in that depth."

"Is there light down there?"

"It's not completely black. They've sent submersibles down there and there's fish living down there. And of course we've sampled at depths greater than six hundred feet with gill nets. Caught scads of lake trout, mostly siscowets."

More recently, Phil says, researchers have netted siscowets at the deepest part of the lake, at a depth of just more than thirteen hundred feet. "Amazing," he marvels.

The *Nature Bulletin* describes the lake trout's spawning activity. "In autumn—usually in late October—the adults come into shallow water and spawn over a gravel or rock bottom. . . . No nest is built, and there is no parental care after the eggs are laid. Lake trout eggs are among the biggest fish eggs known—about one-fifth of an inch in diameter, pale amber in color, and translucent. A twenty-four-pound female may lay fifteen thousand eggs, a small number compared with most kinds of fishes. They develop very slowly and, in late February or March, hatch out fry with large, inky black eyes and a huge yolk sac. They are transparent enough that the heart can be seen beating inside."

They spawn at night in thirty feet of water. When the nearshore water warms up, it drives the hatchlings to their preferred deeper, colder habitat. Those that survive stand a chance of getting caught by fishermen or by biologists who test the waters of Lake Superior with gill nets, which Phil describes as "a wall of twine" with different meshes to catch varying sizes of fish. For scientific purposes, biologists try to net in the same location, at the same time of year, with the same net configuration, and for the same duration.

One of the things they're trying to get a read on is movement. There are two kinds of movement: along the shore and inshore-offshore. "They move," Phil says, but movement is tough to assess. If scientists tag a fish in one management zone (spawning grounds that are considered to grow "distinct populations"), and then catch the same fish in another zone, it means it moved, but that's not necessarily the whole trip. "In the time in between, you don't know where it went," Phil says. In any event, "The chances of getting one back are slim." The work, he explains, "is too new to the Lake Superior scene. The number of tags out there isn't enough to be telltale."

One thing they look at is what Phil calls structure—the numbers of fish at different ages. The structure is supposed to look like a pyramid, with the base representing the number of small trout and the peak representing the number of large trout. Phil explains: "If you all of a sudden found that all you're catching is older fish and no younger fish coming up through the fishery—growing into it—that obviously is a real alarm signal that something is wrong—they're not reproducing, they're not recruiting, they're not growing, they're not living."

In one recent sampling, Phil and colleagues netted 6,362 fish, of which 4,200 were lake trout and 2,162 were other species. In another sampling, they netted 3,950 fish, of which 2,000 were lake trout. They examined the stomachs of 464 fish.

The trip from the depths to the surface can be a problem. Trout are one of the many freshwater fish that are what scientists call *physostomous,* which means that they have an air duct that connects their esophagus to their swim bladder. Says one writer in a publication called *The Fish Sniffer,* "This miracle of God allows these types of fishes to easily and quickly expel air so to swim as freely and effortlessly as needed anywhere in the water column."

Functioning as intended, the air bladder inflates as the fish goes down and deflates as the fish goes up. The deeper the fish, the greater the water pressure and the more gas in the air bladder. The shallower the fish, the less the water pressure and the less gas in the air bladder. The process works like a ship's ballast; Jim calls it "a buoyancy thing." However, when fishermen and researchers bring trout rapidly from the depths to the surface, the fish can't immediately adjust and they blow up like a strutting prairie chicken. "Normally," Jim explains, "the fish will move up at a rate that will allow them to remove gas from the bladder as needed. But if you bring him in a net or on a line, he doesn't have any control. He comes up so fast he can't get rid of that gas. It inflates, and he turns into a bobber." Jim adds, "I don't think I've ever seen a fish with a ruptured swim bladder, but I have seen gulls cause mortality to small fish that were released with an inflated bladder and couldn't sound sufficiently to avoid gull attacks. Sometimes researchers will deflate the swim bladder by inserting a needle or other sharp device. It is likely that these wounds cause some stress, but they likely heal eventually."

Like trees, fish have a growing season and a dormant season, and their growth rings appear on fins, scales, otoliths (ear bones), and vertebrae. Although sometimes reading the rings can be "fuzzy," otoliths are the best structure for aging long-lived fish like lake trout, which grow in all seasons except winter. However, the older and bigger the fish, the harder it is to read, because the growth lines get closer and closer together as growth slows down.

Determining age, structure, abundance—all of it is part of an effort to establish a "year after year" database for proper management. Only continual sampling will yield that knowledge; but researchers' sampling is by no means foolproof. "You can't assume that you're getting a perfect picture of the fish that are there," Phil says. "You know—we're comparing the same place, same time of year, every year, but just think how different things like the weather or anything else could be on any given sampling day. But I would say, in general, we're finding that there are a lot of younger fish—telling you that they are reproducing, growing."

Biologists and fishermen have caught lake trout with empty stomachs and with a mouthful of smelt. Such is life in the inhospitable waters of the grand lady of lakes. Go without or gorge.

5

Coaster Brook Trout

Ahmeek, Michigan, and Ashland, Wisconsin

Bill Deephouse, a retired fishery biologist, has a friendly, forthright bearing that is true—not at all like the compass that he pins to his chest when he wanders to brook or bush. "It's not the best of compasses," he says. "You can almost find any direction you want."

Bill was involved in an undertaking that proved to be equally bewildering—stocking coaster brook trout in the Gratiot River, on the Keweenaw Peninsula, near a little town called Ahmeek, which was Longfellow's name for the godlike beaver in *Song of Hiawatha*. The aim of the work: to reestablish a population that would imprint on the river and return to spawn, as many fish are inclined to do, and become a thriving population.

Coaster trout are brook trout that leave the river and spend time in Lake Superior, where they get bigger than fish confined to a creek or small stream. Brook trout spawn in the fall and hatch in the late winter or early spring, depending on the water temperature; the warmer the temperature, the faster the process, just like a vegetable garden. An increase of nine degrees—from, say, forty-two to fifty-one degrees—halves the incubation from one hundred to fifty days. When brook trout hatch, they are an inch long, live off a yolk sac, and are called fry. By fall, they are fingerlings, two to three inches long; by the following spring, they are yearlings, five or six inches long.

The Fisheries Division of the Michigan DNR has stocked the Gratiot, just upstream from the mouth, with fingerlings and yearlings. Bill was a volunteer on the crew, outfitted with electroshocking equipment, that surveyed the Gratiot each spring, looking for returning coasters. Eight years. Eight stockings. Eight shockings. All in all, nearly 237,000 fish. Nary a one, identified by a clipped fin, found.

"I thought it would be awash with fish," Bill says, "but we've never seen or heard of an adult that has come back."

Predation might be a factor. The nonnative salmonids alone that have been introduced to Lake Superior are steelhead, brown trout, Coho salmon, pink salmon, king or chinook salmon, and splake, which is a hybrid of lake trout and brook trout. These hungry fish make up what Bill calls "a whore's mixture" of big predators, which might make young coasters nothing more than a handy meal.

Some scientists, Bill says, believe there are three distinct populations of coasters on Lake Superior's north shore—those from Lake Nipigon, those from the Nipigon River, and those from Lake Superior—and that the Gratiot work perhaps used the wrong strain. "Don't ask me," this befuddled scientist says.

Native coasters once abounded in the Lake Superior basin. In the 1820s, Henry Schoolcraft wrote about two- to four-pound coasters being caught routinely. The world record is a fourteen-pounder caught in the early 1900s in the Nipigon River north of Thunder Bay, and fish in the eight- to twelve-pound range were not uncommon.

It would be nice, Bill dreams, if coasters, now "reduced to a memory," would, with a little help, rebound in sufficient numbers to sustain themselves

BILL DEEPHOUSE:
He has worked on a coaster brook trout stocking program.
We've never seen or heard of an adult that has come back.

naturally. There are no such prospects on the Gratiot, though, and Bill is dumbfounded. He sums up the results as "a deep silence." He is disappointed. He had dreamed of lunkers.

In northern Wisconsin, they're thinking a lot smaller than that. In addition to planting fingerlings, biologists are planting fertilized eggs. Henry Quinlan of Ashland works on three other coaster projects: on nearby Whittlesey Creek, around the Apostle Islands, and on Isle Royale. Whittlesey Creek is part of a national wildlife refuge popularly called "the little refuge on the Big Lake."

I meet Henry, lean and friendly, one pleasant June evening on the banks of Portage Lake in Houghton, Michigan, his stopover on the way from Ashland to Isle Royale to monitor a coaster population there. He and three colleagues are set to travel the next day to the island on board the *Ranger III,* a cargo and passenger vessel. The foursome is rigged for electrofishing, including boat and generator. Henry works for the Ashland Fishery Resources Office of the U.S. Fish and Wildlife Service, which has embarked on a three-pronged fish-restoration effort: coasters, lake sturgeon, and walleye.

Henry and his team have been doing coaster brook trout surveys on Isle Royale since 2001, concentrating most of their efforts in Tobin Harbor, which he describes as one of many "long finger embayments" that characterize the island archipelago. Henry and his three colleagues electrofish along the shoreline and livetrap randomly in other, deeper parts of the cove. Besides Tobin Harbor, which is on the northeastern tip of Isle Royale, they occasionally survey Washington Harbor (on the west end) and Siskiwit Bay (in the middle).

Henry also works on Wisconsin's Whittlesey Creek, which he calls "a small system." He and his fellow workers started stocking the stream in 2004, but with a different approach. To the question "Which came first, the fish or the egg?" northern Michigan researchers answered, "The fish," while the Wisconsin researchers answered, in part, "The egg," stocking Isle Royale eggs in man-made redds and mimicking the natural process. As a hedge, though, they copied the Gratiot work and stocked fingerlings, trying to determine whether stocking different life stages matters.

Henry says that researchers have the technology to detect genetic differences in brook trout from different rivers, but they cannot detect yet differences between river-dwelling brook trout and their lake-dwelling counterparts—that is, coasters.

They do know that chars—Arctic char, bull trout, and brook trout—have a flexible, what he calls a "plastic," life history. "Some may remain as stream residents, and some may move out to the lake . . . and then return. It doesn't appear to be something that's "hardwired." He says environmental factors are also at work. Low water and warm water in streams might "encourage" fish, or "force" them, to move into the lake, where there are better living conditions and more abundant forage. Whatever the cause of that trip to the lake, coasters apparently don't range far. Sketchy telemetry work indicates that they are "quite homebodies," as Henry puts it, wandering only five to ten miles from their natal stream. And they seem to stay close to the shoreline, inside a depth of fifty or sixty feet.

Around Tobin Harbor, Henry says, there are precious few creeks, and apparently none suitable for reproduction. So the fish from the onset are in the lake environment, where they grow faster but are slower to mature and reproduce. A twelve-incher, which would be an old-timer in a creek, is yet immature in the lake.

It is in the lake that coasters encounter a more fecund—Henry says "softer"—environment than they do in a north woods stream. He compares the scenario to human history. People, he says, had "a much harder life" a century ago, when diets were bare bones, life spans were shorter, and people's stature was smaller. Then came easy street, with "better nutrition, more space—just a healthier environment." So, too, with coasters in Superior. "The lake has more space . . . and is an easier environment for them." They don't have to "work against" the currents, nor do "battle" with otter and mink, nor contend with fluctuations in water temperature and water levels. "It's a very stable system in the lake, and there is, for the most part, abundant and more energetic food. Minnows are certainly going to contain more calories than a mayfly."

A few months after his Isle Royale trip, I meet with Henry at his Ashland office on a cold, wet, and dreary day. He is a deliberate speaker, not given to hasty talk or thought. He is a native of Beaver Dam, Wisconsin, who, as a youth, spent summers "fishing and exploring" the Apostle Islands. He earned a master's degree in environmental ecology from the University of Wisconsin–Green Bay. After two years in the Peace Corps, he worked two years with the Army Corps of Engineers as a wetlands biologist in southern Wisconsin, and three years with the U.S. Fish and Wildlife Service in a lamprey-control program out of Marquette, Michigan. Since then, he's worked in Ashland. "I've got the best job in the world. There are days like today when it's raining and miserable and you're cold, but those days are negated by the many wonderful days out listening to the birds and watching the flowers bloom." He especially likes to work on Indian reservations. "They're on the more pristine parts of the lake."

Henry fills me in on his earlier weeklong trip to Isle Royale. He and his crew netted about twenty coaster brook trout, some twenty inches long and weighing three pounds—"the beautiful ones that some want to see on the wall." They also saw a good number of young adults, eight to twelve inches long, what he calls "the teenage coasters." Typically, on their spring trip to the island, Henry and his cohorts travel the shoreline where the rocks and sunlight warm the shallow water. They work a lot at night with powerful lights and can see the bottom in water that is ten to twelve feet deep. "The number of forage fish out there—lake chubs, smelt, herring, and young white suckers—it's just very abundant . . . so it's a brook trout utopia." Tobin Harbor is six miles long. "We go the whole stretch . . . the entire shoreline. Up and back. Both sides."

Two men net the stunned fish. "There's some skill involved," Henry says. "The fish aren't knocked out. They're not laying there, floating for you. They're swimming. It may be not too different from butterfly netting."

They put the captured fish in a "cattle tank" with an aerator. They pause periodically to gather data—weigh and measure each fish and try to determine whether it is male or female. They mark on the GPS where the fish come from so that they can compile habitat information. They attach a small electronic

HENRY QUINLAN: *I've got the best job in the world.*

tag, two millimeters in length, in the clear tissue just outside of the eye. They take a "little snippet of the fin" and put that in a vial for genetic analysis. They look for parasites. They scrape off a few scales to determine age. Then the fish is released. Sometimes they pick up a fish that they handled the year before. They can tell by the tag near the eye. Henry says, "The recapture is always exciting."

Equally thrilling was an encounter "a few years back" with a pair of large, spawning coasters on a redd along the shore in Tobin Harbor. They spooked the fish off the redd but marked the spot and returned the next day to take measurements of water depth and the size of the redd, and also to gather information on the substrate, which was like pea gravel. That was their one and only observation of spawning fish in the harbor. But they also have captured females that were dropping eggs, Henry recounts, "so all indications are that they're spawning along shoreline areas."

That one redd was in about two feet of water, and Henry believes the currents of Lake Superior would aerate such a site, much like water in a stream coursing over a nest, but he wonders whether thick ice or heaving ice would scour the bottom and destroy the eggs. It is a matter for future inquiry.

Henry and his crew have also surveyed Isle Royale in the fall, the season when brook trout spawn. Most of the female fish they net and handle have between a thousand and two thousand eggs. The crew takes approximately three hundred eggs from each female and fertilizes them with a squirt of milt from a male—thus creating the makings of brood stock. Getting the eggs and milt is simple; a gentle squeeze of the belly, and the stuff of life oozes out. The fertilized eggs are shipped to a hatchery in Iron River, Wisconsin, which then raises the brood stock that Henry needs to stock the Whittlesey.

In 2009, the Isle Royale work yielded as many as seventy-five fish. "There's a nice balance between the young, the young adults, and older fish. We're really encouraged by the range of sizes as they move up through the year class, suggesting there's healthy, natural reproduction."

Whittlesey Creek, just fifteen or twenty feet at its widest, about five miles long, flows into Lake Superior just west of Ashland. It is spring-fed. "It's got wonderful flow, very constant. It's one of the few streams that stays open all winter because the groundwater keeps it warmer and it doesn't freeze." On the Whittlesey, there are brook trout, Coho, and rainbow. At the start of Henry's work, the numbers of brook trout were low—"at best, stable; more likely, declining." Starting in the winter of 2003–4, Henry and his crew have created and stocked the man-made redds. "So we were out there in December and January, scraping away, generally with hands, and sometimes shovel and rake, to create depressions similar to what you might expect a brook trout to create, and brought eggs from our Iron River Hatchery and poured those into the substrate, and then gently covered those up with gravel."

Over the years, they have created perhaps fifty man-made redds and planted as many as fifty thousand eggs. They mark their redds with a brick and check on them throughout the winter without disturbing them. They are encouraged. There is some attrition, but fry hatch. "The eggs are viable," he says. He calls the effort "moderately successful." Since the winter of 2004, they have built redds every other year; in the alternate years, they stock fingerlings, up to twenty thousand.

Henry keeps track of traffic into and out of the stream. He has two electronic detectors at the mouth of the Whittlesey; one tracks fish going upstream, the other tracks fish moving out of the stream and into the lake. So far there aren't many brook trout migrating back and forth to Lake Superior, but the resident population in the creek has gone from thirty to three hundred. These fish, apparently, aren't coasters yet, but there are "greater numbers, absolutely," and twice as many "young of the year" than they counted before stocking.

Henry has also worked around the Apostle Islands. It's tough duty—wind and waves, as opposed to the narrow, sheltered coves of Isle Royale. All of the islands are fairly flat, without much relief, but Oak Island does have a few streams on it, so most of the research is focused there. Henry has helped with some baseline surveys in the islands—once again to determine numbers, sizes, dispersal, and movement in and out of the streams. No follow-up since that exploratory work, but his office continues to provide technical support for the tribal work.

On a clear day, looking north from Chequamegon Point, northeast of Ashland, the Apostle Islands look inviting. I tell Henry about a man I know who says he loves to fish for trout because they take him to the most beautiful places in the world. "Well, that's right," Henry says. "That's the key here, isn't it? I guess I enjoy working with them for the same reason. Yeah." He says of the northern Wisconsin shoreline, "It's a wonderful place. I guess anywhere around Lake Superior is a lucky place to be."

6

The Wildflower Child

Isle Royale National Park

You can tell Joan Edwards by the flowers in her eyes. They grace her labor, life, and spirit, and she feels fortunate that they do. "I'm lucky," she says. "I feel privileged to do the work I do." A botanist, Joan studies wildflowers, including *Sagina nodosa,* the knotted pearlwort. She tracks a community of them on a rocky stretch of shoreline on Isle Royale. "They're so tiny, we call them belly plants," she says. "You have to get on your belly to see them, and they smell wonderful."

This is a world where Joan Edwards is Paul Bunyan; where the harebell flower, the size of a dandelion, is a towering white pine; where a four-inch-high facet of rock is an escarpment; where a crack is a canyon. Angels could not dance on the knotted pearlwort. "These flowers are smaller than shirt buttons," Joan says. "When you look across the rock, it looks barren. It looks like there is absolutely nothing growing. And then, if you get down on your hands and knees and really look carefully, there are these rare plants growing in the cracks, and they're so small you need a magnifying glass to see some of them. I think it's a pretty amazing world."

Knotted pearlwort, one of Michigan's rarest wildflowers, is one of twenty-one arctic flowers in North America that grow on Isle Royale which, along with a scattering of places on the north shore of Lake Superior, is their southernmost range. Lake Superior "helps shape Isle Royale" and provides a favorable habitat for arctic flowers. The cold lake, Joan explains, "acts like a big refrigerator all around the edges of the island. That's why these little rocky shoreline communities have these arctic plants."

Joan, a professor and researcher at Williams College in Massachusetts, has been studying the knotted pearlwort on the south shore of North Government Island near the northeast tip of Isle Royale since 1998. Her thirty-foot-long work area is neither pebbles nor boulders—rather, it is a mass of fractured rock that rises gently from shoreline to crest. The higher up on the land, the more vegetation: arctic flowers give way to scrub cedar and other bigger plants, and then, on the high point of the island, trees take root. The knotted pearlwort ekes out its existence on the cold shoreline, Joan notes. "Glaciers, the theory goes, left behind pockets of these species in suitable habitat."

As with all plants that attract her attention, Joan simply wants to learn more about the knotted pearlwort; she suspects that the fate of this species might be linked to global warming. "On Isle Royale, we have these arctic species that love cold temperatures, and with global warming, this plant is right in the line of fire. I think those might be the first species we'll lose. But no one will know if we're losing them unless we track them."

Isle Royale, about forty-five miles long and nine miles wide at its most far-flung points, is a national park located fifty-five miles north of Copper Harbor, Michigan, and about fifteen miles south of Thunder Bay, Ontario. This archipelago is comprised of one big island and hundreds of little islands—a total of half a million acres. Indians called Isle Royale the "lone isle of the sea," and Minong, which means place where there are good berries. According to an engaging little book, *Place Names of Isle Royale,* published in 1999 by Smitty Parratt and Doug Welker, French Jesuit missionaries and fur traders reached the island in 1669 and changed the name from Minong Island to Isle Royale, after King Louis XIV of France. Fur-trading companies established fisheries on the island before 1800. The U.S. government bought the island from the Ojibwe in 1842, on the eve of Upper Michigan's copper boom, which lured mining ventures to the island. It wasn't unusual for the mining operations to burn off trees and other vegetation on the various islands in order to expose the copper-bearing rock. As well, there were lightning-caused fires. But it was human activity that was especially devastating, destroying half of the island's plant and animal species, including the woodland caribou. Nevertheless, as early as 1921, there was a call to make the island a national park, which it became in 1939. It has reverted to wilderness and is visited by a mere seventeen thousand adventurers a year.

One Fourth of July, I embark on the *Ranger III,* the park service's passenger ferry and cargo vessel that motors between Houghton, Michigan, and Isle Royale's Rock Harbor, seventy miles distant. The trip takes about six hours. The *Ranger,* built in 1958, makes its way west and north along Portage Lake for ten miles, leaves the embrace of two breakwaters, and enters Lake Superior.

I go to the coffee shop where Theresa, a friendly, buxom, dark-haired woman, serves coffee. She has worked on the island for two years and on the

Ranger for three. "This is like summer camp, except you don't have to grow up," she says.

Theresa likes the passing company of strangers of every ilk. "All kinds of guys come out of the woods," she says, handing me a register in which park visitors have written their impressions.

"I love wilderness but I also love civilization."

"The pretty heavy rainstorm kept nipping at our heels."

"Overly tired, out of water, we found our next enemy—ourselves. Bickering back and forth, exchanging multiple unmentionable words."

"Isle Royale is a pretty cool place. . . . I thought about writing something with deep meaning and insight but I'm just too tired now."

"You're going to die out there."

The *Ranger*'s first stop is at Mott Island, where the park headquarters is located. Parratt and Welker say that Mott Island is named after Charlie and Angelique Mott, who sat on a mining claim and stayed on the island in the winter of 1845–46. The book gives this account of their ordeal after a promised boatload of winter supplies never arrived: "Charlie slowly starved to death. Toward the end, it is said he sharpened a knife while looking longingly at Angelique. Thinking he intended to eat her, she was on guard until he passed away. She barely survived the winter. She caught snowshoe hares by making snares from her hair. Legend has it that Charlie is buried under the present location of the men's restroom at the park office building at the main dock."

After an hour on Mott Island, during which I tread on Charlie's ignoble grave, the *Ranger* departs for Rock Harbor a few miles west. Scores of people mill about the dock. Joan welcomes me. She is in her fifties, trim and youthful looking, with short hair. She proves to be soft but not weak, enthusiastic but not zealous, single-minded but circumspect.

Joan is with her husband, David Smith, a zoologist who studies frogs, and two college students, Galen, a senior from Alaska—who describes the whole experience, not the weather, as "a little too cool"—and Ellen, a sophomore from Kentucky. The students help with the couple's research. The four of them go to Rock Harbor once a week to pick up groceries. They also pay $3 for a five-minute shower at park facilities, for there is neither running water nor electricity on Edwards Island, where they live and work in the summer.

Joan earned her PhD in biology at the University of Michigan. These days, she is mainly focused on biogeography, which she defines as "the distribution of organisms"—in her case, terrestrial plants. In search of wildflowers, Joan has ranged far afield—from China to South Africa to Antarctica—but she conducts most of her work on Isle Royale, where her family is one of the few remaining who have a life lease on island property—in Joan's case, Edwards Island, which is about three-quarters of a mile long and about one-eighth of a mile wide; it is shaped like a horseshoe, the open end to the northeast. The Edwardses' lease is in the name of three family members who are now in their eighties. When they die, the lease will end. Joan is of two minds about that: she will be sorry to lose her enchanting niche on the island, but she will be happy the land will remain wilderness.

Joan started studying plants on the northeast end of Isle Royale in 1974. The rich floral life is "really amazing," she says, with dozens of varieties of flowering plants. She focuses her attention on *Cornus canadensis,* which is called the Canada dogwood or bunchberry, on Edwards Island, and on the knotted pearlwort, the bloom of small stature, on North Government Island.

When I join Joan and David on the Fourth, the two are winding down their work, which usually lasts six to seven weeks. We trek over a small hump of wooded terrain to Tobin Harbor, several hundred feet north of Rock Harbor. We fit five people and supplies into a fourteen-foot runabout with a fifteen-horse outboard motor. The water is bluish green, ripply, and clear to the bottom. "This should be a tropical paradise," Joan says.

Tobin Harbor is long and narrow and full of cubbyholes. Joan points out landmarks. We pass Bailey's Island, where there is one small shack. "One year, a man named Captain Bailey overwintered there," Joan recounts. "To keep his canned food from freezing, he cut a hole in the ice and kept his cans in the water. All the labels fell off. He didn't know whether he was getting beans or canned peaches for dinner." We nudge up to a small dock on Minong Island, where there is a little building to drop off and pick up mail three times a week. We push off and make our way to Edwards Island, from where we can see more small islands to the northeast and the lighthouse on Passage Island, five miles distant, that guides ships going to and from Thunder Bay through a four-mile-wide strait off the end of Isle Royale.

The Edwards cabin sits thirty feet back from a ten-foot bank overlooking the water and faces north. Joan allows that, all in all, it's a run-down and primitive array of facilities—a place for research, not cocktails. "Everything up here is old." The compound comprises three small buildings, all painted reddish brown. Besides a two-room cabin, there are a storage shed and a small screened-in summer kitchen. A lean-to roof hangs from one end of the storage shed and protects the cooking area, where there is an old wood cookstove. A kettle and three pots of water that constantly sit on the stove can definitely call each other black. Outside of the cooking lean-to are two rickety wood tables that have seen better days. There are two plastic pails for garbage and a small compost pile, which are not an invitation to unwanted visitors because there is little wildlife on this island. No bears, no raccoons, no skunks, no coyotes, no wolves, not even any snowshoe hares—only birds and red squirrels. Lying about are several kayaks, four wooden boats, and a birch-bark canoe that Joan's brother made. Joan especially likes a cedar boat, appointed with brass, made in the 1950s. "Beautifully done," she says. People don't craft like that anymore, she laments. "It's sad. It's very, very sad. It's a push-button world."

As she prepares dinner, Joan describes her work. "It's not high-tech, it's careful observation. A lot of research is doing something over and over, and you start noticing things. There's still a lot to be described by a careful, trained eye. The details about how flowers are put together are really gorgeous, remarkable. There's a discovery to be made right under your nose. The flower world is unbelievable. People walk right by it and don't see it." Isle Royale gives her pause—what she calls "a connection" with a natural world that she believes is disappearing elsewhere.

The main vegetation on the island is spruce and fir, sprinkled with some white birch, cedar, and mountain ash—along with wildflowers, lichen, fungi, moss, and algae. The lichen is "conspicuous" around the edges of the island, but not on higher ground inland. The reason may be the recurrent fog that hangs low over the shoreline, Joan speculates. "There's a lot of moisture." She doesn't know whether the lichen is a parasite or just a boarder. "There is so much we don't know. Isn't that awful?"

Joan cooks grilled onions and Polish sausage, Ellen reads *Zen and the Art of Motorcycle Maintenance,* and Galen reads *Elmer Gantry.* "It should be good, it's thin," Galen says. He reminds me of a fellow I know who says he buys only thick books because he wants to get his money's worth.

Dusk now. The temperature is fifty. The mosquitoes are bad. After dark we retire. David and Joan are in the small bedroom, and I'm in the main room with Ellen and Galen. Ellen reads and writes letters by a flashlight strapped to her head like an old miner's carbide lamp. In the distance, the foghorn at Passage Island moans every twenty-seven seconds.

The next morning David and Galen go to search for frogs. I follow Joan and Ellen as they walk a trail from camp to a low spot in the middle of Edwards Island and then up and over a small bump that slants down to the rocky shore on the south side. Canada dogwood flowers line the trails. Individual plants are marked by a small orange flag on a stiff wire stuck into the ground and by a number inked on a leaf. On other plots, a one-foot-square swatch of fine mesh is draped over a wire frame to keep insects off small groups of flowers; bugs sometimes trigger the flower's pollen-release mechanism, and Joan wants to study them undisturbed. The Canada dogwood typically has four white petal-like bracts, the size of quarters, that capture your attention—but Joan shows me the tiny flowers in the center of the bracts: a world of stigmas, styles, filaments, and pollen-carrying anthers, twenty to forty flowers, each a little larger than the head of a pin. She says of the dogwood, "Even though it looks like one large flower, it's an inflorescence with many tiny flowers."

Using magnifying lenses, Ellen counts and describes the flowers that open each day. She wants to determine if there is a pattern. So far, all she knows is that the first four flowers usually open like the points of a cross; beyond that, a pattern, if one exists, is yet a mystery.

From her lab work, Joan knows that Canada dogwoods can't self-pollinate. She calls them "explosive flowers." Most flowers open gradually, unfolding in slow motion. "It's very unusual for flowers of any kind to explode open," Joan explains. Those that do, like the Canada dogwood, do so suddenly. She says that the first descriptions of exploding flowers cropped up in the late 1800s, but no one knew how they exploded, how fast they exploded, or why they exploded. "We seized onto that," Joan says, "and I think I know how they do it." She figured it out over the past winter in her lab, when she studied the flower structure under a scanning electron microscope. She also took pictures, at ten thousand frames per second, of the flower opening. Inside the tiny flowers, the pollen-covered anthers, each measuring three millimeters in diameter, bend as they grow in the confined space, coil up with energy, and then unloose "ballistically, like out of a cannon." "It's catapulting, actually," Joan explains. "It's nature's trebuchet." The tiny flowers pop open in less than half a millisecond and project their pollen up to two and one-half inches. "Isn't that incredible! I like discovering things." Her work on this flower has been published in the scientific journal *Nature.*

Joan's pants are tucked into her socks to rebuff bugs. She wears a big, broad-rimmed white hat that looks like a sou'wester, with the brim upturned so it doesn't get in the way when she bends down over a flower.

As we work from the more wooded north side of the island to the rocky south side, Joan notes that there are few flowers in the middle, as it is too dark. "You have to have a tree-fall happen, and the flowers appear." Whatever stakes out turf has to be hardy, for the soil is spare. The root mass of one windfall has uplifted as much rock as earth. Here, Joan and Ellen have an eye out for the little picture. On knees, noses to the ground, Ellen counts, and Joan alternately inspects and takes notes. In the background, the lake, only slightly stirred, whispers. Storms must batter the island, for there is driftwood fifty feet inland.

Much of the vegetation is scrubby, but the land is not at timberline, Joan says—just exposed and with poor soils. Joan explains that this land mass was scoured by glaciers, so the ecosystem started as bare rock. "Things don't decay here very quickly because it's cold," she instructs, "so you don't have a lot of rich soil." She wonders, "How can this whole forest grow on a few inches of soil?" It's fascinating to her that, in this lean environment, "There is just this profusion of flowers."

We return to the cabin area and sit on benches in a little clearing overlooking Tobin Harbor. A blue jay flits about. It's the first one Joan has seen in two weeks. Here, the breeze knocks the mosquitoes down, but the flies are bad. To the northeast, we can see the three humps of Passage Island. Also to the northeast, a half mile away, a rock mass on the shoreline of another island glows red in the sunlight. Joan explains that seagulls congregate on the rock, and orange lichen flourishes on the nitrogen in their droppings.

It is warm in the little clearing. Around us, Joan points out, are buttercups, wild raspberries, and wild sarsaparilla. A pigeon hawk, which Joan says is really a small falcon, glides overhead. Just offshore there are two red-breasted mergansers and a black cormorant. Joan has seen an eagle nail a cormorant sitting on the water and swim to shore with it. Raucous sounds come from above. "The raven and pigeon hawk are having a fight," Joan explains.

At seven o'clock, Joan starts to prepare shepherd's pie for dinner. While David uses an old bow saw to cut firewood, Joan boils water and fills the two thermoses. The wood smoke smells good. Now overhead there is birdsong. "How many people get to eat dinner to the song of the Swainson's thrush?" Joan wonders. It's chilly, and Joan wears a frayed red sweater that she knitted in college. The sun casts a golden glow on Tobin Harbor. A loon laments; some people mistake the sound of a loon for a wolf howling, David says.

After dinner and after dark, Joan and I go to the quiet cabin. I sit on the floor with a flashlight to read my notes; she sits on a cot. Faint, moody light from my flashlight plays on her face.

Joan tells me she started coming to Isle Royale in the 1960s when she was a teenager. She liked to hike and fish and pick blueberries and thimbleberries, which grow on the island profusely. Raspberries, though, are scarce and late blooming. It's early July, and they haven't yet formed. "Everything is late out here," Joan says. Her childhood visits led to what she calls "a connection with nature." She says she's been interested in plants ever since she was a little girl. Now she's immersed in plant pollination systems.

"Why study on Isle Royale?" I ask.

"It's a wonderful natural laboratory." First of all, she elaborates, it's relatively little influenced by humans. She notes, for instance, that there are no honeybees on the island, as they aren't native to North America. Therefore, she says, "You can be assured that the plant pollination systems on the island are pretty much native insects and native plants, and those are systems that have coevolved after many, many years. Throw in a honeybee, and it can mess up the whole system." Further, she notes, the Isle Royale ecosystem is simpler than most because it's so far north. That simplicity makes it easier to understand, but even such relative simplicity is complex. "One of the communities I study," Joan says, "is the rocky shoreline, and it's even simpler, and we don't even understand that."

Biodiversity is the watchword of her work. "It's particularly critical right now because I think humans are spreading over the Earth in a way that's never happened in the history of the globe. Ever! And in doing so, we're causing lots of species to go extinct. And I think one of the reasons I do the research I do is that I hope if I find out more about how a flower works or how different species are interconnected in nature, I can share that with other people, and other people will see the importance of all these different species coexisting—how, really, we have to have them in order to survive ourselves."

She notes that the forest floors filter our water, and fungi and bacteria yield medicine. She calls these "ecosystem services" that hinge on interaction in natural communities. "If we don't maintain that biodiversity, it's not going to be there for us when we need it. We think we can restore nature. How do you do it? You can't re-create it. You can't transplant it. It would die, even if I were the best gardener in the world."

Nature shapes her attitude and outlook. She talks of biologist E. O. Wilson: "He refers to it as *biophilia*—love of life. If you live and respect life of all kinds, I think you're a better person and it makes life fuller." She talks now about the big picture. "Look at those harebells. They're eking out their existence, and yet you look at it and it's this vibrant flower, it's electric blue, and it's growing out of virtually nothing. Now that's telling you something about life. You see how fragile life is, but also how tenacious life is, and how ingenious life is."

All of it puts her in awe. She says she is not particularly religious, but she is spiritual. Her church is the open air, her pew the forest floor, her prayer the island rock. But she also is grounded in pure science. "One of the big questions in botany: Why are the flowering plants so successful? When they evolved, they took over the plant world, and they exploded in diversity. There are more flowering plants, plants that produce flowers, than any other group

Joan Edwards:
If we don't maintain that biodiversity, it's not going to be there for us when we need it.
(Photo by David Smith.)

of plants that exist on this Earth. So one of the big questions is, Why? One of the ways I'm trying to tackle that question is, I'm trying to understand what makes a flower successful—how does it function, how does it work?"

She calls the inquiry her "little projects." In the 1990s, she showed that the anthers of the wood lily open and close depending on moisture in the air. "It closes in the rain to protect the pollen supply." No one had ever shown that flowers could do that, she says. "This is the only documented case of such behavior among all the flowering plants. Stunning! Here's a little piece of a very, very big puzzle on why flowering plants are so successful. They have these little adaptations that allow them to increase their reproductive output."

"What good is that knowledge?" she asks, and then answers herself, "I think it does satisfy just a curiosity. Darwin said the flowering plants were 'an abominable mystery.' He couldn't figure out why there were so many, so suddenly, so diversely. It gets back to the whole question of, if you understand all the little intricacies and how amazing plants and animals are, other species are, I think then you have a greater respect and a greater desire to protect them and preserve them and explore them."

In 1995, Joan traveled to New Zealand and stumbled upon another discovery. She learned that the native New Zealand mistletoe, a flower always believed to be exclusively bird pollinated, was also insect pollinated. This big flower, an inch or more long, has four petals that come together on the top. The flower can't open on its own. Prodded by her husband, Joan and a colleague took a closer look at the flower and saw that "tiny, tiny bees," native to New Zealand, were able to open up the flower to get at the pollen, while big, chunky nonnative wasps couldn't. She explains, "The native bee that's been with it, and coevolved with it, can open it, and the introduced German wasps are clueless." That, she says, is evolution at its finest. "Evolution is very simple. It's genetic change. And if you can get genetic change in a population, you've got evolution. It's that simple. I don't see how anyone can say evolution doesn't occur. I mean, to me, it's beyond the pale."

Science is her lifeblood. "I feel like we're on the cusp of new discoveries all the time." She tells me that the knotted pearlwort, for instance, grows in the Arctic and on Isle Royale (and on a few places on the north shore of Lake Superior) but not in between (in southern Canada)—just in the two extremes. Botanists have a name for this phenomenon: the Great Lakes–Arctic Disjunct. Lake Superior country also is a part of the Great Lakes–Western Disjunct, evidenced by thimbleberries and a flower called devil's club, both of which grow on the Keweenaw Peninsula and on Isle Royale and west of the Rocky Mountains, but not in between. Joan says scientists have no explanation for these disjuncts: "How do species separated by huge distances still remain the same species? They're not interbreeding with each other, but they're still maintaining the distinctive features of that species. It's a huge question."

The next day, Sunday, I stay by the cabin while Joan and Ellen revisit the Canada dogwood. I fish awhile, get skunked, and then read in *Place Names* more stories of people and island. The highest point on Isle Royale, Mount Desor, is at 1,394 feet. The Ojibwe named one promontory Ishpeming Point, *ishpeming* being a native word for "high ground" or "heaven," but they miscalculated; it is only 1,377 feet high.

It doesn't take an inventive eye to note that Lake Superior is shaped like a wolf's head facing west, with the Keweenaw Peninsula the jaws, Isle Royale the eye, and Duluth Harbor the snout. Somebody with a lot of time on his hands figured out that if you reorient the map of Isle Royale 180 degrees, the land mass looks like a *windigo* (or *weendigo*), an evil spirit that the Indians believed lived on an island in Hudson Bay and roamed the north woods, eating humans. The windigo were much feared by the Ojibwe and other tribes of the Michigan-Ontario region.

Malone Bay and Malone Island, which are a few miles southwest of Rock Harbor, are named after John H. Malone, the second keeper of the lighthouse on nearby Menagerie Island. He had thirteen children, and the whole family lived on Malone Island. The book notes, "One son died after slipping on the rocks. Some say he is still at the light, making occasional ghostly appearances." The Malones were known for picking and consuming vast amounts of seagull eggs. They also relied on gardening, fishing, and raising a cow, which they would transport in a rowboat from island to island for grazing.

Place Names reveals that stories abound of "Jesus rocks" on Isle Royale. These were places around the island where people would stand on reefs that were just under water so that, to incoming boaters, it appeared they were walking on water.

Joan and Ellen return from their outing, and we prepare to kayak the mile from Edwards Island to North Government Island, which is just beyond Scoville Point, the east end of Isle Royale. Joan readies equipment, including a one-meter-square, collapsible, wooden frame with a four-inch gridiron made of twine. Wrapping up the device in big plastic garbage bags, she asks, "What did we ever do without plastic?" We carry our modest amount of gear a couple hundred feet from the cabin to the shore, where the kayaks are pulled onto the beach rock.

I have never been in a kayak. After outfitting me with a life jacket and a skirt to keep the water out of the craft, the group puts me in the kayak while it is still on the beach and pushes me into the lake, with the charge to stay close to them and to shore. I am as tense as a liar.

The rest of the group follows. We parallel cobble beaches. Rock palisades line the watercourse. Some outcrops are thirty feet high or more—some bald, some with stubby growth, some with trees. The lake is ten feet deep and clear. The water is crinkly and looks green up close and deep blue in the distance. After ten minutes, I relax a little bit in the kayak, but then Tobin Harbor opens up to the lake proper, the waves get a little bigger, the kayak bounces around, and I proceed gingerly. Soon, though, we are again in protected waters and beach in a little cove, and I'm pulled out of the water and then out of the kayak, high and dry and safe, to my surprise.

Just a few feet from the pebbly beach, we encounter a twelve-foot rock face. Joan points out a man-sized devil's club against the base. It's a warrior—armed with long spines on stem, branch, and leaf. The small rock face above the devil's club has a few footholds and handholds. Joan goes before me, turns back at the top, and lends a strong, steady hand. We make our way down a shallow slope. The air is cool. Little waves lap the rock where she studies the knotted pearlwort. They are largely without competition. "If they weren't flowering, you'd never notice them," she says.

While dominant along the shore, the knotted pearlwort are not alone. Higher up, there is a sketchy presence of wild elderberry and shrubby cinquefoil. Lichen, moss, and grasses grow on the gray granite lump. Joan encounters a pink wild rose. "A wonderful smell." A wood lily stands out "like fire." "It belongs in someone's garden." A goldenrod. A willow. A magenta primrose.

On a dozen sheets of graph paper, Joan has drawn maps of the site she has plotted. By positioning her portable string gridiron and referring to her penciled maps, she can locate individual plants from year to year. One reason she likes to work on rock—"one of my favorite habitats"—is because it's a stable laboratory. "Dirt moves," she says, adding that "some cracks are more nutritious than others." She notes that some pearlwort, nestled deep in cracks the size of a playing card, get sunlight for only moments a day, when the sun is directly overhead.

Noses to stone, magnifying lenses in hand, Joan and Ellen peer intently at the knotted pearlwort. One spot, one and a half centimeters long, is home to thirty flowers and buds. When Joan and Ellen pinpoint features of the rock and recognize a flower, they put a thumb-size piece of colored tape on the rock, on which they record the name of the plant, its size (the diameter if it is round or the length if it is oval), its status (seedling, vegetative, or flowering) and, if flowering, the number of flowers and buds. They use waterproof pens to record the information, and the tape is impervious to rain or waves. They will return to transfer the data from tape to paper; the data will be analyzed back home. Meanwhile, their commentary is instructive:

"It's gone, so it died."

"There it is. It's bigger now. It survived from last year. It's just incredible."

"This crack goes out of the plot."

"I think I know where we are now. Is there a triangle?"

"Oh, phooey, we goofed."

While the two of them work, three ships, leaving or heading to Thunder Bay, pass by the strait between North Government Island and Passage Island. They are two to three miles away, and we can hear the deep thrumming of their engines.

A few hours later, Joan and Ellen are finished. They have used sixty-six pieces of pastel tape to mark a trail of wildflowers thirty feet long and as crooked as a lightning bolt.

We make our way back to the kayaks and paddle back to Edwards Island. I'm an old hand now. Kayaking has gone from a worry to a pleasure. Halfway back, Galen spots a piece of driftwood the size of a fence post onshore, beaches, and fits it into his kayak. Back at the cabin, Joan starts cooking spaghetti. In the shade, away from the breeze, the mosquitoes are bad. David saws up the driftwood for firewood. A little later he spots an eagle in a tree a quarter mile across Tobin Harbor, and we watch it through binoculars.

Then, as darkness falls and all sound but that made by the breeze, the waves, and the lighthouse is snuffed out, Joan and I once again visit by flashlight in the dark cabin. She has nine plots where she tracks her arctic flower.

Why study one flower? I ask.

"I figured out a way to follow it. To follow individuals. That's a really hard thing to do. A tree you can mark and you can follow through time. But little herbaceous plants that grow on the ground, it's very hard. So I figured out a way I can mark them or map them so that I can actually find them the next year. You saw us trying to find them this year. We're pretty good at it, and I think we have a very high degree of accuracy in terms of pinpointing the exact same plant the following year. So you can actually follow them from one year to the next and get an idea of what they're doing.

"And the second reason I'm really following them is that when we started to worry about global warming—for the past twenty years, ecologists have been saying global warming may be a problem—I think we have started to document now that it is changing the distribution of species." Thus, they measure the size and count the numbers to see if they are reproducing or not.

Healthy plants reproduce; unhealthy ones don't have the energy. Determining whether they are reproductive or vegetative, Joan says, "is a measure of how robust the population is."

After several years of study, she has a sense of the health of these arctic flowers. "I think the population is doing pretty well." She hasn't yet analyzed all the data but, she says, "Generally, you lose a few every year, and you gain a few every year. I think the population is staying even. But in 2008, a year the lake level was low, it was too dry and I saw more dying."

Joan tells me she has traveled the world with an eye for the flora. "I've been on every continent, all seven, and most of the places I've been to are natural areas. I've been to Africa. I've been to Antarctica. What does a botanist do in Antarctica? Well, you really are hungry for plants because there are only two native flowering plants in all of Antarctica. I saw one of them—it's a grass. And I think the other one is some kind of primrose. I didn't see it. I only saw the grass. We saw lichen, and we saw algae. We were in Antarctica for two weeks, and I was really starved for plants.

"Everything is huge and it's such a harsh environment. There's ice everywhere—and not a little bit of ice. It's tons of ice. Huge amounts of ice. And then you run into these little areas where there's land and it's teeming with life. You don't just see one penguin. You see tens of thousands of penguins. But only two species of flowering plants. You miss them.

"When we left Antarctica, we came back to Cape Horn. The kind of plants that grow on the tip of South America have aromatic oils in them and it gets carried offshore, so I could smell them. And finally we landed, and I was so excited. We got there and we had to climb up this steep cliff, up to this lookout." It was summer in South America, and flowers abounded. "I wanted to roll in the flowers and I wanted to go over and look at them and explore them. But there were big signs all over: 'Do not leave the trail. This area might have land mines.' Because that piece of land has been fought over by the Chileans and Argentineans, so it's all land-mined. Isn't that outrageous? Outrageous! I suppose it protects the plants, though, from people like me that go over and look at them and sniff them."

She has been to Asia, too, and reveled in the wildflowers of the Tibetan Plateau—"where there were magical wildflowers, wildflowers that were turquoise and magenta and yellow and white and just amazing." From there she went to Szechwan, near the Thai border, in China's tropics, and that was also fabulous. "So I've been there, and I've been to Europe, some. I haven't been to as many natural areas in Europe. I'd like to go to Scandinavia. I think it would be like here. Some of the plants would be exactly the same. They occur all around the Arctic, so they'd be very interesting. The knotted pearlwort occurs there."

She has done genetic studies of this diminutive plant. "The little subpopulation we studied today is very inbred because they can pollinate themselves. And I don't think the seeds travel very far, so a lot of those babies that get established are probably from the parent plants right there. And if you just go a little farther down the island, you get another group, and if you go over to South Government, you get a different inbred group. Each little tiny population has its own distinctive genetic fingerprint, and I think that's important because, if you want to preserve the species, one idea is to have a lot of diversity, and if you have a lot of diversity, then if something happens like global warming, you're going to have some individuals that maybe deal with the warming better than others, and so, in the long run, you preserve the species. The genetic structure of the population is very important."

Earlier, in daylight, I noticed on the wall of the cabin a linen with these words embroidered on it: "Chance favors the trained mind." Joan tells me it's a quote from Louis Pasteur. The slogan inspires her. "It's a wonderful symbol," she says. "I think teaching gives me the opportunity to train young people. If I can help train their minds, I can hopefully make chance come their way."

Rock of Ages lighthouse. (Drawing by Sandy Slater.)

7
Rock of Ages
A Reef West of Isle Royale

Lighthouses have been called "America's castles." Thirty-three of them were built on Lake Superior. The first two, at Whitefish Point and Copper Harbor, date back to 1849. Five more are near Isle Royale. One of these, Rock of Ages, was first manned in 1908. Rock of Ages is about two and a half miles west of Isle Royale and was one of four lighthouses on Lake Superior where the keepers were isolated on reefs or islands for an entire shipping season, which lasted as long as the open water.

The lighthouse keeper has gone the way of the milkman, the coalman, and the iceman, but I tracked down one, Albert Stridfelt, who worked at Rock of Ages in 1939. This beacon pokes up from a chunk of granite just big enough to accommodate the tower, which is 50 feet in diameter at the bottom and 130 feet high. At other lighthouses on the mainland, Albert was part of a crew of three. At Rock of Ages, there was a crew of four because one man was always getting away from it all on Isle Royale, where the lighthouse service had a small cabin. "We'd stay there a week, take turns," Albert says. "It was very livable." While there, the men socialized with the commercial fishermen who lived on the island. "It was good fellowship," he recalls.

Like sailors, the men worked four-hour watches: four on, eight off—noon to four and midnight to four, for instance. A lighthouse tender, which Albert calls "a good-sized piece of boat," routinely came with supplies. It couldn't tie up at the lighthouse because of a long string of reefs, so it anchored a couple of miles away and shuttled supplies and newspapers in a smaller boat. Another supply boat, the *Winyah* from Duluth, went regularly to Isle Royale to service the commercial fishermen, and it would deliver mail, which the lighthouse men would pick up by motoring to the island in a twenty-one-foot boat every few days.

They also used that boat to carry back the moose they poached on the island. "That was the style," is the way Albert describes the practice. The men stored the meat in the subbasement of the lighthouse, right on the cold water. "It was an icebox," he says. "We had meat all year."

They also gathered seagull eggs. The keepers would go by boat to rocks where the gulls nested, mark all the eggs with a crayon or aluminum paint, then go back to the nests the next day. They left the old, marked eggs alone and picked the fresh, unmarked ones, because old seagull eggs taste fishy. Albert says of the marked egg, "That was like a tattletale." A fresh egg, he remembers, "made a pretty good meal. They have an odd taste, but you get used to it. It's a good egg."

"Who did the cooking?"

"We took turns. Everybody cooked, but the keeper, he didn't cook. He was a big shot."

Albert describes the fare: "We had eggs and bacon in the morning . . . moose meat. . . . Stews was easy. . . . And we made pies, too. We had apple by the barrel. Then we had fish. Good lake trout."

"How about speckled trout?"

"Yah, we went in the harbor. Into Isle Royale. We got them nice little speckies and, oh, they were good. Get about ten or twelve of 'em and put 'em in a pan with some butter. That was top shelf." They trolled along the reefs or anchored and sat. "We'd still fish," he says. "Go on a reef and be quiet. Maybe you've done that, have you?"

After Rock of Ages, Albert spent the rest of his working days at Eagle Harbor lighthouse, on the Keweenaw, which was in town and easy duty. Come and go as you please.

Albert enjoys talking about his working days, but when I meet him, he is a forgetful, foggy ninety-year-old man. "Too bad I don't have pictures to give you a bigger idea," he apologizes.

I manage to get that bigger idea from the Rock of Ages logbook for the year Albert was out there, 1939, which I find at the National Archives in Arlington, Virginia. All the entries are concise and constitute a litany of routine. A typical weekday entry: "General station duties." A regular Sunday entry: "Observed the day." A daily notation: the weather report. Other entries show the men scraping, scrubbing, painting and varnishing, cleaning the lens, polishing brass, maintaining the station boat, cleaning the dock of wood and coal, and splicing lines. There is not one word about food. There is one reference to washing clothes. There is mention of only three people—not the keepers, though, but temporary laborers. The 1939 season lasted 219 days. The log notes that the signal and beacon were sounded forty-six times; the keepers picked up the mail fifty times; boats brought visitors or inspectors half a dozen times.

The 1939 season began with the crew landing at the light at eight thirty in the morning on May 2. The men commenced to store supplies; put into commission the engines, station boat, beacon, and radio; and chop ice from the dock.

MAY 5: *They made their first trip to the island for mail.*

JUNE 1: *The tender Marigold arrived with a two-man repair crew to replace the engine in the signal room.*

JUNE 29: *"Tender Tamarack arrived with oil."*

JULY 16: *A coal tender arrived. "Scow tipped over and injured three men."*

JULY 17: *"Learned one man died from injuries received here yesterday when scow turned over."*

AUGUST 8: *"A great number of flies around station. Reflection of Passage Isle Light visible at 10 p.m. on the clouds."*

AUGUST 11: *"Northern lights at this writing 11:00 p.m."*

AUGUST 16: *"Swept flies out of tower."*

AUGUST 17: *"Flies bad."*

In early October the handwriting changes in the log but there is no mention of a crew change.

OCTOBER 12: *"Light Snow first of the season."*

OCTOBER 15: *"Gale of wind. Raising temperatures."*

OCTOBER 25: *"Sounded beacon for mist."*

OCTOBER 26: *"Sounded beacon for fog."*

OCTOBER 27: *"Sounded beacon for snow. Very cold."*

NOVEMBER 7: *"40 degrees."*

NOVEMBER 9: *"19 degrees. Making ice on dock."*

NOVEMBER 28: *"Repaired kitchen chair."*

NOVEMBER 30: *"Repairing shelves for paint and nails. Making hanger for blocks and chains."*

DECEMBER 6: *"Station closed at 6:30 a.m. Strong SW winds [signed] M. M. Miles."*

Miles's name is the only one mentioned in the whole log. It appears the work was important, not the workers.

The logbook offers only a bare outline of life on the rock. It depicts no boredom, deprivation, yearning, or fun.

But I meet a younger man, Don Nelson, who fills in some details. Don was a lighthouse keeper; now he is a chronicler. He is a jovial fellow and he and his wife are the only wintertime residents of White City on the south shore of the Keweenaw. In nearby Jacobsville, there are a dozen other stalwarts. The two little settlements are about sixteen miles from Lake Linden, a town halfway up the Keweenaw, and eight miles from a tavern named Dreamland. Between Dreamland and White City there are only three or four homes, a roadside cemetery no bigger than a minute, and lots of deer yarded up. I count nearly thirty when I first go to see Don. He lives on Portage Lake, which is twenty-five miles long and cuts the Keweenaw Peninsula in half. Where Portage joins Lake Superior on the north side of the peninsula, it is called the Upper Entry; where it connects to Lake Superior on the south side of the peninsula, it is called the Lower Entry. At each entry there is a breakwater and a lighthouse.

Don, who grew up in Marquette, worked on commercial fishing boats and sailed on the ore boats. In the early 1950s, he joined the Coast Guard, which had taken over the work of the Lighthouse Service, and spent nine years as assistant keeper at the Lower Entry lighthouse, which was built in 1919. The light, which is at the end of the breakwater, was operated from shore, thirty-eight hundred feet away, where the buildings and equipment to support the operation were located. The crew at the station checked things out on the light itself maybe once a month—and it was handier to reach by boat than on foot. Besides operating the light, radio beacon, and foghorn, the crew was responsible for fifteen canal or river lights on Portage Lake, each powered by twelve eighty-three-pound batteries that had to be charged and changed routinely. In addition, two sets of range lights had thirty of the cumbersome batteries. Using a twenty-five-foot boat, Don and his coworkers tended these guides to navigation during the shipping season. These lights were needed because the first three miles of Portage Lake, inside the Lower Entry, are sinuous.

Don knew Albert Stridfelt in passing. He recalls him as a gentleman who carried himself well. Don allows that his duty at Lower Entry pales in comparison to Albert's time on Rock of Ages. His real interest these days is not his own work but that of keepers like Albert, who were the last remnants of the storied age of lighthouse keeping. The years "1850 to 1940," he muses, "that's when the real stuff was going on."

Rock of Ages, Don informs me, had a dock and crane to take on supplies. Above the basement and a subbasement, there were an office, a galley and dayroom, two levels of keepers' quarters, a watch or duty room, a service room, and the two-story lens room. "Wherever you went, it was either upstairs or downstairs," Don says. There was a coal-fired boiler and steam heat, fuel tank, water pump, engines to run the air compressors and, later, generators. The men drank from the lake and flushed their sewage in the lake. "That's the way it was in those days."

The beacon at Rock of Ages, which is 117 feet off the water, has been called "a masterpiece of glass prisms and brass." The lens mechanism, called a Fresnel, was made in France and cost about $35,000. It was called a clamshell lens, which describes its shape but not its size, for it was eight feet in diameter and in height. The lens comprised hundreds of glass prisms and four circular pieces of magnifying glass, called bull's-eyes, which were about eighteen inches in diameter. The prisms gathered the light from the kerosene-fueled lantern and directed it to the bull's-eyes, which in turn intensified the light twenty-thousand-fold and redirected it as a single beam. The lens sat upright on a disk that floated on a bed of a ton and a half of mercury. Don says the mercury was a "frictionless" turntable. "You could take and move that lens with your little finger."

The light flashed twice—by one account every fifteen seconds, by another account every ten seconds. The mechanism weighed more than three and one-half tons. The light was the largest of its kind on Lake Superior and the most powerful light of all those on the Great Lakes when it was built. According to one account, it could "shine through twenty-one miles of murky weather—that was the power of the Rock of Ages Light." On a clear day it could be seen from Keweenaw Point, seventy miles distant.

Don has a litany of praise for the lens makers: "These guys weren't stupid. This was a precision piece of equipment. . . . I'm constantly baffled—not baffled, amazed—at the intelligence. . . . Who would drum up a mechanism like this? . . . I have great respect for what they did. . . . People look at it as being a simple thing: Go down there. Throw a switch. The light goes on. That's it. That's a whole new world in there."

Don is a member of the Great Lakes Lighthouse Keepers Association and has been studying lighthouses since 1979. He has visited every one on Lake Huron, Lake Michigan, and Lake Superior. "I've read and read and read, but there's so many things I don't know. Everything regarding a lighthouse has to do with one thing, and that was the keepers, the humans. A lighthouse today, it just sits. It's automated. Nothing goes on. What do you talk about? What do you write about? Nothing. It's there. So everything that took place in the history of a lighthouse involves the keepers. Everything."

Don says they had easy duty—he describes it as "cushy." Although many keepers maintained it was a rough job, "Don't kid yourself," Don warns. "That lie in the beginning becomes gospel." The truth of the matter, he says, is that the work was neither glamorous nor hard. He doesn't embellish the reality of his eight years at Lower Entry. "We didn't work hard, believe me. You didn't work all day long." Cut the grass. Shovel the snow. Paint. Play cards. "Always fishing—fish, fish, fish."

The attraction of lighthouse work ebbed and flowed with the economic tides. "When times are good, nobody wanted to be out there. Keepers were quitting. When times are bad, everyone wants the job." In the early 1900s, a keeper got $600 a year; assistants, $400. (There was higher pay for isolation duty.) When Don worked in the 1950s, he was making $60 a week. That was good money. I know one old-timer who recalls making $38 a week in the 1950s, and another $48 a week. To supplement wages, keepers at lights on the mainland commonly sold fish and pickled seagull eggs on the side.

Don has a 1902 instructional booklet for keepers issued by the U.S. Lighthouse Service detailing everything from how to paint to complicated mechanical drawings of the lenses. It lists every man's weekly allotment of food, including "2 ounces of apples (evaporated)," "1/4 ounce of mustard," "1/2 pint of pease (split)," and "1 pound of mutton (fresh canned)." It even has "directions for restoring the apparently drowned."

Lighthouses serve two purposes, Don explains: In harbors, canals, and entry ways, they say, "I am here. Come." In places of danger, they say, "Stay away from here. This is problems."

Time seals all fates, and the manned lighthouses succumbed to automation. Rock of Ages was automated in 1977 and switched to solar in 1984. The lens and pedestal and clockwork mechanism were dismantled in 1985 and put on display in a museum on Isle Royale.

In the 1960s, Don says, when the first automatic fog signal came out, the question was: "How do you turn the fog signal on and off without a man doing it who can see the fog coming in?" The Germans developed a device that "recorded a combination of humidity and what-have-you." He adds, "It was a crude thing. They invented it and, like all inventions, it takes time and refinement." At the start, though, "It was accurate enough to satisfy." An automatic fog signal turned out to be the beginning of total automation, a process that would end with solar power. Technology built lighthouses and then was their undoing as far as providing a livelihood. The men to run them became expensive and expendable. With radar, radio beacons, computers, and the Global Positioning System, ships know exactly where they are at all times. "No more sextants, no more nothing," Don says. All lights, he says, are obsolete for commercial shipping. These days, he notes, "the lights and horns are there specifically for small boats."

Rock of Ages has been called an "isolated, lonely promontory." It shares that distinction with three other Lake Superior lighthouses: Passage Island, Manitou Island, and Stannard Rock—all accessible only by boat. Rock of Ages and Passage Island direct traffic around Isle Royale, which, one mariners' guide advises, "should not be approached nearer than two miles from ashore, as it abounds in ledges and rocky spots, rendering the coast very dangerous." So much so, that one chronicler wrote: "The 'song of the Sirens' beckoned more than one hundred vessels with the alluring melody of misfortune to the rugged shores of Isle Royale." Nevertheless, the route near the island was busy with traffic going from Duluth and Thunder Bay to Sault Ste. Marie and back. When bad weather blew out of the north, Isle Royale was a buffer, and vessels would hug the lee of the island—a calmer ride than the open water to the south, which is "restless" with wind and wave. The Rock of Ages Reef stretches its jagged reach for a mile and a half. Three ships have "fetched up" on the reef over the years—the *Cumberland* in 1877, the *Chisholm* in 1898, and the *Cox* in 1933—so that the rock is also called "the Reef of the Three C's."

The light was on from sunset to sunrise and in fog. While the light could be seen from afar, the foghorn was more problematical. "Sound carries crazy on the water," Don remarks. "In fog, weather, or snow—'every weather,' as they call it—the air is thick, and sound trying to get through, it's pretty tough. Sometimes you can hear a horn one day twelve miles out. Another time you can't hear it a mile away, due to the thickness and atmospheric conditions. Sound will reflect, too. Sound will come out and hit a wall of fog and *zingo!* head the other way. So you can't get a true direction from a foghorn. You can't do that 'cause it deceives you. So now you got the light, and now you got the horn, and they're still not perfect. They're good, but they're not perfect."

Don is interested in artifacts—lenses and logbooks and pictures—from bygone lighthouse days. "Stuff doesn't stay around long," he says. "The things of history are something to be held onto."

But history isn't lighthouses, he asserts again. "History is people." And the people who kept the lighthouses, especially the isolated ones, were a resilient and interesting breed, in Don's view. They had easy work but a tough time. The routine entailed "a hermitlike lifestyle" that served up a steady diet of "isolation and boredom, boredom and isolation." The Lighthouse Service had stringent rules and frequent inspections. Why? Keep the place clean and keep the men busy. "Idle hands, you know, lead to trouble," Don says.

He has written extensively about lighthouses, including Rock of Ages. Here is one entry: "When the foghorns were blowing with all the engines running, or the winds buffeting the tower, it was not a pleasant place to be. With all this, you had better get along with your fellow man and have no problems ashore with family. It's a lifestyle that only someone who has served here or at a similar light station can explain. Many have said it's a lost time in their life."

A spooky time, too, if one man is to be believed. In 1972, a newspaper reported claims that the Rock of Ages lighthouse was haunted. Local keeper Chuck Middleton maintained that one of the doors in the tower "would open and close of its own volition." Although he allowed that no keeper ever came in contact with an apparition on that small rock, "[i]t's . . . that gol'darn door. If only that could be eradicated, things would just be swell on ol' Rock of Ages."

I ask Don whether he knew Chuck Middleton.

"I heard the name."

"He said Rock of Ages was haunted."

"Well, every lighthouse was haunted, according to the keepers. That's a hoax as far as I'm concerned. They'll tell you, 'Oh, I hear doors closing. I hear this. I hear noises.' When you're stuck out in an isolated place, your mind plays funny things on you. I don't believe this type of hokeypokey, but those that do swear by it."

When Albert Stridfelt talked about gathering seagull eggs, I pictured the men getting just enough for a meal. Don shows me one log entry that notes men at another light got seventy-six eggs on one day alone. And, although "alcohol was not allowed—absolutely under no uncertain terms"—it was common and plentiful. He says that some keepers even had stills.

Don has an 1869 mariners' guide that lists every single light and buoy on the Great Lakes. It and another guide from 1916 include maxims:

"Enough blue sky in the northwest to make a Scotchman a jacket is a sign of approaching clear weather."

"A red sun has water in its eye."

When it comes to remembrance of times past and people past, of lighthouses and keepers, the sun also has a tear in its eye.

8

The Lakehead

Thunder Bay, Ontario

"Lake Superior truly is an ocean," says Bill Dunlop, who knows what he's talking about, for he has crossed and recrossed the big lake for sport and recreation, and has sailed five thousand miles on the Atlantic Ocean.

If Dunlop can say that about Lake Superior, then I can say the hills along Highway 17 between Sault Ste. Marie and Thunder Bay, Ontario, are mountains. They remind me of Colorado, minus only the bare peaks. For four hundred miles, Highway 17 alternately hugs the shore and wanders inland as it connects these two ports. It cuts through rocks of many colors—white, cream, tan, brown, pink, red, and black. Some are smooth, like scoops of ice cream; others are faceted, like chunk coal. Beyond the rocks that wall in the road, there are escarpments that bring out my wife Marilyn's whimsy. "There's a dead dinosaur," she says. "See him laying down with his tongue hanging out." The road pushes through vast forest. The evergreens, some of them standing high on the ridges like sentinels, are deep green; the aspen, which shimmer in the sun and quiver in the wind, are pale green. The hills are gentle here, precipitous there. There are only two flat stretches. Near Pukasqua National Park, by the Pic River, the emerald hills fall steeply to a pearl lake. "Forget Bethlehem," Marilyn marvels. "You can have a vision right here."

The road goes north and then bends west and then south. No guardrails: just posts and three strands of cable. Three kinds of pullouts: for travelers to deposit trash, for truckers to check their pulp loads, and for snowplows to turn around. Two surprises: along the whole route, not one scrap of litter, not one dead animal.

This is bilingual Canada. The signs at the animal crossings display a black image of a bull moose with the words "Night Danger" and "Danger de Nuit." We see just one moose, outside of Pays Plat. It looks gangly but runs gracefully.

We count fifty creeks and rivers and eighteen inland lakes along the way. Many cairns, a foot or two high, sit on the flat rocks that crowd the highway. They are as numerous as the names of young lovers painted in white on the rock faces. We are told later that natives call the cairns *inukshut*. In Ojibwe, that means "We were here."

The City

Thunder Bay, the city, population 109,000, sits on the banks of Thunder Bay, the harbor, which is home to Thunder Bay, the port. The city of Thunder Bay, which is called the lakehead of Superior, straddles the Kaministiquia River. *Kaministiquia* is Ojibwe for a river with islands, two of which are located on the delta, separating the big river into three braids: the McKellar River in the middle, the Mission River on the south, and the Kaministiquia, which locals call the Kam River, on the north. The name Thunder Bay harks back to the first Europeans who arrived in the area in the seventeenth century. Local Indians called the location *Animikie,* which means thunder. The French explorers, then, called it Baie de Tonnerre, or Thunder Bay. The bay runs northeast to southwest. Pie Island, which one local calls "a meat pie with a big bite out of it," anchors the lower end. The Sibley Peninsula, sixteen miles long, extends a protective arm on the upper end. The sweep of the mainland of the bay is about twenty-three miles. A half mile from shore there is a five-mile-long breakwater, with three or four openings for ships; five miles beyond the breakwater are two small pieces of land called the Welcome Islands.

The dominant feature of the landscape is the last four miles of the Sibley Peninsula. With bluffs up to seven hundred feet high, it's a dead ringer for a person lying face up. It reminds me of Colorado's Sleeping Ute Mountain. This lump of land, called the Sleeping Giant, is the subject of an Ojibwe legend recounted in the Thunder Bay Historical Museum:

> The Ojibwe were leading a "peaceful and industrious" life so that the Spirit of the Deep Sea Water wanted to reward them. The Ojibwe were known for their silver ornaments, and the Spirit revealed a rich silver mine. If a native were to tell the White Man of this mine, he would turn into stone. A Sioux scout tricked the Ojibwe, learned the location, and led two white men to the lode. There was a terrific storm near the mine, which is called Silver Islet. The white men drowned, and the Sioux scout became crazed. After the storm, there

appeared the great sleeping figure of a man. The star-crossed Sioux had been turned into stone.

The sounds of thunder are evident in white culture, too. In the historical museum this story is attributed to Catherine Moodie Vickers, describing a storm in 1873: "Ribbons of fire ran up the sky in all shapes, more like rockets and fireworks, whilst the thunder leaped in a continued roar, like nothing I ever heard before. If I were an artist, I would choose Thunder Bay in a storm as the grandest representation of the end of the world."

The Port

The city of Thunder Bay was formed in 1970 with the merger of the twin cities of Port Arthur and Fort William. The port of Thunder Bay, which spreads over twenty-two miles of wharfs, elevators, freight sheds, railways, and terminals, comprised the biggest grain port in the world in 1983. Now it is one-third of what it was in its heyday, with but eight elevators in use, down from thirty-two in the 1950s. Similarly, 425 ships a year visit the port, down from 1,400 in 1983. And there are 68 boats in the Canada fleet, down from 120 in 1993.

Canada has always been an exporter of grain. These days it exports 25 million tons a year. Thunder Bay constitutes less than one-third of this commerce. The reason for the decline: world affairs, says Tim Heney, head of the Thunder Bay Port Authority. It is said a hummingbird beating its wings in the Amazon affects the breezes in Indonesia. Likewise, the Canadian grain market has been affected from afar, Tim explains. For the first half of the twentieth century, the biggest market for North America's grain was Europe, where the land—and thus agriculture—was devastated by the world wars. Farmers in the northern prairie states of the United States and the prairie provinces of Canada, then, fed the needy of Europe. Then three things happened: peace came; Europe rebuilt and replanted; and taste buds changed in Asia, where the masses acquired a taste for hamburgers—and the buns to go with them—instead of rice. "Nobody predicted that switch," Tim says.

The result: the destination of most of Canada's grain exports has shifted from Europe to Asia. That, in turn, means that Canada's railroads now haul the grain west to British Columbia, rather than east to northern Ontario, leaving Thunder Bay somewhat high and dry. "Transportation goes wherever it's cheaper," Tim says, and British Columbia is in Asia's backyard while, in comparison, northern Ontario is Asia's lower forty. The seaway, he says, is operating at only 50 percent capacity.

Thunder Bay used to have a trump card: the Great Lakes–St. Lawrence Seaway, which Tim calls "one of the great wonders of the world." Locks were built to facilitate the movement of grain from the Canadian prairie to Europe. The locks at Sault Ste. Marie are about 1.5 miles long and they raise or lower ships 21 feet. Contrast that with the Welland Ship Canal, between Lake Erie and Lake Ontario, which is 26 miles long and raises or lowers ships 326 feet. The Welland accommodates ships up to 740 feet; the Soo locks can handle thousand-footers. There are thirteen of these, built between 1972 and 1981, and they are limited to Lakes Superior, Michigan, Huron, and Erie.

"They didn't envision the markets totally shifting to the other side of the world," Tim says. "Things change, and lately they can change pretty quickly. We're going to see dramatic changes in world patterns, trading patterns, manufacturing, all kinds of things. And maybe a return to marine." For that to happen, retooling Thunder Bay as a port is a must. Up to this point, he notes, "It never happened because it never had to." Now it has to. Tim reports that no new ships have been built for Great Lakes service since 1985. "You need those new vessels with new capabilities to move forward," he says. "Renewal of the fleets is a big issue."

He refers to a 2007 study of the Great Lakes–St. Lawrence Seaway system that addressed a range of improvements—especially a switch from bulk cargo, like grain, coal, and iron ore, to container cargo, like tractors and windmills, along with the ships and port facilities to go with them. Then Thunder Bay could cash in on trade with, say, China, which, the report says, "is already the world's largest single exporter of containerized cargo and is soon expected to become the fastest-growing importer of containerized cargo."

That could bode well for Thunder Bay and the heartland, for the two provinces and eight states of the Great Lakes–St. Lawrence system contain 25 percent of the North American population—not a small market, either as an importer or exporter.

Resurgence would befit the town. Thunder Bay's whole history is based on maritime commerce. "Everything we did was by shipping in this part of the country," Tim recounts. "The ports were here before the highways. It can go back that way if we use more modern thinking. Once you get on a ship, you can go anywhere in the world, eh? That's the magic of it."

The Coast Guard

Sitting in the early morning sun, which casts long shadows, Phil Hayes and I sip coffee and talk on the open front porch of the Canadian Coast Guard's

TIM HENEY: *Things change, and lately they can change pretty quickly.*

Thunder Bay station, which is on the edge of a slip that opens up to the bay. This slip accommodates a tug service and the Canadian Coast Guard on the south side and a high grain elevator on the north side. A hundred geese float on the calm waters. Phil tells me that some of the geese stay year-round, while countless others only pause on their journey south in the fall. "Oh, goodness, they're steady," he says. "I sit here and watch these birds a lot. They're a story in themselves. They mate for life. They'll look after each other's young."

Phil has the leisure to learn their ways because in his work, a search-and-rescue operation, he is on call always but idle sometimes. He works two weeks on, two weeks off. When he's working, he lives at the station, which looks more like a home than an office. Outside, the green lawn is well tended and accentuated with flowers that bask in the sun. In contrast, there's a big black bollard squatting on the porch. The crew of four here are the commanding officer, two seamen, and Phil, the engineer. "I've always been engine room," he says. He earned the certification, with both sea time and exams, over a period of ten years. "I didn't need ten years," he explains. "I took ten years."

Phil joined the Coast Guard in 1988. He's an Irishman from Newfoundland and speaks with a strong brogue. He's lived in maritime communities all of his life. "Paddle around as a kid—that's all we had to do," he recalls. As a teenager, he worked on fish trawlers on the Grand Banks and in a fish-processing plant. As an adult, he worked onshore for one month, which he characterizes as "the longest ten years I've ever spent. I couldn't wait to quit." He's also worked as an oiler on lakers. "I knew I was going to end up on the water. That's all I can do. It looked very dangerous to be on the deck, so I decided if I'm going to do this, I'm going to do something on the inside. Go below." He attended St. John's Marine Institute. He says of that education: "Career development, I suppose, would be the proper term."

As we speak, a heavy fog creeps in. The geese glide into it and disappear. The station has two vessels that are docked about one hundred feet away: one is a 22-foot rubber raft with twin-150 outboards; the other is a 47-foot craft with twin-350 diesels. The men serve an area with a fifty-mile radius, or two hours' run time. Prior to his Thunder Bay duty, Phil worked in the Northwest Territories and on Lake Winnipeg. Besides search and rescue, he also works on a Coast Guard icebreaker. It's a 230-footer with almost 9,000 horsepower. The frame members in the bow are mere inches apart. "Ice breaking is noisy," he says. "That's probably the worst part. . . . We could sit like this, but we wouldn't be able to talk. . . . Thunder Bay is heavy ice. Freezing cold. Too cold for too long, and windy."

PHIL HAYES: *I knew I was going to end up on the water. That's all I can do.*

Phil's search-and-rescue work is based on the fact that, as he puts it, "misfortune happens." Typically, boats break down or run out of fuel. Helping people is gratifying. "When we pull up alongside of people, they're scared. Nervous and scared. We make them feel secure and safe. It's a big thing. Just our presence, they feel better. It's nice to see the relief on their face. Sometimes we have trouble getting to them in really bad weather. Our biggest thing—we try to not get in the same predicament they're in." He doesn't single out one or another venture. "You're just doing your job. You don't think about it. There are little rewards along the way—when a guy gives you a sincere handshake. That's all you need—a meaningful handshake and an acknowledging smile."

As he speaks, the fog lifts and the sun reappears. The water is so drowsy-calm it's hard for me to imagine it rough. Phil warns, "It can go from like this and, by two o'clock in the afternoon, you've got three-foot seas."

The big mistake of the inexperienced: ignorance. "Not knowing what can happen." The big mistake of the experienced: cockiness. "They feel more competent in challenging nature." He adds, "I've found that the experienced ones, when we find them, they're usually dead." Phil says of the bad stuff: "The result is usually not as good as you'd want it to be. . . . Sobering is probably a good word."

Humbling, too. He tells of a sailboat that overturned, resulting in two people drowning. "I read the obituary. They sailed around the world. They were very experienced people. When you realize they died, that kind of makes you realize that there's a big force here—the water. You can never let your guard down. You find you're not as good as you think you are." He struggles for words. "Hopefully you get the gist of what I mean, anyway."

"Have you ever been scared?" I ask.

"I can honestly say I have been maybe once." In very bad weather they hit the breakwater. "For a second or two, which seemed like a lifetime, I thought, 'Maybe we'll sink right here.' I thought I was going to die that night." The rescuers needed rescuing. A tugboat came for them. "We were concentrating on what we were looking for, not what we were doing."

He knows now that fear is not a portent. "I've been out when I thought the other people were going to die and they didn't."

The geese come back, in an arrowhead formation. They flap their wings furiously and roil the water. Phil says they won't fly off because they're molting.

He has a black bracelet on his right wrist; it's for helping out at a shelter home. He has a silver bracelet on his other wrist; it's for good health. "I come from an Irish background and everybody's superstitious." He also has an earring in his left ear. He likens it to "pennies on dead people's eyes." "It's supposed to get you to the other side—heaven, I suppose. One form of life to the other. You pay for everything. As they pull my body out of the water, I've got payment. There's always a ferryman and you've got to pay the ferryman, and this is what's going to do it for me."

He doesn't practice a faith. "I don't believe in what I was raised to believe. I don't believe heaven is a place where everybody is friendly." He suspects, though, that he'll be part of some good energy.

Then, out of nowhere, he interjects: "You should have a pipe. Everybody has something to enjoy, eh?" Part of his enjoyment: he doesn't have to contend with rush hour and time clocks.

Some people romanticize what he does: "Wow, you've got the greatest job in the world." For his part, "I think I have a nice job. I never get bored waiting around because there's always people. People fascinate me. The most interesting part of life is people." He wonders why so much is written about the minds of evil people. "Why don't they try to get into the minds of good people?"

Meanwhile, he has a job to do, and it's based partly on everlasting storms. "People who say, 'I love rough weather' have never been in rough weather," he says.

There is not a ripple in the slip now. The only thing moving is the geese, and they're in no hurry to get anywhere.

"It's just been a windy, rotten summer," Phil says. "We don't need wind. Smooth sailing is the best for everyone."

The Mission

Ed Swayze, an Anglican priest or curate (curer of souls), engages in a "ministry of service" on the docks of Thunder Bay—for "the fellas on the boats." Ordained in 1987, Ed has worked in Thunder Bay since 1994. He serves St. Stephen's Anglican Church, a congregation of about fifty people, and the Mission to Seafarers, a nomadic bunch from around the world, mostly eastern Europe, India, and the Philippines. "We're here for the people of the port and the seafarers in the port," Ed says. He doesn't work much with lake sailors. "I just found that looking after oceangoing sailors, that consumes most of the time I've got to give." The mission's guest registry reveals the names of sailors from India, Myanmar, China, Holland, Russia, Estonia, Croatia, Ukraine, Germany, Poland, and Liberia.

The port mission, founded in 1961, is one of about eight hundred around the world. Most are Roman Catholic; three hundred are Missions to Seafarers affiliated with the Anglican, or Episcopalian, Church. In Thunder Bay, Ed and thirty volunteers work out of a mobile home near the port authority, the Coast Guard, and a tug service—all of it in the shadow of tall grain elevators. Ed devotes two days a week to the mission.

It is said that youth will build a stairway to the moon; old age, a woodshed. Although not old, Ed is the woodshed guy. "What we do for them is little things," he says. He and his helpers pick up sailors in a van and bring them where they need to go, typically Wal-Mart. "They have limited contact with shore, and they need assistance with transportation, they need assistance getting in touch with family." They're not flush with money. "The lowest paid make a thousand U.S. a month."

The sailors also can visit the mission to relax; use telephones and computers; get warm clothing; buy postcards and long-distance phone cards; play foosball; have coffee, pop, and lunch; watch television; use outgoing mail service; and enjoy magazines and books for the taking. "The Internet is getting more popular," Ed observes. He bought a webcam so the sailors and their families can see each other online. The mission also distributes pamphlets with information on local churches. Once in awhile he brings the Eucharist on board, and now and then he and his helpers transport people to a mass. "Most of the seafarers are Catholic."

He says of their needs, "I talk about it like a business trip. What do you want to do? You want to touch base with family and see how they're doing. You want to go buy toiletries and some stamps. That's what these guys want to do." Plus, because they're cooped up for days on end, "They want to get off the ship and stretch their legs or want to see some different people." No time to dillydally, however. "They've got four hours to go ashore and do their business." There are some language barriers, but "English is the working language in ports around the world." Nevertheless, a rack on a wall of the mission has Bibles in twenty-four languages. In the back of the structure, there is a chapel, with eleven chairs and a small altar that Ed, a woodworker, built. They have services once a month for the volunteers and other people around the port.

The logo of the mission is a flying angel, and there is a nautical feel to the décor of this refuge. A picture of "the last lake boat of the season inbound in December at sunset, with ice-fog and mirage." A display of different flags used as maritime signals (presumably before radio) and what they mean. A yellow, black, and white one: "I am on fire and have dangerous cargo on board, keep well clear of me." A yellow and red one: "I am dragging my anchor." A chart of thirty-six different kinds of clouds: eight from on high, sixteen from low in the sky, twelve from in between.

Ed, just shy of fifty, is of medium height and build, with glasses, dark hair, and a beard. He is deliberate and soft-spoken, pausing for long moments when speaking.

"You're the opposite of a preacher in a tent revival," I suggest.

"You've got to be calm when it storms," he replies.

He serves sailors going from the deep into the harbor, and he describes their "trade route": pick up cargo in the Great Lakes ("They're up here looking for grain"); take it to Europe or the Middle East; then they get steel from Europe and bring that into the Great Lakes. Round trip—six weeks. So there are two discharge ports and two loading ports. An average of two days in each port, in each berth. So that means that in a six-week period, there are potentially eight days they can get off the ship. But that doesn't mean they can go ashore eight days. Sometimes they're not allowed ashore for security reasons. Sometimes they're needed on the ship. "So in a six-week period," Ed says, "they're lucky to get ashore two days."

The mission meets every oceangoing ship. Sometimes nobody wants to go ashore; sometimes half a dozen sailors want to; other times it takes two trips in the van to accommodate everybody.

"They're very grateful for what we do for them. Every now and then they end up in the hospital and we go visit them. Sick or hurt, the ship leaves without them, and they have to be flown home."

What manner of man chooses this labor?

"They're a lot like us," Ed says. "They're concerned about their kids. They're concerned about their wives. They're concerned about having enough money to retire on. . . . Their contracts range from six months to fifteen months. They get a month leave, and they're back to sea again. So it's a hard life. You have to be basically happy with yourself and able to get along with people. One of the ways I liken it is, imagine yourself being in an apartment building and you have to stay there for a month at a time, and if you want to go outside, you can go stand on the front porch, but you can't go any further. And that's the life of a seaman, so if you aren't able to cope with that, you don't survive."

He and his volunteers are ever ready. "We're set up; if somebody calls, we respond. If a ship comes in, we're there to meet the ship." His annual budget is $30,000. He gets financial support from the Diocese of Algoma and the Thunder Bay Port Authority.

The biggest demand of his work? "Remain flexible." The schedule of the ship can change as quickly as time. Once he made arrangements for three pickups; all were cancelled within minutes. He knows better now: "A ship doesn't come in until it comes alongside." On average, there are two a week, but sometimes there are four a day. "The port here follows the grain trade, so the busy

Ed Swayze: *You've got to be calm when it storms.*

months are May, October, and November. October and November because the harvest is starting to come in. And May, you're selling last year's crop."

He himself is a recreational sailor, and he has a twenty-two-foot boat called the *Blue Angel.* In both his recreation and his work, he has found that people who work close to land or water are more in touch with nature and spirituality than people in the city—"Just the vastness. It causes you to meditate. Sometimes people who live in the city lose touch with creation."

Ed was a forester before he entered the clergy. "A lot of values, they share," he says.

"Like what?" I ask.

"Caring for things. Stewardship of forests. Stewardship of people."

He sums up his mission work: "One of the things from the Gospel of Matthew, when Jesus is talking about the judgment of nations, what's important is the verse that says, 'I was a stranger and you welcomed me.' That's one of the big things here—we extend a welcome to the strangers. What we're about is—we're providing hospitality. That's an aspect of loving your neighbor."

The Welcomeship

From 1974 to 1994, Jack and Norma Gurney owned an excursion vessel, the *Welcomeship,* that took visitors from the Marina Park to Fort William, a historic encampment reconstructed from voyageur days that is a few miles upstream on the Kaministiquia River. They also offered harbor tours on the *Welcomeship,* seventy feet long with capacity for two hundred passengers. Norma and two partners ran the business; Jack ran the boat. His was a seventeen-hour day during the season, May through September. "Big days, but worthwhile," he says. Like many cruise-ship operators, he had a clever spiel with which to entertain his passengers. His best line: "The Kaministiquia River has three mouths. They should have named it after my mother-in-law."

Jack paints, mostly pictures of ships. When he was young, he was a competitive swimmer. At age thirty, he rubbed himself with a coat of lanolin and swam from the Welcome Islands to the shore, a distance of a little over five miles. It took him three hours, fifteen minutes. It was in August, but he says the water was near freezing. "He finished strong," according to a newspaper account, "coming from the water without assistance and asking first for a 'smoke and my shirt.' He was the only person in eighty-degree heat who was truly shivering."

The Gurneys and my wife, Marilyn, and I enjoy coffee and cookies in their backyard, graced with flowers and a warm breeze, on the banks of the Kaministiquia, with cannon fire sounding from Fort William just upstream.

Jack, who is "a couple of heartbeats from age eighty," alternately folds his arms and then gestures expansively when he talks. He has gray hair and a resonant voice. "He's cute, eh?" Norma says. She looks nice in a white jacket and slacks and a light-green blouse—"all dolled up like a brand-new broken arm," my old aunt would say. She and Jack are natives of Thunder Bay. They've been married sixty years.

Jack was born in 1931. His father was a railroad man; he took to the water. He worked on a tugboat for a dredging company as a deckhand, wheelsman, and then captain—"pushing ships," he says. As well, he hauled stone from a quarry to beef up the break wall, which always settled and shifted from ice and waves. He says the breakwater was 125 feet wide at the bottom, about twelve to fifteen feet on top. Jack also towed booms—he calls them "rafts"—of pulp logs, twelve thousand cords at a time, for the paper mills (five then, three now). And he dredged silt from the harbor bottom, especially at the delta. Those were the days, he recalls, when one man's winter job was to chop ice around the many pilings that dotted the harbor's docks. He poured oil on the water to keep it from freezing around the pilings,

JACK AND NORMA GURNEY:
JACK:
I whistled all the time. I used to get in nothing but trouble from that dredge captain.
NORMA:
I've lived here all my life. I still think, "Wow."

because the ice tended to grab them, raise them up, and make them unstable. "One guy did that all his life," Jack recalls. "That was his job—a thing of the past, like everything." He remembers when twenty-four ships anchored in the harbor at one time, many of them lined up for the iron-ore dock. "Now there is no ore dock," he says. "It's gone. Times change, things change." Jack enjoyed his work on the tug. "I whistled all the time," he says, which is a no-no among mariners. "I used to get in nothing but trouble from that dredge captain. 'Shut your mouth, Gurney. You're whistling again.'"

He's been very ill for more than a year. "I should be dead," he says.

"Are you afraid of dying?"

"No. I've had a good life and I could go tomorrow, no problem."

Norma—who had a grandfather who lived to 104 years, had five wives, and died working in his garden—is ready to go, too. She'd prefer it not to be on an airplane. "I'm not a good flyer," she says. "I need a double rum and a gravel."

"What's gravel?"

"Dramamine."

She says the water is more inviting. "We share the largest freshwater lake in the world. You could put the British Isles in Lake Superior. How lucky to live here. I've lived here all my life. Nearly eighty years, I've seen that now. I still think, 'Wow.'"

Norma says the lake will be a good cemetery. "He can bury me at sea," she says of her husband, "because captains, they know how to bury people at sea. They wrap you in canvas and the last stitch goes through the nose."

"Why do they do that?" I ask.

"I don't know. Isn't that awful? They can just shoot me in the river."

Jack interrupts. "That's some kind of superstition that sailors have. Yah. Keep you from drowning. Sew up your nose. Make sure the guy is dead. Sew his mouth shut, too."

The Gurneys are kind. They came to town to lead us back to their home, about ten miles distant, they fed us, and they indulged our questions. "Kindness," remarks Marilyn on the way back to town, "you have to develop it through years. I love old people."

The Rescue

Norma Gurney says Gerry Dawson is a hero. "Above and beyond," she asserts emphatically about the time he saved two sailors, adrift in dark, rough seas—a rescue that she says was characterized by "bravery and seamanship."

Gerry Dawson demurs.

What did the rescue really take?

"A lot of luck."

Why did he do it?

"I must have been crazy."

Gerry, who is in his fifties, owns Thunder Bay Marine Services. His father, a former oceangoing sailor, started the business in 1952, when he bought a thirty-eight-foot boat, moved to Thunder Bay, and started a bumboat business: a floating store that served the ships coming into the harbor with everything from cigarettes to boots.

Gerry started working for his father as a lad, "doing dishes" and "offloading" cargo. He was tying up lines for the big ships when he was fourteen. He started working on his captain's papers when he was eighteen. At nineteen, he wrote his certificate as a master of minor waters—handling ships of any size inside of the harbor. Then, in short order, he earned the certificate that allows him to work on tugs of any size anywhere around North America.

Gerry and his father offered a wide range of services: a little dredging in the elevator slips; linesman service (helping tie up the boats and shifting them up and down the docks as they load); diving services that included inspection, repair, and construction as well as checking the pilings in the grain elevator slips; disposing of garbage, galley waste, and dunnage; sportfishing on the Bateau Rocks off Isle Royale; and sport diving on shipwrecks. (The deepest he's been: 165 feet. He sounds like Yogi Berra talking about it: "It's a long way down when you're looking back up.") Gerry sums up, "Anything for a buck on the water we'd do. We'd even deliver Christmas trees to the ships." In 1983, at age twenty-six, he bought the business—"two boats and a barge and all the goodwill"—from his dad.

In 1989, he got into the tug business. Thunder Bay Tug Services has six tugs, several small launches, two barges, and a forty-ton crane for salvage work and dock repairs. Right after Gerry bought the tug business, there was a marked downturn in business, and ever since it's ranged from rocky to smooth sailing. The fluctuations confuse him. "We just hope from year to year it stays good. Last year it was slow. This year is even slower. And three or four years ago it was booming. So you just don't know from one year to the next. Still, we were able to keep our head above water, so to speak, but it was tough sledding. There have been many trying years. I don't think a lot of people see that side of it."

He employs six men full-time, ten or twelve part-time. "We try to keep our tug guys going through the winter," he says. They do maintenance, engine repairs, and ice breaking. It typically takes four to six hours to break the ice in a thousand-foot elevator slip. He has broken up as much as fifty inches. "You don't walk through it. You have to keep bashing at it." It's not really what he calls "a good moneymaker" because he does a lot of damage to his tugs—to the tune of $100,000 last year to the *Point Valour* alone.

He also pushes a lot of ships around in the harbor. Sometimes ships can maneuver on their own; sometimes it takes two tugs for one ship. The situation varies depending on wind and ice and whether a ship has a bow thruster. He's proud to be "reliable." He can usually muster a crew and be on the way to help a disabled ship in an hour or two.

He did that on October 30, 1996. "There was a storm coming on the lake," he recalls, "so we had to move our two tugs, the *Point Valour* and the *Glenada,* up the Kam River overnight because the waves were too high at our dock where we were tied up."

Then Gerry's wife, Sharon, took a distress call from a man named Dana, who, with a partner, was stranded on the *Grampa Woo,* a 110-foot excursion vessel adrift off Grand Portage. Dana and his partner had gone out to the *Woo* in a small craft to make it fast, but it was dragging its anchor. Then their small craft broke down, they were stuck, and they rode the *Woo* into open waters. "A calamity of errors," Gerry says. Later, Dana called Sharon again to report that a freighter had picked them up and was towing them east. The plan: rendezvous off Pie Island, eight miles south, and transfer the tow from the freighter to either the Coast Guard cutter or Gerry's tug, *Glenada,* which is seventy-eight feet long, with 1,200 horsepower. The distress call came at four thirty in the afternoon. Gerry and the Coast Guard took off separately at six o'clock and went to Pie Island. "We could see the lake freighter towing him," Gerry recalls. "When they got close to us, the wind shifted and the tow line that the lake freighter had on him broke." The freighter, loaded with fifty thousand tons of coal, sought shelter in Thunder Bay. "So then we had to head out into action." The winds were seventy knots. The seas, from the southwest, were up to eighteen feet. "We were also getting freezing spray, so my wheelhouse windows were pretty well covered with ice. I couldn't see very much." All the vessels had running lights, and Gerry had spotlights, as well as a small heater that he situated to keep the window clear.

Waves were breaking over the tug. He didn't know it until later, but his deckhand, Jim, was hanging on for dear life. "The bulwarks on the *Glenada* are four to five feet off the water—and he said the whole back deck was underwater, and so he was holding on to our towing bits, and his legs were floating out behind him. That's how close he was to being washed overboard."

The job: connect the two vessels with a ninety-foot, lightweight heaving line and use it to bring across a stout, three-inch towline. Jim hit the target with the heaving line. "We were just getting ready to send my big line to him when the small line snapped. We lost our opportunity in a matter of seconds."

Meanwhile, Gerry had worries. That week, he had bought six thousand gallons of diesel fuel that had 150 gallons of water in it, so stalling was a danger. Also, the towline from the freighter was trailing behind the *Grampa Woo,* so he was worried about it getting tangled up in his prop. "That was my biggest concern—that that line was going to get wrapped around our propeller and we'd be dead in the water too." The plot thickened: his engineer was overcome by fumes in the engine room. "So now I've got nobody keeping an eye on the engines." He thought, "If the engine quits, we're done."

They tried unsuccessfully to get a line to the *Grampa Woo* two more times. Gerry had radio contact with the Coast Guard, three-quarters of a mile away. They decided to forget the disabled vessel and just get the two men off. "The Coast Guard, we asked them, 'You guys want to go in and get them off?' They said, 'No, we're just barely holding our own. There's no way we'll get close to them.'" The Coast Guard radioed the helicopter service of the U.S. Coast Guard station in Traverse City, Michigan, and alerted it to the trouble. Then the Coast Guard cutter disappeared from Gerry's sight and from his radar. "I thought they'd flipped over. I thought we'd lost 'em."

He tried to get close to the *Woo.* "We hit the back of the boat once and did a little bit of damage to it." They tried again, and he put his big bumper tire "right up tight" against the disabled boat. "I don't know what happened," Gerry says. "The sea went calm. The two men jumped. Jim grabbed them by the seat of the pants, pulled them over the bow fender, and they were floating, or sliding, down the icy deck. Then Jim got 'em up in the galley and we started looking for the Coast Guard cutter and found out they were okay."

With everybody safe and sound, they called Traverse City. "We told them that we had the men—but the boat, we're letting it drift, letting it go wherever the lake will take it. That was one of the toughest things—to actually watch the boat go, let it go, and not get a line on it. 'Cause I'm a boat owner, and that's your pride and joy, and you don't want anything to happen to that."

They sought shelter at Tee Harbor, which is just off the east end of the Sleeping Giant, and waited out the storm for two days.

Gerry is incredulous yet. "It was a fluke, I think, that we were able to get that close in those conditions and get them off there without anybody getting hurt."

"Jim must be a bruiser?" I suggest.

"He's a pretty big guy, but, I mean, they jumped at the same time that we were dropping in the trough of waves and their boat was coming up, so it evened out enough that we were able to get them on board and get them off there."

I offer, "You've bumped alongside a lot of ships. You knew what you were doing?"

"Yeah, but we're not used to doing it in fifteen- to eighteen-foot seas. It's usually a gentler landing than that."

The *Grampa Woo* washed ashore a quarter mile from Passage Island lighthouse, east of Isle Royale, about twenty miles from Thunder Bay. "We went out there four or five days later to see what damage there was. It looked almost like it was floating, but then we took a good look at it and there were big holes in it. It was sitting there for good." On that first trip out, they found life jackets jammed in the rock crevices twenty feet off the water.

Due to bad weather, they couldn't get back out to the wreck for twenty more days. "By the time we got out there the second time, it was completely demolished. It was just the back end of it sticking up out of the water, and the rest of it had been broken up, broken apart."

It took two years for the park service and the insurance company to decide to scrap it. Gerry got the salvage contract. "That was another adventure in itself, because you're exposed to the open lake. We ended up nineteen days out there, salvaging it. We were able to get eight good working days out of nineteen."

They lifted big sections onto barges by crane. The park service also wanted all the bits and pieces off the lake bottom, so Gerry sent divers down to do that cleanup. "They actually found a couple bottles of wine that weren't broken and a jar of pickles and, oh, a couple of coffee mugs. You'd see stainless steel shafting, three inches in diameter, twisted like a pretzel and here you find a jar of pickles and a bottle of wine. It's just unbelievable."

Gerry and his men were honored for their deed by the Coast Guard, the International Shipmasters Association, and the City of Thunder Bay. The rescue has been widely publicized.

What's overlooked?

"The lives that were at stake." He means the three people on the Coast Guard cutter and him and his two men.

He says things happened so swiftly they were a blur, but there was time to worry, too. "You wonder if you're going to get home."

"Are you a hero?" I ask.

He's not having it. "Help out a sailor that was having a problem. It's an unwritten law of the sea. Somebody might help you someday."

He is absolutely without bravado. The closest he gets: "We were tested to our limit that night. That's for sure."

Is his a romantic life?

GERRY DAWSON: *Anybody can take the helm when the seas are calm.*

"It is fun on a day like today. Like they say, anybody can take the helm when the seas are calm."

The best part of the business?

"You never get two things the same from one day to the next."

The worst part: "The ice is the worst."

All in all, he says, "Sometimes it's not how much you make, it's who you help out."

A Tug at Work

Gerry Dawson's brother, Stan, who is in his fifties, is a bulkhead of a man, with hams for hands and a big belly. His job today: help a laker, the *Canadian Providor,* out of a slip on the south end of Thunder Bay. The job is at once yeoman's duty and a delicate maneuver, but Stan, master of the *Point Valour,* is up for both.

On a sunny late afternoon, Marilyn and I board the *Valour,* and Stan welcomes us into a spacious pilothouse. With the ropes off the bollards, he powers the craft away from the dock and heads south through the opening of the breakwater, despite which the elevator slips are "vulnerable" to storms. "It can get ugly. A northeast or east wind around here is the worst. It comes right off the lake and smashes in."

Shy of the Welcome Islands, Stan turns southwest and parallels the breakwater. He puts the tug on automatic pilot, opens drawers, and shows me charts of this part of the lake. Deep water is white, shallower water is light blue, and even more shallow water is dark blue. Stan doesn't get tangled up in the blue. "I like to play it safe," he says, adding that the inner harbor and channels are dredged to a depth of thirty feet.

Stan started working for his dad when he was twelve, chipping and painting. In his late teens, he went to British Columbia for five years, working on tugs that delivered gas and equipment to the logging camps. He started out a deckhand and ended up with a tug master's certificate. He calls it "a ticket." That required five or six written exams on seamanship, other courses on firefighting and emergencies, and three years of sea time. He studied at Vancouver in the winter. Like Gerry, he's certified for tug work in waters anywhere in North America. He also has a shipmaster's certificate but has never used it.

"Was it tough?" I ask about his studies.

"It depends on how hard you partied. Chart work could be tough."

His biggest problem was staying focused. "I was only twenty-one years old," he offers—enough said. Now he is all wise. He gestures to a dark line on the horizon, near another dark line on the horizon that is Isle Royale. "I see we've got a little mirage working today," he says. "That usually means east weather is coming."

He's been all around the Great Lakes and the St. Lawrence Seaway. "I can't remember where all I've been with these things," he says of tug boats—"all I ever worked on."

On this day, he's headed for Mission Basin, on the southwest end of the bay. He points out a sawmill and pulp mill; the red range lights that guide ships into the channel; two grain elevators; and two ships, one just tying up, the other, the *Providor,* topping off its load. It is old, has no bow thrusters, and needs Stan's help to get out of the slip, which is a tight fit. The *Providor,* 730 feet long, is registered in Toronto. It has a black hull and white superstructure and a black and red stack with a white triangle. It's a straight-deck vessel, not one with a self-unloading conveyor and boom.

There are green and red buoys outside of the slip. Inside their perimeter is what Stan calls "good water." As he speaks, the water turns brown. "I kicked the bottom up," he explains. His tug has a fourteen-foot draft and his propellers are ten feet in diameter. The laker will load to just over twenty-six feet. "You'll see some mud when he gets going," Stan predicts.

He positions himself bow to bow—what he calls "stem to stem"—with the *Providor.* While he waits for the laker to finish loading, we talk. I mention that I've noticed people call oceangoing boats "salties" and lake boats "lakers." I've also noticed that people call saltwater sailors "salts." "What do you call a freshwater sailor?" I ask Stan.

"Sailor," he replies, then adds, "It depends on who you're talking to. His wife probably calls him a pain in the ass."

He has mischievous blue eyes. He smokes Canadian cigarettes, a brand called Vantage, and uses a stubby plastic holder. "It cuts the good stuff out of the cigarette," he says. "It's better for me." The window and door to the pilothouse are open. The sun glints on the water, and the bow waves are as rhythmic as breathing.

He's not at all superstitious. Marilyn asks him if he believes in the legend of the Sleeping Giant. He guffaws. "I don't believe any of these old wives' tales."

"But isn't it interesting?" Marilyn persists.

"Not in my world," Stan says. "I could make up better stories than that when I was in kindergarten." He pauses. "It's a nice rock formation."

Two of the crew join us in the pilothouse. They work a steady six hours a day and then are on call for any amount of time, at any time. Nobody makes plans for shore life. The engineer says that he tells people, "If I'm there,

STAN DAWSON:
We've got a little mirage working today. That usually means east weather is coming.

I'm there. If I'm not, I'm not." These hands don't get much of a break. Stan checks his log and reports that the last season ended on January 15 and the new season started on March 20.

The *Providor* has a routine. Load grain in Thunder Bay, take it to Quebec; load iron ore in Quebec, take it to Hamilton, Ontario; run empty back to Thunder Bay and reload with grain. Stan says that the last time in, the skipper said that his load of 26,800 tons of grain—five trainloads of one hundred cars each—was worth $23 million. The grain comes from the Canadian prairie provinces of Alberta, Manitoba, and Saskatchewan.

The *Providor* is loaded and has winched itself to the end of the pier. Crewmen on the tug and on the ship attach the towline. Then the tug begins its work. It has big heavy-equipment tires chained to the bow, smaller truck tires along either side, and two 675-horsepower engines. The tug muscles into the laker, pushing the boat backward and at the same time pulling on the rope, so that the bow comes off the dock. Stan calls it a "slingshot" maneuver; it's like being parallel parked, backing into a driveway, and then heading back out in the opposite direction. It's close quarters. Connected by radio are a mate in the bow and one in the stern. The mate in the stern calls out the footage to the green buoys that mark the shallow water. "Hundred . . . seventy-five . . . fifty."

The tug nudges the ship backward. Stan provides running commentary.

"I can twist this guy around like a pretzel."

"It's basically running heavy equipment."

"You get a little wind involved and it really gets interesting sometimes."

"Sometimes you don't have time to do the finesse. You go hard."

He's in constant radio contact with the captain. "She's a heavy old girl today, sir," Stan says to him.

"Oh, yes," the captain says.

"Get him headed in the right direction and then we can all go home and have a drink," Stan says. He's just bought a new motorcycle and is anxious to get on it.

Soon the job is done. "It's a good thing, too—I'm getting hungry," Stan says. He lingers, though. "We're staying alongside in case he needs another shove."

Then black smoke billows from the big ship's stack, and it begins its journey to Baie Comeau, Quebec. Stan gets on the radio.

The *Valour:* "That'll be it, Captain. See you in sixteen days."

The *Providor:* "You've got it, my friend. Thanks for the help."

Stan moves ahead smartly. The tug goes about twelve knots. Stan blows his horn: one long, two short. The laker does the same.

"What's that all about?" I ask.

"That's a salute," Stan explains.

He goes beyond the breakwater, turns left, parallels the breakwater, then enters one of the openings and heads to the dock in the bay. We disturb a pelican. Stan says there are many around. Eagles, too. He's counted up to twenty-three on the ice.

Headed for the dock, Stan remarks, "You've probably heard it said that the only difference between being on a ship and in prison is that you can't drown in prison."

He is only jesting. "I love it," he says. "You get to see some nice sunrises and sunsets. Last night there was a full moon shining on the water."

The Road Back to Sault Ste. Marie

Marilyn and I backtrack southeast to Sault Ste. Marie. Between Thunder Bay and Wawa—one dead black bear and one dead moose. Two women, with a flatbed truck and a winch, are loading the moose. I stop to talk to them. Picking up roadkill is their job. One says they average one dead moose a day along just a fifty-mile stretch.

We stop in Wawa for gas—about $5.50 a U.S. gallon. But if they clip you on the gas, they seduce you with service. Attendants man the pumps, wash the windshield and side-view mirrors, and check the oil. "Your oil is right on," reports one man. "Nice and clean, sir. I'm going to put an air gauge on that tire just for fun."

Inside, we make purchases, including maple sugar candy the size of a quarter and in the shape of a maple leaf. This is 13 percent sales tax country.

Continuing south, we pass Old Woman Lake, Dad Lake, and Baby Lake.

A change of directions doesn't change the scenery. "The luster and prettiness—where did that come from?" Marilyn wonders. "If you miss the beauty of this, you're a fool."

Spotted on the whole return trip: one trash bag and one plastic bottle.

We approach the Canadian Soo. Counting the Soo, there are sixteen locks between the outlet of Superior and the Gulf of St. Lawrence. There are also four rivers: the St. Mary's, the St. Clair, the Detroit, and the St. Lawrence. Stringing them all together makes for three major seaports—Superior, Duluth, and Thunder Bay—that are more than two thousand miles inland.

We cross the International Bridge and stop at the locks on the American side. I have told Marilyn I'd like to see the size of the pumps in the locks; I learn there aren't any. The water merely seeks its own level. Close the lower end of the lock, and it fills up with water to raise the ships; close the upper end of the lock and open the lower end, and the water drains to lower the ships. It takes less than an hour for one ship to make the passage. "Something else, eh?" a fellow observer says. While we watch, the *James R. Barker,* owned by the Interlake Steamship Company, passes through. It's hauling fourteen thousand tons of canola seed from Thunder Bay to Windsor.

We leave town and head east, going from the big hills of Canada to the flatlands of the eastern Upper Peninsula. Marilyn says of Canada, "They got the pretty end of it."

9
The Start of Something Big
Duluth, Minnesota

It is early January 2006, a mild winter that was preceded by a hot and dry summer. From the bluffs overlooking Duluth Harbor, Lake Superior is flecked with whitecaps, what oceanographer Jay Austin calls "lots of cotton." "We're in the ice season, supposedly," he says.

Instead, it's a season of discontent. The talk of the town, Jay says, is how low the lake level is. "Because it's important for commerce," he explains, "people get very worked up about it. This is the big thing that is going on in Superior this year. It's at its lowest level since 1926, the lowest seasonal level, and it'll probably drop some more over the next couple of months, so we'll have the lowest absolute level in the last eighty years." He notes, for instance, that the average precipitation the previous year was seven inches short of the norm, twenty-four instead of thirty-one inches. "And it was a really hot summer, so you get a lot of evaporation and we lost another three or four inches."

Whom does that affect at this seaport?

The maritime industry, Jay answers. "They dredge the channels coming in, and they dredge all the channels inside the harbor. I don't know exactly, but they dredge it to, like, thirty feet, and those sailors want to have twenty-nine and a half feet of draft. They don't want any extra space under that boat because the more taconite you put on, the fewer trips you've got to take. So it costs huge amounts of money when you suddenly have to put three-quarters of a load on the boat. The cost of everything goes up. So, yeah, it's a foot or a foot and a half below where it should be for this season, and that's a big deal to these people who are counting on being able to get in or out of the harbor."

The lake level may be topical, but it engages Jay's attention only in passing, because, he says, "It doesn't affect the overall behavior of the lake."

His abiding attention is to collect data on water temperature, research for which he and colleagues received $1 million from the National Science

Foundation. "I'm relieved and busy," Jay reports on my second visit with him in 2009. Data on Superior's water temperature has proven difficult to come by, but Jay has enough information on surface temperature to know that the lake is warming up much faster than the atmosphere. However, he has no data on subsurface temperature and avows that it is high time to rectify that. "There's a saying, 'The best time to plant a tree is twenty years ago, and the second-best time is today.' We might not have long records of heat content on the lake, but if we're going to start measuring it, we may as well start now."

Jay is a friendly, dark-haired man, lean of frame, rich of gesture, fluid of speech. He is enthusiastic about his work. He came to the western shore of Lake Superior in 2005. He teaches physics at the University of Minnesota–Duluth and does research at the Large Lakes Observatory, where scientists study large lakes around the world, including the Great Lakes. Jay, who previously worked on the East Coast, has shifted his research from oceans and estuaries to Lake Superior, which has not been well studied; the flow of existing data is a trickle. He guesses that is the case, in part, because the lake is "big—and away from everybody."

New to the area, new to limnology, and new to the scientific community studying Lake Superior, Jay probes the science and secrets of the lake. Courtesy of the National Science Foundation grant, he and colleagues have outfitted seven moorings—cables that are affixed with instruments along their length and deployed in deep water. The cables have an anchor and a buoy that is fifty feet below the surface, lower than the draft of any ship. Twice a year, the caretakers of this equipment venture out, locate the moorings via GPS, and send an acoustical signal that releases the setup, which floats to the surface with an ocean of information. Scientists—including those who piggyback on the operation to collect other data—then "interrogate" a total of 130 instruments and collect information, which includes water temperature throughout what Jay calls "the water column"—from top to bottom.

Jay's work was preceded by other inquiry. Since 1980, the National Oceanographic and Atmospheric Administration has placed three buoys in the lake—on the west end, in the middle, and on the east end—all in open water. They set them in April and pull them in November before the lake ices over. The buoys record water and air temperature, wave height, wind speed, and other meteorological information. Lastly, there are a dozen "surface moorings" spotted on land around the lake, usually at lighthouses, that record data on the weather. This shoreline monitoring was begun in 1979.

Jay has also found water and sewer department reports for the City of Duluth with all kinds of data, including monthly water temperatures, going back as far back as 1929. "This is a very good thing," he says. "It's really rare to measure things that carefully, that long."

Jay also has stumbled upon what he calls "an amazing resource"—a daily recording of intake water temperature, going back more than one hundred years, at a power plant on the St. Mary's River in Sault Ste. Marie. He was elated to find it. "It's not clear to me why anybody should care about what the water temperature at some plant intake was in 1907, but boy, it's a nice thing for me to have. One man's trash is another's treasure."

People like Jay, who grapple with the whys and wherefores of water, encounter a situation that is difficult to get your arms around. "Everything depends on everything else," Jay says. Ingredients in the mix include sunlight, wind, cloud cover, current, runoff, turbulence, humidity, temperature, rain, and the fluid mechanics of water. "It's a difficult environment to make good observations. It seems like such an obvious, easy thing. Here's this big chunk of water and it's getting warmer—how hard could it be to figure out what causes that? It turns out, pretty darn hard. Ferociously complicated. People have been working on this lake for decades, and our level of understanding is still really, really basic. But it's exciting. There's work to be done. What I'm interested in doing is getting a profile of temperature over a very long time. I want to understand how the lake works and how the lake might respond to long-term changes in climate."

He plugs all this data and more into computers. "The nice thing about a numerical model," he says, "we can observe the whole lake at once, and we can impose any force we want on it. Say we wanted to know what happens if the wind blew from the west. Okay. In the lake, what we'd have to do is sit around and wait for the wind to blow from the west. And then you have to worry about, well, the wind really was blowing from the east for the three days before that, and it was blowing from the north before that, and how did that affect it? It gets really complicated. Whereas with a numerical model, I can simulate any condition I want—well, within reason—and look at how the lake responds to meteorological forces. You can sort of play God and decide how you're going to force the lake and observe that. Okay. You can see where that would be a really handy thing to be able to do—your own little toy lake to play with. It's impossible to do that in the world."

Jay says computer modeling has largely replaced physical models: scientists used to blow wind over a large tub shaped like Lake Superior and try to deduce from that the lake's behavior. "It doesn't happen anymore," he says. "Very, very rare."

Understanding the lake, Jay says, hinges in part on a salient feature that he calls the "thermal cycle." He explains that warm water weighs less than cold water; therefore the two don't readily mix. So in the summer, the lake becomes stratified—the top two hundred feet of the lake might be fifty degrees, while the water below might be forty degrees. Then, what Jay calls "a weird anomaly" kicks in. Cold water, on its way to becoming ice, actually gets lighter for an interval—from thirty-nine to thirty-three degrees. In the winter, then, this lighter, cooler layer sits atop heavier, warmer water, resulting in another season of stratification. In between the two seasons of stratification, there are two counterpart seasons of mixing—when the surface layer warms to forty degrees in the spring, and when the surface layer cools to forty degrees in the fall. Then the temperature of the water column is uniform and the water readily mixes. "So the whole idea," Jay sums up, "is the lake, twice a year, overturns." This thermal cycle, unique to freshwater, "is not a trivial concept." It refreshes the lower layer, sustaining aquatic life in the deep water.

There are other dynamics in the lake. There is a current that goes counterclockwise in response to the Earth's rotation. "Technically, there are tides," Jay says, "but they are miniscule—so small nobody pays them any attention." A more pronounced phenomenon is called a seiche—what scientists refer to as the "bathtub effect." Jay explains the physics behind the seiche: "If I have a bathtub, and I blow wind over it, the water stacks up on the windward side, and then when I take the wind away, the water will slosh back and forth." This happens in Lake Superior, and with a sustained easterly wind, the effect in Duluth Harbor can be a marked current. "The entrances into Duluth Harbor are relatively narrow. The changes in height might be relatively small, but the velocity in the channel can actually be quite large, and ships have to be careful to time their entry into the harbor—you want to go against the currents in order to maintain steerage. The Army Corps of Engineers has an instrument in the channel that acoustically measures which direction the water is flowing, and a set of lights that informs ships. If it's red, you want to think real careful before going through."

The behavior of the lake is largely due to the weather above the lake, and air temperature and water temperature are inextricably linked. "The lake doesn't want to be a different temperature than the air," as Jay puts it. "If the lake is colder than the air, the air is going to give heat to the water. If the water is warmer than the air, the water is going to give heat to the air." Jay says the two are always trying "to come into equilibrium."

He continues, "The main thing that puts heat into the lake is sunlight. Okay. Sun comes up every day, heat rains down upon us. If you're a lake, if you've ever flown over a lake, or an ocean, it looks really dark. Dark things are very good at absorbing heat. Ice, on the other hand—we've all been outside on a nice snowy day, and you can barely keep your eyes open because ice and snow are really good at reflecting sunlight back up. So if you form ice, what you do is, you sort of cap off the lake so that it can't absorb any sunlight. If you form ice, it delays the start of summer. In fact, it dramatically delays the start of summer—by months. If you take ice away, or ice gets less and less, it means summer starts earlier and earlier every year, and we are observing that as well. If summer starts earlier, the lake has more of an opportunity to catch up with the atmosphere. Half the warming of the lake is due to the air temperature getting higher in the summer, and half of it is due to reduced ice cover in the previous winter. So, if air temperature goes up by a degree, you expect the lake to increase by a degree. The trick is, what we're seeing is, the air is increasing by a degree over time, a number of years, and the lake goes up by two."

At this stage of his inquiry, based on surface data, Jay knows that the lake is warming up about five times faster than the global atmosphere and about two times faster than the Upper Midwest atmosphere, which is heating up twice as fast as the global average—"Don't ask me why." He describes the lake's warming as "spectacular." Regional air temperature is warming at a rate of 0.12 of a degree per year. The lake is warming up by about 0.22 of a degree per year, or two degrees per decade.

JAY AUSTIN: *Why is Lake Superior getting so warm so fast?*

Jay says that the length of the summer-stratified season has gone from 150 to 180 days over the last century, an increase of 20 percent. That constitutes a warming of eight to ten degrees in a century—a rate of change that cannot be explained solely by Earth's atmosphere.

It is a mystery that stirs his curiosity. Exactly what it means is uncertain, he tells me, but there is no doubt that, if the situation persists, "the lake will be different." He remains the detached scientist. "I can't tell you whether that's a good thing or a bad thing."

He continues, "Right now, I only have information about what's going on on the surface. I know the surface temperature is increasing, but I have no idea how much the water column is being affected by this change. I don't know how extensive that heating is." He hopes measurements on the various moorings will describe the situation.

In the meantime, he wonders, "What is it about the lake that is so sensitive to changes in climate? Why is it getting so warm so fast? That's the big question. What makes the lake the canary in the coal mine?"

10

"Madmen, Mysteries, and the Pursuit of Jacques Cousteau"

Houghton, Michigan

When I was a greenhorn backpacker in Colorado, I tested my equipment half a mile from a dirt road, on a small creek no bigger than a borrow ditch, at an elevation of about eight thousand feet. I dug up a worm, as flat and flaccid as a wet egg noodle. I put it on a hook, tossed it in the water, and promptly caught a small brook trout. It was about five inches long, and its head constituted two-thirds of its body. Like the worm, I surmise, the fish didn't have the nourishment to sustain itself.

Although not to that extreme, Lake Superior is a hardscrabble body of water: stingy with nutrients, lean of life. So much so, says Marty Auer, scientist, engineer, and teacher, "It makes you wonder. How do you grow lake trout out there with so little stuff to support it?" He points to the middle of the lake on a map. "If you lived out here, you'd be hungry."

It's an extreme condition in an extreme lake, and Marty calls Superior "a real end-member." He elaborates, "If we were to lay out all the lakes of the world in whatever fashion, Lake Superior is at the end. It's one of the poorest lakes, nutrient-wise. It's one of the coldest lakes. It's one of the biggest lakes. It's one of the most violent lakes. It's one of the more unpolluted lakes. So Superior is really special."

He adds, "You really can't appreciate how big that lake is until you get out in the middle of it and you go, 'My goodness, this is deep. My goodness, this is wide. This is a big lake.' You go out to that lake in the middle of June, when everybody's got the barbecue going, they're sitting in shorts, they're playing Frisbee and softball, shooting nine holes of golf, and you're out there in your snowmobile suit. In the middle of the lake in July, it's in the forties."

The cold is one reason Superior is nutrient-poor. Marty likens it to a garden. "A garden is regulated by temperature. The garden doesn't grow until

MARTY AUER bundled up for a day on the lake in May. (Photo courtesy of Michigan Technological University.)

the sun comes out and the snow melts. Winter holds that lake in its grip right into July, until it finally warms." He says the average temperature is less than forty degrees.

The condition of the lake is also noteworthy. "For those who appreciate unspoiled natural ecosystems, this is one," Marty says. One benchmark is clarity. Researchers measure this characteristic with a Secchi disk, a round white piece of metal the size of a dinner plate. Attach a rope and lower it in the water until you can't see it anymore. That's less than three feet down in Lake Onondaga, a small lake in New York State that is extremely polluted; that's six feet down in Lake Michigan's Green Bay, which is also badly polluted; that's sixty feet down in Lake Superior. "That's how crystal clear Lake Superior water is," Marty says. "This lake is really, really clean."

There are four reasons: not many people in the Lake Superior basin, not much agricultural runoff, not much industrial contamination, and the land that the lake drains is relatively small compared to its size.

These circumstances limit the amount of phosphorus, which drives the food web in most freshwater lakes. Phosphorus is the limiting nutrient; an algal cell is one hundred parts carbon, fifteen parts nitrogen, and one part phosphorus. There's plenty of everything that algae need to grow in Lake Superior except phosphorus. More of it, and Lake Superior would sustain more aquatic life. But there can be too much of a good thing when it comes to phosphorus. With excess phosphorus, algae go crazy, grow like weeds, deplete oxygen, and the bottom of the lake becomes a virtual coffin. A sewage-treatment plant, farm runoff, septic drainage—"All of these things shoot phosphorus into the lake, and away it goes," Marty says. "That's why Lake Erie gets green." The opposite is true of Lake Superior: little phosphorus means the lake is undernourished.

In these austere waters, Marty and several colleagues probe the lake to discover its secrets. Superior, he laments, has historically been "very poorly" studied because it's huge and remote. What research is being done is simply to study the resource and answer one question: "How does this lake work?" In fact, adds Marty, "There are a lot of questions out there that we'd like to answer." It's his calling. "Some of us get a big kick in learning how things work. Discovery is always exciting."

He calls it "pure research" as opposed to applied research—that is, "exploring the unknown" as opposed to applying engineering know-how. The engineering, he says, will come with the understanding. "The applications of the future are built on the science of today."

In the summer, then, Marty and company venture unto these waters on a thirty-six-foot research vessel, the *RV Agassiz.* While the lake may be enticing, the undertaking can be forbidding. "You're aware of how deep it is, how unforgiving the shoreline is, how quickly the weather changes," he says. "It's not canoes and loons and a pine-laden, forested shoreline. It's a great big, cold, tough place."

A native of Syracuse, New York, Marty studied ecology, sanitary engineering, and water resources. Now he is at Michigan Technological University.

He has coal hair and a silver mustache, and is ever the teacher as he explains the biology of the lake. He paces, talks, and writes on a whiteboard to illustrate his observations. He is as enthused as a boy catching his first speckled trout.

We start with the base of the food chain, plankton. The term *plankton* means free-floating. "That doesn't mean it doesn't have flagella and might be able to whirl around in a circle for awhile, but it's not going downtown." Rather, plankton go where the currents take them. Marty describes their movement: "If you start in the cockpit of an airplane and walk to the tail while it's flying from Chicago to San Francisco, you're plankton. You're moving but you're not going anywhere."

There are two types of plankton: phytoplankton, which are plants, and zooplankton, which are animals. The phytoplankton are microscopic algae. "What are we talking?" Marty asks rhetorically, as is his professorial way. "Scum in the birdbath. That's the algae. The free-floating ones—that's the phytoplankton, and they're out there in Lake Superior." Phytoplankton grow like a garden. "They're simply plants. So whatever your garden needs, that's what they need. They need phosphorus, they need sunlight, and they need reasonable temperatures. This is all very much like things you understand. Because out in the woods or around your backyard, all of this stuff is happening. The leaves die and fall to the ground and they decompose, and then the little worms and whatever eat that stuff, and then the robin comes. This is just like your backyard, only it's happening in the lake."

Zooplankton are plant eaters. "You can think of them as freshwater shrimp, but they're not as big as shrimp. They're only a couple millimeters long. You have to have magnifying glasses to see these critters; they're all through the water."

Plankton live and die in two environments and are part of two food chains: the benthic and the pelagic. Benthic means the bottom of a body of water; pelagic means the open water.

What is benthos? "When you go out in the woods and roll over a log, there's all sorts of little creatures running around under there. These are terrestrial representatives of the creatures that live on the bottom of the lake. But instead of eating leaves when they fall down, they eat this rain of detritus—phytoplankton and zooplankton, which, when they die, fall to the bottom. So we talk about the food chain, about a benthic food chain and a pelagic food chain, and some fish that we're aware of in the lake are very much dependent upon one of those food chains or the other."

In the pelagic world, zooplankton eat phytoplankton; herring eat zooplankton; and lake trout feed on herring. In the benthic world, sculpins live by pecking at the different organisms that are living right down in the bottom sediments; lake trout feed on sculpins.

Marty says these are small examples of a more complex life in Lake Superior, where there are hundreds of species of phytoplankton, dozens of species of zooplankton, and dozens of species of fish.

"We can talk about suckers, we can talk about sturgeon, we can talk about king salmon, we can talk about coaster brook trout, and they will all have a place in this as well." Many are not native, including, in part, salmon, steelhead, brown trout, and smelt. For all the variety, Marty says Superior supports only one-tenth the fishery of Lake Michigan, which has warmer and more nutrient-rich waters.

Neither does Superior attract as much money for research, for there is a downside to work on this lake, Marty explains. "The shortfall of this lake is that everybody has the impression that it's a big bathtub of sterile, distilled water. It doesn't have any problems, so why care about it? It doesn't get the respect from the people who have the resources to support investigation. When you've got the Cuyahoga River on fire or the cormorants with their beaks twisted sideways, or beaches closed due to sewage pollution, that's where the money goes. So we have a hard time encouraging the people with the money to support research on this lake.

"There's a lot of work to be done because, again, harking back to something that may be familiar to you, gardening is not a simple thing. And we don't know exactly how this garden grows, and if we don't know how the garden grows, then how can we address threats? How can we manage human population pressures? How do we know how much phosphorus? How do we know how long it'll be before the PCB concentrations in the lake trout go down? How do we know what the effect of an invasive species will be? How do we know how many lake trout we can take out of the lake? How can we manage, protect, and remediate a lake when we don't understand how it works?

"You don't take your car to be fixed by the milkman. You need somebody who has studied that car, and knows how it works, and has the manuals. We don't have the manuals for Lake Superior yet. We don't understand the lake. It is so big and so extreme in many ways, we're just going to have to go and learn, step by step."

Scientists know some processes. For one, just as Superior stratifies top to bottom because colder deep water and warmer surface water don't mix, it also stacks up side by side for the same reason. The sun can warm shallow, nearshore water, because there's less of it. Expansive deep water, Marty says, "just laughs at sunshine." The result: a temperature difference of several degrees between nearshore and offshore water. Different temperatures mean different densities, and the twain meet but don't mix. This zone—the thermal bar—lies about one to two miles from shore. At this interface, the warmer water, like clothes in a dryer, hits the cold water, tumbles over, sinks, returns to shore, and recirculates back out to the thermal bar. Nutrients coming from rivers and runoff are trapped along this bar. Marty says, "Let's say you were a big delicious mayfly and you were kind of sitting on the water—where would you end up?" At the thermal bar. "So if you were a steelhead, where would you like to hang out? Right there. And in fishing terminology, this thing is called the 'scum line,' because you can actually look and see bits of foam and pieces of leaf and bugs and stuff." Along this boundary, sport fishermen cast their hopes and scientists their curiosity.

One part of the inquiry: a benthic organism called Diporeia. "You ever see pill bugs?" Marty asks me. "Those little bugs that roll up into a ball?"

"No," I reply.

"You haven't seen that? You should roll over some logs. Think of them as small shrimp. Diporeia feed by scraping around on the bottom. The detritus. They are vital to the food web because they are the primary food of the lake whitefish. As well, lake trout feed on sculpins, which feed on Diporeia. This organism is disappearing from all the Great Lakes except Lake Superior. And one of the beliefs—there is no widely accepted solution here—is that it's in competition with zebra mussels that simply filter out, suck in, all of the phytoplankton that are settling to the bottom, and nothing ever gets there for the Diporeia. This is a crisis in the other lakes, and it's beginning to impact fish populations—whitefish, for example, in Lake Michigan and Lake Huron. In Lake Superior, the Diporeia populations have not been impacted by anything, and they remain very abundant."

But not everywhere. Scientists divide Lake Superior into three regions. From shore to three kilometers, the shelf region is fairly shallow. Beyond that, there is a slope region. And then, farther out, the deep is called the profound region. The Diporeia are all on the slope—five thousand to six thousand or more to a square meter. Shallower or deeper, there are mere hundreds.

"Why do you find something more at one place than another?" Marty asks and then answers. "Let's talk about food for a minute." Their food is phytoplankton, which grows where there is sunshine. The phytoplankton settle to the bottom sediments where the Diporeia "hop around and eat it." In the shallows, where there are waves and turbulence, "You've got big trouble if you want to live there," because food doesn't settle; it's churned around. In the profound region, the water is comparatively quieter, "so things settle beautifully out there." But the Diporeia are vulnerable all the way down, as they are preyed upon by zooplankton. So in the nearshore and in the deep, "There's nothing for Diporeia to eat."

Marty and his colleagues can describe this dynamic because they have plumbed the depths with sediment traps and a small clamshell dredge. "We collected samples from the deepest spot of the lake last summer, and what you'll find down there is clear, clean water"—plus bedrock, and some fine-grained material that Marty calls "silk clay." Diporeia are down there, Marty says, but have just a toehold.

This team of researchers hopes to make a mathematical model of Lake Superior to predict how many organisms, like Diporeia, are at a given place. "If we have the capacity to predict that, then it must mean we understand how the thing works. And what we hope to be able to show is that the whole story is how much food they get. The more food you get, the more of them you can grow. If that can be shown in a mathematical framework, then we can go back to the lakes where they've lost these things and we can say, 'If the zebra mussels are getting this much of their food, then that population there should have gone down'—and we can prove it's zebra mussel competition."

It may be, Marty speculates, that circumstances have "diverted the energy of the lower lakes away from what we value as an ecosystem, say, lake trout, to one dominated by a prolific exotic of no apparent use or value." He hopes not.

His interest in what he calls "this lakes thing" was the result of a watershed encounter in his college days. "A couple of people that came into my life when I was a student showed me how exciting this field could be. This crazy guy had the fire in him, and he gave the fire to me. I had always wanted to be an explorer—all my young life—and he said, 'You can be an explorer of lakes.'"

The quest is its own reward. "Sherlock Holmes had this thing he used to say to Watson. 'Come quickly, the game is afoot.' And off they would go into the mystery. And when I see a signal in the lake, like the peak of Diporeia, I know how important Diporeia are to the fish in this lake. I know the problems they're having in the lower lakes with Diporeia. I know there is a mystery that would help us understand that organism—and may help us to do something to bring back the integrity of the lower lakes. So when I see that mystery, I hear, 'Marty, come quickly, the game is afoot.' And that's what the excitement is, whether it's contamination in Onondaga Lake, or the quality of the New York reservoir system, or Diporeia in Lake Superior. These are mysteries, and I get to find out how this system works." So he sums up his life story: "Madmen, mysteries, and the pursuit of Jacques Cousteau." Marty is immersed in an endeavor that is as mysterious as a fog, and as engaging as a riddle. "This is more fun than you could ever want to have," he says.

II

Looking for the *Edmund Fitzgerald*

Whitefish Bay, on the East End of the Lake

On the night of November 10, 1975, on the way from River Rouge to Duluth to pick up a load of iron ore, Don Erickson, captain of the SS *William Clay Ford,* reached Whitefish Bay at about four o'clock in the afternoon and hunkered down in the lee of Whitefish Point. This is the gist of his story, related over three interviews.

"The wind was blowing from 290 degrees, which is a little bit north of west. Not much. The worst storms are from the southwest. We get really bad storms outta there. I don't know why that is. You'd think out of Canada would be worse. But they actually aren't. We went to anchor. The closer you can get up to the land, you won't swing so much. We were maybe a half mile from the land, swinging 180 degrees, back and forth, and that's a strain on the anchor.

"I figured I'll just sit here all night, maybe all the next day, depending on the weather. We're in a safe place. I'll sleep all night because I don't have any worries. I went to talk to the guys in the pilothouse and tell them what to do—'If the wind shifts, if it lets down, let me know.' I was sitting up there with 'em when all this stuff comes over the radio. I heard them talking."

By "them" he means Bernie Cooper, skipper of the SS *Arthur Anderson,* and Ernest McSorley, skipper of the SS *Edmund Fitzgerald.*

"Cooper asked McSorley how he's doing.

"'We're doing fine. We're holding our own.' Because, before that, McSorley had called up Cooper and said they were taking on water and had a list. Bernie was pretty well worried about him.

"So this is getting close to seven o'clock at night. It's dark out there at that time. In November, Lake Superior is dark early.

"Cooper on the *Anderson* says, 'I just lost sight of the *Fitzgerald.* I couldn't see him on the radar, and there was a snowstorm, and he never came outta the snowstorm. I can't see him anymore.'

"So he called me up and he says, 'Eric, did you see anybody come around the point?'

"I said, 'No,' because we were watching.

"At that time, they had intermittent snowstorms, and when a snowstorm was there, you probably couldn't see much farther than the ship. And then after the squall went over, you could see maybe fifteen or twenty miles.

"Cooper kept trying to tell the Coast Guard, 'There's something wrong with the *Fitzgerald.*' The Coast Guard really didn't believe it. One of the biggest boats on the lakes at that time. Vanished.

"That went on for an hour or so. Finally, it got through to the Coast Guard that something actually had happened, so they started calling. Twelve ships were anchored on the Whitefish, under the point. And the Coast Guard called up everybody and asked them if they would go out to see what happened. See if they could find anything. Everybody, everybody said no.

"By this time, the *Anderson* is getting down close to Whitefish and the Coast Guard called the *Anderson* up and says, 'Would you go back out there and see what happened?' And Bernie says, 'Geez, if I turn around and go back out there—you got one on the bottom now, you'll have two on the bottom.' So he kept coming down the bay and I'm up in the pilothouse listening, and I know all these people. A lot of these people. Personally. Everybody said they wouldn't go out there. I go down to my room, and we're still anchored in a good place. I figured somebody got to go out there. There's them guys I know. So I went back up to the pilothouse and I called up the *Anderson* and I told him, 'Bernie, those guys are in trouble. Somebody has got to do the best they can. I'm going to pick up the anchor and go out there.' So Bernie says, 'If you go, Eric, I'll go.'

"We picked up the anchor. You can't go around close to Whitefish Point because you get a backset off of there. The sea hits the point and goes back out again, you know, like a boat going down the river—the wake hits the shore and comes back out again. With that much storm, you get a big backset. You have to get five, six miles off of there to go around that point. Anyway, the *Hilda Marjanne,* a Canadian boat, says, 'Well, we'll come out there, too.' Most of the Canadian boats at that time didn't come up in Lake Superior that often. The *Hilda Marjanne* didn't. So he doesn't know about this backset. We went down a little ways, far away enough from Whitefish Point, and we were doing alright, and the *Hilda Marjanne* came around real close because they're not as fast as we are, and they're going to cut the corner and get out there with us, and he got in that backset. He really rolled and pitched and rolled, and no matter which way you're going, you have seas coming from both ways. He decided no way could he make it. He turned around and went back into Whitefish. We kept going out there and got alongside the *Anderson*—between a half mile and a mile is about as close as we got to him. We can pretty well make him out. He knew just about where the *Fitzgerald* was, the last time he'd seen him. Now it's at least ten thirty, eleven o'clock. We were light. We didn't have any cargo, so we had it full of water, ballast. You wanted the boat down in the wind so you won't be blown sideways. The *Anderson* was better off than we were because they had cargo—it strengthens the boat.

"Everybody on the ship, everybody, was up and looking out the portholes. A whole bunch of them were up in the pilothouse because you can see better. It was a nasty night. It was really rugged, the seas coming right over the pilothouse. It's probably thirty feet up there.

"We got over just about where Bernie said he lost 'em and we checked down. You are going against the wind and the sea, and you check her down, you'll stay right there. You don't go anyplace. I called the Coast Guard at the Soo. 'Okay, now you got us out here, what are we going to do if we find anything?' A sea running like that, you couldn't launch a boat to pick up anybody. You couldn't do much of anything. And the Coast Guard says, 'Well, don't worry, if you see anything, let us know, and the helicopters'—they had two helicopters in Traverse City—'they would take care of it.' They had a C130 out there, and they were dropping flares down, so we could see. We wanted them to try to drop the flares closer. They were afraid to burn through the deck, afraid to get too close. I didn't expect to find anybody, but we were hoping.

"We stayed there all night until it was getting daylight the next morning. It's eight o'clock before it's daylight around that time. We stayed right in that area. After two o'clock in the morning, three o'clock in the morning, someplace like that, the wind started going down a little bit, abating. Then the other ships that were down in the bay said—'Well, the wind is going down,' they'll come out and do what they could, too. So we're talking to the Coast Guard, and he says, 'You guys did as much as you could. These other guys are all going to come out there now, so you go ahead and proceed wherever you're going to go,' so we went up the lake.

"We met the Coast Guard cutter *Woodrush,* out of Duluth, right around Keweenaw. And by the time we got up to Keweenaw, there was pret'near dead calm. So we went on up to Duluth, and by that time another storm had come through, and I couldn't get in Duluth. The wind was blowing right across the piers. That was the next storm to come down. The *Woodrush* didn't get down the lake until the second storm. The captain of the *Woodrush,* he said that's the worst storm he'd ever been in. He was in the second one that came down there."

Outside of Duluth, it was too deep to anchor, so Don went back and forth for twelve hours, perhaps a mile offshore, beneath the bluffs northeast of the city. "It's high land, see. You got a good lee there. In all the years that I sailed, that's the only time that I couldn't get into Duluth on account of the weather."

Five days later, Don was back in Duluth at the same time as Bernie Cooper of the *Anderson*. Cooper told Don that he thought the *Fitzgerald,* ten miles ahead, went too close to Caribou Island, where there's a long shoal, Six Fathom Shoal, which is thirty-six feet. Cooper decided not to go that close and altered his course ten degrees.

Don continues: "Just after that, McSorley called up Bernie and says, 'We're having problems, we're making water.'

"So it has to be that's what happened. That he got in too close and, in my opinion—there's all kinds of opinions, you know—that there's no other thing in my mind that would make that *Fitzgerald* sink. Touching that shoal. Probably didn't touch it really bad, but just put a hole in it. Three hours later he was gone.

"After all the years of thinking about this stuff, it's one of those things that happens, and you feel bad about it 'cause they're people you know. We decided all we could do is go out there and do the best we can.

CAPTAIN DON ERICKSON has a picture of the SS *Benson Ford* gripped in ice in December of 1984. He has crackled through ice on Superior in June. I knew a wheelsman, now gone, who told of ten inches of snow from a lake squall in early July.
(Photo by Brian Parmeter.)

"Somebody else would do the same thing, but they don't happen to be there at that time. You don't do any of this stuff on purpose. If you happen to be there, you do the work. You try to help 'em as much as you can. That's just normal procedure. That's the law of the sea. You're supposed to help anybody as long as you're not endangering the ship.

"We have a storm like that two or three times a year. It wasn't really anything out of the ordinary. The longer you're out there, the more storms you get. Lot's of 'em."

Don Erickson is part Swede, part Norwegian. He was born in 1927 and raised in Superior, Wisconsin, a maritime community just east of Duluth. He went from high school dropout to able-bodied seaman to captain. "Everything I'm telling you is my opinion, and it's true," he assures me. "I'm not telling you nothing I wouldn't sign my name to."

As a lad, he worked at the grain elevators. When he turned fifteen, he had a birth certificate forged to get his seaman's papers. "The notary public would sign anything," he remembers. A year older on paper, he went down to the docks.

"You need a deckhand?" he asked a mate.

"Go home and get your clothes."

It was like that, back then. Lots of ships, lots of jobs. "You could get a job pret'near all the time in them years."

Don is a short man with wispy white hair, a gravelly voice, and a calm bearing. He recalls his years of sea duty as he sits in an easy chair at his summer home, which is on a cove on Huron Bay off Keweenaw Bay, ten miles east of L'Anse, Michigan.

He was seaman for six years. During the off-season, he studied to be a pilot and was diligent about it. Others in the class weren't. "They're all sitting most of the time, telling stories about what boats they're on, and then go down and drink their lunch. Go back up, and tell some more stories. After a week of that, I figured I'm not learning anything here. So I got one of the other guys. We got together and studied by ourself."

He earned his first-class pilot license and served as a helmsman for a year, even though that was lesser duty for his new capabilities. "As a wheelsman, you learn the docks and how the boat handles. That's where you start. Originally, all the guys went up that way. I went up quick." After one year as a first mate, he wrote for his master's license. His wife, whom he married in 1956, helped him study. "It hasn't always been easy," he says. "I wouldn't say I'm very smart as far as academics." In 1962, at age thirty-four, he was a skipper; he served twenty-five seasons, all on the *William Clay Ford,* a 647-footer with a straight deck built in 1953.

In one respect, it was like being all by oneself in a crowd. He says, "To a certain extent, no matter what happens, the captain is the captain. It doesn't matter who or what the captain is like—they all just treat him that way. He's 'the old man.' In that sense of the word, it gets lonely."

Most of the time he guided his ship from Ford's River Rouge works to Duluth and Superior to pick up iron ore. They made eighteen knots an hour light, fifteen knots full. It took five days and eight hours to make the round trip from River Rouge to Duluth and back. It took twenty-four hours just to cross Lake Superior. He also went to Thunder Bay, as well as Escanaba and Marquette, Michigan. When workers on the Mesabi Iron Range were on strike, he hauled ore out of Labrador.

Sailors are a superstitious bunch, but as a captain, Don adhered to only one of these notions: after the winter layover, never leave dock on the first trip of the season on a Friday. "It was bad luck. If they wanted to leave Friday, they might leave the dock on Thursday night, get a hundred feet away from it, and go back in."

Out on the water, he sounded the very depths of life. "I'm not very religious at all," he says, "but there's no place that you would be closer to God than being out there by yourself. We had a passenger on board. He would come up in the pilothouse with me on Lake Superior. He said, 'Don't you feel important when you're captain on a boat here like this?' I said, "No, you look over there, there's another boat there. All you can see is a light or two, and there's people just like we are on that boat, and what is that? A small little light you see over there. That's all it is. So you're not important. You're not a whole bunch of anything. You're just—it shows how small you are compared to what some people think.'"

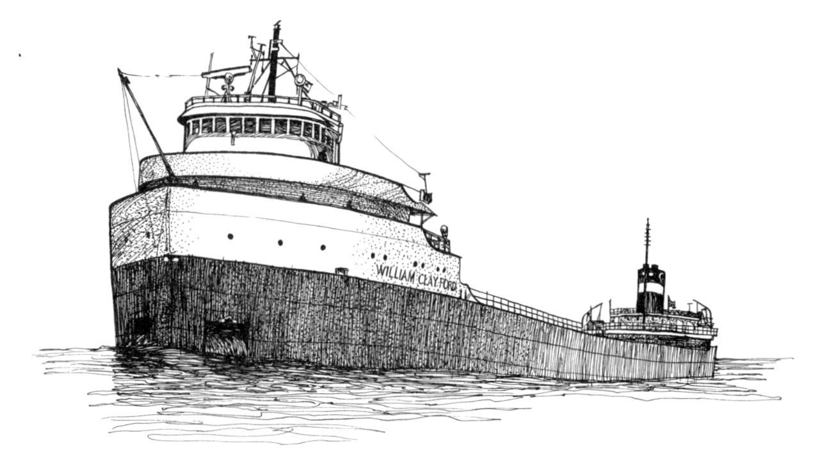

The William Clay Ford. (Drawing by Sandy Slater.)

Why does the fate of the *Fitzgerald* have such an enduring hold on the imagination? Compare it to a day in 1912, when twelve ships went down during a storm on Superior and 249 sailors were lost. In light of that, I ask Don, why is the *Fitzgerald* so storied?

"That song." (He means Gordon Lightfoot's 1976 "The Wreck of the *Edmund Fitzgerald.*") The mariners' chapel in Detroit tolling the bell twenty-nine times every year, one for each man lost. ("Touching.") The mystery of why the ship went down. ("Nobody will ever know.") It adds up, he says, to a legend: "Once it's started, it's mystic."

Don has a metal plaque on the wall of his workshop. "Presented to the officers and men of the Ford Motor Company vessel *William Clay Ford,* by the Great Lakes Maritime Institute, in appreciative recognition of their heroism. On the night of November 10–11, 1975, these men voluntarily left a safe harbor to face the dangers of gale-force winds and vicious seas, in the blackness of a storm which had already claimed as a victim the steamer *Edmund Fitzgerald,* to search for possible survivors of that disaster, exemplifying the finest traditions of the maritime profession." Listed are the names of Captain Donald Erickson, master, and his crew of twenty-eight.

He remembers all those men supporting him on that fateful night. "They said, 'Anytime you want to go, we'll go with you.' That was a pretty nice feeling—no matter what we did, they were on my side."

Don says of his days learning to be a helmsman, "You always look behind you to see the snake you're making. That's where you learn it's crooked." These days, looking back, his wake is straight.

One man who will attest to that is Dale Lindstrom, who Don says was the best mate he ever had. Dale, who went on to become a skipper, is retired now and lives just down the road from Don in L'Anse. I go to see him. He says of Don, "I learned it his way, and that was the best way. He was one of the best guys I ever sailed with, and I've sailed with a few."

Dale was Don's third mate on that fateful night when the *Fitzgerald* wouldn't see morning. "If we were from me to you, we couldn't have helped," he says. "It wasn't anything heroic. It was just something we had to do. What we did wasn't that interesting," he adds, gesturing emphatically. "I could tell you an interesting story, but it'd be all lies." Truth be told, people have been down there, on the bottom, and Dale is amazed that nobody has seen any bodies. "It's awful weird that they all stayed inside," he says.

Meanwhile, come November every year, Don gets phone calls from the curious and the media. Too many of them. "It almost makes you wish you hadn't done it," he says.

12

"This Is Home Now"

Hancock, Michigan

Gilmore Peterson, seasoned and savvy, navigates the restive waters of Lake Superior in search of a livelihood. Day after day, he plumbs the depths to net fish to sell in his market on the hilltop above Hancock, Michigan. He deals with the vicissitudes of his trade stoically, the weather bravely, the routine doggedly. He has two boats, oilcans both—stocky and unhandsome. They are called gill net tugs and are for toil, not pleasure. "Yachts are for a ride," Gilmore says. "Boats are for work."

Gilmore, who is in his early sixties, is six feet tall and hefty, but a bad back slows him down. He speaks softly and surely—without a hint of the proverbial "chattering mind." Instead, he has the calm air of somebody who knows what he's about. He is patient with my questions but has little faith in my ability to write about his work. "You'll glamorize it," he tells me. "You'll make it seem interesting." I right off get the drift that this business isn't all song and sunshine.

Gilmore, who is part Indian and part Scandinavian, is a member of the Red Cliff Band of Lake Superior Ojibwe. He grew up in Bayfield, Wisconsin, where the workingmen were tied to nature, laboring as loggers, farmers, and fishermen. He himself is in a line of fishermen that goes back three generations to one of his great-grandfathers. His grandfathers were "fishermen and everything else that you can be." His father was a fisherman, too. Gilmore recalls days when one hundred boats plied the waters and reefs around the Apostle Islands in pursuit of herring, which they caught by the ton.

"Were there more fish then?" I ask.

"No," Gilmore answers. "That's why Dad had to go on the ore boats."

His dad put Gilmore to work when he was nine. He worked in the summer and early fall in a twenty-eight-foot open boat. When he was young, he freed fish from the net. When he was older, he lifted nets by hand. When the fishing was slack, he picked berries, picked beans, picked rocks, and peeled pulp. "Little here, little there, little this," he describes his working youth. "You did all kinds of things to make a little money when you didn't have any. Sometimes there wasn't no work." Gilmore doesn't remember the hardships of his child labor, only the lessons. "You got to learn how to work," he says. "A kid don't know how."

That attitude appears to be an adult perspective, though, because at age seventeen, figuring his dad worked him too hard, Gilmore quit school after the eleventh grade and went to Milwaukee looking for adventure. "You have to try other things," he explains. "You don't know what you'll do."

How you gonna keep 'em up on the lake after they've seen Milwaukee?

Easy.

Gilmore worked in a warehouse and operated a forklift. The wages weren't bad, but the work was boring and a bit out of plumb. "A lot of times you're done and they tell you to go hide," he tells me. He means out of sight, out of the boss's mind. "I didn't like that."

Lake Superior started looking pretty attractive—"a little more diversity," Gilmore recalls, and "you have to use your wits." So, after two months in the big city, Gilmore was lured back home by his dad's ways. He says of his father: "He didn't monkey around. You always had to work, and you had to work hard. Dad wouldn't let you do anything but. 'C'mon, now. Let's go.'" The ethic rubbed off on Gilmore. "I can't see myself retiring. You work 'till the day you die."

Gilmore worked with his dad for several years; then his dad worked for him. In the early 1980s, there were twenty-three other fishermen working the waters around Bayfield. Then, in 1985, after a long limbo—twenty-five years or more—commercial fishing reopened off of the Keweenaw Peninsula. Gilmore commuted for three years, then moved up permanently in 1988. He calls the Bayfield area "up there," and the Keweenaw "down here." "This is home now," he says.

I get nosy and fish around for details on how successful Gilmore's business is.

"I hate to tell you everything," he says. He adds that the price of doing business—fuel, nets, hired help, and wear and tear on the boats—"drives everybody out." He remarks, "You have to catch a lot to make a living."

His is the only full-time operation on the Keweenaw, and he is the only Indian with a fish market. He opened it in 1994. It is both savior and devil. He eliminates the middleman, so he makes better money, but it's a tough go. "The hard part is when you got all these orders," he says. "They depend on you. You have to have the fish." So when the times are good, he fishes hard, and when the times are bad, he fishes hard. "I have fished Christmas," he says.

He fills orders and worries about filling orders. Sometimes he has to buy fish to meet the demand. The idea behind the business is simple: "You do something that people want." But the work is anything but simple. He has to find fish, catch fish, lift fish, gut fish, clean fish, fillet fish, smoke fish, package fish, and ship fish. "Some days you don't make any money," Gilmore says, "some days you do. Some people think that fishing is dropping a net. I work harder now than I did when I was younger."

That, of course, goes back to those days when he labored before he shaved. When he first tells me he started working at age nine, it is within earshot of two of his sons at the filleting table in the fish house.

"How old were you when you started fishing?" he asks the two, both big strapping young men.

"Nine," they chorus.

"Coincidence," Gilmore says.

The man who put him to work when he was a small fry has passed on. "Dad was a hard worker," Gilmore says. "The whole town knew that. Everybody liked him. They don't come around but every hundred years like him."

Six types of fish occupy Gilmore's time and attention—chubs, herring, whitefish, salmon, lean lake trout, and siscowets. The siscowets are junk. When Gilmore catches them, he throws them right back in the drink. "They're the biggest thing in the lake, probably. They shouldn't be."

"Were there fat trout when you were young?" I ask.

"Been around forever, yah."

I can't tell the difference between a lean trout and a siscowet. Gilmore can at a glance. He says they have a fatter belly, whiter skin, more fat in the meat, and a pug nose. "They look like they run into a building."

If there are too many siscowets, Gilmore says, there are too few chubs. There used to be loads of them in the lake. Not anymore. "The fat trout eat 'em up." Now he has to buy chubs to smoke. He also has to buy salmon because they are top feeders and Gilmore fishes the bottom and catches them rarely.

Gilmore calls the lake trout "an incidental catch." He says, "If you were just catching trout, you'd be a part-time fisherman." He's allowed to take two thousand trout a year, but he never fills the quota. He's not allowed to set for trout in November when they spawn because they school up and are "too easy to target." Herring also spawn in November, when Gilmore goes after them in earnest. That leaves whitefish. "That's our main fish, anyway, that we depend on," he says.

The trout are primarily a local sell because "nobody wants them," Gilmore explains, noting that many people are scared off of trout because of PCBs.

Gilmore doesn't believe that fish in any way contribute to poor health. "Fishermen ate that fish all of their life," he says. "I never knew one to die of a heart attack." He quickly corrects himself: "One fisherman I know of died of a heart attack. He was picking apples. But then he was ninety-two."

I accompany Gilmore, who is the rudder of this operation, on two trips to Lake Superior. One time, his son Chris is the lone hand. A second time, there is extra help: Ray, Chris's cousin. There is no mistaking that Chris has the brawn for the bull work on the boat. He has bulky shoulders, thick arms, and meaty hands. I ask him whether he likes fishing. "It's okay," he answers. "I missed a lot of summers, but I had money."

Gilmore's gill nets are three hundred feet long and four feet high. He sets gangs of six nets. He's allowed to set up to twelve thousand feet a day. On a typical day, this crew deploys nets and then lifts the previous day's set. When the raise is on, Gilmore tends the mechanical lifter and steers the net to the picking table, where Chris frees the fish from the net, and Ray fills up tubs at his feet with nets, guts, and herring eggs.

Chris fills tubs with whitefish, herring, and lake trout. The tubs are behind him but he doesn't need to look to toss and hit the mark. Each tub holds about one hundred pounds of fish. I count the contents of one tub: thirty-nine fish fill it. Some of the fish are lifeless, some flap desperately, some gape, and many are streaked with blood. All have eyes like shiny black and silver beads.

It takes an hour to lift the nets. The first half of the gang is a steady diet of fish, one every five or six feet, sometimes three or four together. The second half of the net is almost empty. I comment on this to Ray. "It just works out that way sometimes," he says. "It has its short days; it has its long days." After the net is all in, Gilmore climbs to the pilothouse and heads the boat for home, slowly, on automatic pilot. Then he climbs back down to help gut the catch. I notice that Chris is putting aside the livers.

"Why save them?" I ask Chris.

"Ray likes 'em."

Ray says, "Batter 'em up and fry 'em—they're good for the masculinity."

Chris doesn't like them. "They taste like liver to me."

Eggs and livers excepted, the picking table is a mess of blood and guts and scales. Styx must look like this.

It takes the men less than an hour to gut the roughly 240 fish—about seven hundred pounds. One hundred pounds is a bad catch; two thousand pounds a good catch. Gutting done, the men wash their rubber gear, the deck, and the picking table. With Gilmore back at the wheel, the boat muscles along. "It's powerful," Ray says. "It can push you right through ice." It is like this crew's work: absolutely no fumbling.

On another trip I take with him, Gilmore can't find a set, although he searches and searches for it.

"Do you lose many?" I ask.

"Oh, yah. You lose 'em. Not too often, though. I actually think when you can't find 'em, they're stolen."

I tell him what an old Maine lobsterman told me long ago. "Sonny," he said, "the waterfront is full of cutthroat and jealousy."

"That's basically true," Gilmore says of some fishermen. "A lot of 'em are hungry. They want every fish in the lake."

But Gilmore has a tranquil nature, and he doesn't let a lost net rankle him. "I got enough to worry about without worrying about that," he says, but allows that greed, well, "It don't do anybody any good."

His search for the missing net fruitless, Gilmore heads to a second net, ten minutes away. After lifting it, he returns to the area of the lost net. With GPS as a guide, Gilmore drops a grappling hook on a line where the net should be. A few minutes later, in 150 feet of water, he snags it, and then he gives the line to Chris, who pulls it in, hand over hand, looking for the end of the net so they can attach it to the lifter. Over and over Chris pulls, his face contorting into a grimace. After a long fifteen minutes, he has the end of the net up. Gilmore looks at the rope that was affixed to the lost buoy. A clean cut—no fray, no tatter.

"What happened?" I ask.

"I have no idea." He pauses, then says, "That's the trouble. People think they're being smart. They don't know you got to find the bugger." Gilmore confides that he has taught many Indians how to fish over the years. Now some of them want him out of the area and out of business. "I guess there's people like that all over," he says. "Every religion and every walk of life." That is a mouthful for this man; it's as sore as he gets.

Peterson's Fish Market sits atop Quincy Hill, ten miles south of North Entry. There is a sales area and an adjoining room for work, which involves mostly cleaning and filleting as well as processing herring eggs. The filleting is an art. Standing to Gilmore's right, I marvel at how fast he is. "If you weren't standing next to me," he remarks, "I could go a lot quicker."

The fillets are sorted—some for sale, some for smoking. The smoker, just outside the side door to the fish house, is like a metal closet: six feet high, six feet wide, and three feet deep. The fish are on racks or hooks, beneath which a hard maple fire smolders in a shallow, cut-off barrel. The fire is warm and the wood smoke smells good. The setup "does a good job," Gilmore says. "We just do old-fashioned slow cooking." They smoke the fish one and a half hours longer than required by the State Health Department.

Customers can buy whole fish, fillets, smoked fish, and herring caviar. As well, Gilmore's wife, Pat, makes and sells a fish spread made from "onions, relish, fish, and a secret ingredient."

The rest of the afternoon, Gilmore idles about, having a smoke, drinking pop, and munching on smoked chubs, which are golden brown, wrinkly, and big-eyed. A few customers come in. One wants fish carcasses. He'll put them in water to grow leeches that he'll sell for bait. Gilmore gives him the carcasses, and then we talk fishing.

"Do you have a map of the lake bottom?" I ask.

"No." Then he gestures to his head: "Up here, yah."

"Do you have good spots that you keep quiet about?"

"Eventually, everybody finds out anyway. They can see you there lifting."

"How long did it take you to learn the trade?"

"I'm probably still learning."

Then his net mender, an old Finn, comes in. He charges $125 a gang. Gilmore pays him.

"You're paid in full," the man says.

"You're never paid in full—just for a little while," Gilmore answers.

Summertime and the fishing is easy?

Not for Gilmore. He says fall and spring are the best seasons for fishing. There are more fish around.

"Why?"

"I don't know. There just is. They must school up or something. Sometimes there's no rhyme or reason to it. You can't pinpoint it."

In contrast, in the winter and summer, fish are "spread out."

Gilmore generally fishes from one hundred to five hundred feet deep—seldom deeper. "Too deep in the water, you start hitting the fat trout," he says. "You don't want them."

Gilmore fishes on both sides of the Keweenaw Peninsula. The one constant: he fishes the bottom. As the fish roam, he follows. "You just find 'em," he says. Experience—what he calls "knowledge from years ago"—helps.

"Do you have secrets?" I ask.

"Oh, we probably got a few," he answers. He will, for instance, set his nets different ways, perhaps southeast instead of northeast—"stuff like that." Still, he says, he's learning all the time. "My dad said, 'You learn something every day fishing.'"

Whatever his strategy or whatever the season, Gilmore has to contend with the current. It can be especially strong on the north side of the peninsula, although "it's all over," he says. "It can be different top and bottom. It can move those nets. It can drag them a long ways." It can be so strong that sometimes logs are moving on the bottom. Along with snags and rocks, they account for big tears in his nets. "You want the fish to wear out the net—not the sticks and stuff," Gilmore says.

When on the water in winter, Gilmore sometimes can't see land. With cold air and warm water, the lake "steams," he explains, and that steam hangs in the air like a shroud. A ferryboat captain told me once that old-time fishermen could smell the land in the fog. I ask Gilmore about that. "No," he says. "Their nose ain't better than no one else's."

If the current is hard on nets, wind wears on Gilmore. "Rolling around is hard. Never used to be, but it's getting there. Little aches and pains become big aches and pains." His dad had to quit fishing because "his legs went to heck"—"He couldn't stand it anymore," Gilmore says. "It's the odd angles, plus it's throwing you this way and throwing you that way. It's probably worse than working."

"Ever caught in a bad storm?" I ask.

"Yes."

"Were you afraid?"

"No. You go out there long enough, you don't get scared. Scared don't do anybody any good." He allows, though, that with big waves—some higher than his fish house—"you know you're out there." It has to blow pretty hard for him not to go.

"Are you superstitious?" I ask.

"Probably not. You just go. You gotta go, you gotta go. Catching lots of fish? Go."

I tell him I've heard that old-time sailors didn't want women on a working boat.

That wasn't superstition, Gilmore says, it was practicality. "A lot of men needed work." Anyway, in earlier days, Pat, who now runs the store, often helped him on the boat.

Chasing fish can be chancy. "They might be out here one day and ten miles up the lake the next."

Fishing "probably isn't like any other thing," Gilmore says. He contrasts fishing to logging. A logger, he notes, can count the trees on the back forty. "On the lake you don't know. You can't say, 'I'm going to go out and catch a thousand pounds.' One day you'll catch a thousand, the next day three fish."

"Does the barometer affect fishing?" I ask.

"No."

"Wind?"

"Sometimes, I suppose."

GILMORE PETERSON: *You gotta go, you gotta go. Catching lots of fish? Go.*

"Temperature?"

"I wouldn't know. I don't think so. It's where the feed is. They gotta eat."

The bottom of the lake is a world he can only dimly discern. "It's a long way down there. They don't even see the sun."

His work is tiring. "It's all hard," he says. "There ain't nothing easy. Hurry up and go as fast as you can. That's about it." Although the fact that it's hard does lend job security. "If it was easy, everybody would be fishing."

Experience helps with the pursuit.

"Did those old-timers know the ropes?"

"Probably, yah. You learn on your own, too. You learn other things—kind of add to the knowledge. You can kind of think, too."

It beats driving a forklift. Gilmore has traded "the same thing to the same place" for "different year, different stuff," by which he means his encounters are as changeable as the weather.

Despite the downsides, he is aboard for good.

Would he ever quit?

"I couldn't if I wanted to. That's all I know." He adds, however, "Most of the time I get tired of it."

Gilmore is one of seven children—the youngest of four boys. He has two doses of Scandinavian blood—Norwegian and Swedish—and also Ojibwe. When he was growing up, the mix didn't matter. "You're considered Indian," he says. "The Indian part was hard. It was a bad thing to be." But he never denied his heritage. "I never lied about it. You are what you are. You can't change it." Nor can you get around it. "There's prejudiced people all over." The ill feeling he encountered was subtle but sure. "They never tell you. You just, oh, you don't believe as good about yourself. They think you're inferior. You could tell."

Gilmore attended Catholic school for nine years, and he doesn't speak kindly of that upbringing. He wasn't allowed to practice native traditions or speak the language. "You couldn't be anything Indian. They made me feel bum."

"Were you able to shake it off?"

"I don't think it's all shaken off yet, actually. You kind of realize you're not as bad as you thought you were. At least for me. I couldn't say about other people."

"Are you still Catholic?"

"No. I don't think so."

"Do you follow native ways now?"

"No. I'm aware of them."

I ask him about dream catchers in the fish house.

"I don't know," he answers. "Ask the wife." He says Pat dances in the annual powwows and makes native costumes for the grandkids. "She wants them to know that they're Indian and be proud of it."

Gilmore went to the funeral of his godmother, an Indian-language teacher, recently. The funeral lasted two days, and she was buried on the third day. "No crying. You can't cry. No glasses. You have to see her with your own eyes." Somebody had to keep a fire tended, and somebody had to sit with her. "That was interesting," Gilmore says. "I don't remember everything."

One tradition Gilmore knows about is called a giveaway. "If they honor you, you give stuff to people." It's an exercise in material detachment. "You give something close to you, not junk. It's got to be something you cherish."

I remark that I've read that some Indians believe the lake is a spirit.

"That's the way the Indians believe. I'm not very religious at all."

"Do you believe the lake is a spirit?" I ask.

"Nah, I don't think so," he answers. "But if there was a religion to believe in, it would be Indian. They honor what they see. Their God is what they see. It's a good religion, I suppose. Better than most. It's more of a giving religion than a taking religion." He is kindhearted about those who believe the lake is a spirit: "Some people might need that."

What he values most are his family and his work. His philosophical stance: take responsibility for your own actions. His business, then, is based on accountability. "You're your own boss," he says. "You can't lie—to yourself, even." Truly, he's a practical man.

The job can become wearisome, but never the lake. "I just love being on the water and working on it. It gets in your blood. I just enjoy it. I always did—ever since I was a kid. Maybe it was an adventure or something. I don't have to grow up."

In harsher days, Gilmore, part Indian, part white, would have been called a half-breed. But there is a better way to describe him. For in the ore-rich Keweenaw, there is another thing called a half-breed: a nugget that is part copper, part silver.

13
The Ricer
Odanah, Wisconsin

According to Ojibwe oral history, five hundred years ago the spiritual leaders told their people, who lived on the Atlantic Ocean at either Hudson Bay or the mouth of the St. Lawrence River, to move west for survival—as far west as "where food grows on water." That food was the wild rice of the Lake Superior basin, including northern Wisconsin west of Ashland—an area called "the Wisconsin everglades" that is on and around the Bad River Indian Reservation. Some Indians call the Bad River Tribe "the bog people" because of their close ties to the wetlands and the wild rice that grows there.

A member of the Bear Clan of the Bad River Tribe, Sharon Nelis is a ricer. Each late August she and her sons venture by canoe into the expansive Bad River Sloughs to harvest the wild rice, which rises from the water like wheat in a field. It's easy to get lost here, but Sharon knows her way around.

Sharon is savvy, especially about nature and its bounty. Partridge and muskrat are her daily fare. She knows how to make maple syrup and how to brain-tan deer hides. She cans venison and makes a dozen kinds of jellies. She makes moccasins, knife sheaths, and parfleches. She likes to ice-fish for lawyer on Lake Superior and for walleye in both the lake and the sloughs. All of these activities please her. "I think I was born a century too late," she says.

Sharon, who is in her fifties, also does magnificent beadwork, as delicate as sand painting. She has beaded everything from salt and pepper shakers to a priest's stole. She shows me her dancing skirt, which is simply stunning. She's been beading since she was eighteen and describes the activity as a "long process, a lot of work." She says, "I've got to work hard for these things that I want."

"Are you known for your beadwork?" I ask.

"I feel it's a gift I've been given. I've only charged for it once for one little piece—one time I needed money real bad. But I usually barter. I get a lot of stuff like that—trading."

SHARON NELIS: *I've got to work hard for these things that I want.*

Sharon recently made three pairs of moccasins for a man. She used moose hide—she has eight of those stashed away—thick for the sole, thin for the tops so "you could bead on it." In return, she received enough walleye to fill her freezer.

Sharon explains that beadwork is distinctive. She can distinguish the products of the Iroquois, the Winnebago, and the Seminole. She characterizes her work as an art, not a hobby or craft. The Ojibwe word for bead means "berry from the Great Spirit." Beadwork, then, is a spiritual exercise; Sharon compares the beads to rosaries and worry beads. Beading is also a "tranquil" exercise. For colors and shapes, she takes inspiration from nature—sunsets, sunrises, flowers, leaves, and water. According to Sharon's culture, the beader must leave a mistake in each piece because nothing is perfect except the Creator. She doesn't particularly worry much about that because she always spots something wrong with her work.

She gets her beads from a warehouse in New York City and especially likes what she calls "cut beads," which are faceted and reflect light nicely. She has trays and bowls filled with beads. "Severe punishment to the person who spills any of my precious stock," she has said in writing about her work. She concludes, "Beading will either drive you insane or sane, depending on what you are."

I ask her about hunting.

"I don't think of it as hunting," she responds.

"What is it?"

"Dinner."

Sharon's father taught her how to hunt for rabbit, deer, and partridge. "Now I got boys, so I don't have to do it anymore. One of these years I'm going to hunt rabbits again. I love rabbit. I don't care how you fix it. And muskrats. I like all that wild game. I don't care for beaver much. It's too rich." She has eaten beaver but not beaver tail. "I like the muskrat a little better. The small ones. It's not greasy, and it's got a very mild flavor. It's very, very good. It doesn't have that gamy, wild taste. You wouldn't even know you're eating it."

"Do you like bear meat?"

"I can't eat bear. I'm Bear Clan."

In the summer of 2004, she shot and killed a nuisance bear on her property. "A great big bear." After she shot it, she stayed in the house. "I was home alone and didn't know if it was wounded or not, or if it was dead." When her son Andy came home, he right away put tobacco out for her, which is an Indian gesture meant to square matters with the spirit world. "I felt really bad. I'm Bear Clan so that would be like my brother. It was one of those things. You had to shoot. It couldn't be helped. I had grandchildren and he was getting too close to the house." Andy buried the bear and put more tobacco down. "I probably could have used the hide, but I didn't want to do a bear hide, cause it's so heavy and hard. I've never done a bear hide." She did save the claws. They will be a gift for others for dancing regalia.

Sharon has long, dark hair, a soft, soothing voice, and a generous nature. She grew up in Milwaukee. Her father was Ojibwe and English; her mother was Ojibwe and Swedish "and something else in there." She moved to the Bad River area in 1978. She married her second husband, Marv, in 1987. He died of cancer in 1996. He was "quite wild in his day," Sharon says, and an outdoorsman. "He knew every berry, every foot of the reservation. He knew every tree. He knew his woods." He taught Sharon and her children how to rice.

She says her husband was very traditional—"He didn't just talk about it. He did it. . . . He loved old people and kids. And he would always share what we had. We weren't rich, but we'd have boxes of jellies and he would take a case and give it away. He always said, 'I've got to take care of these old people because someday I might have to be taken care of.'"

Marv was raised Catholic but as an adult took to native ways, so he wanted a funeral that combined the two traditions—a mass in church and a native ceremony at home. Sharon says the native ritual contained nothing "weird" or "secret," but she is disinclined to talk about it. "It's not something you discuss." She relents, though, and talks about the funeral a little bit. Inside the home, all the mirrors were covered, so Marv's spirit couldn't see itself still in the world and be reluctant to leave. When the ceremony was over, the casket was passed outside through a window rather than the front door—"so the spirit will start the journey and not look back to see our sorrows and tears." Outside the home, friends and relatives tended a fire, stoked with purifying cedar and tobacco, that burned until the ritual was over. People stayed up in shifts throughout the day and night so the fire wouldn't go out and the body be left alone. Sharon explains, "That's why they call them 'wakes.' You stay up with the body." Everybody told stories. Everybody feasted. "Feed everybody who comes to the house," Sharon says. "Scads of food." The ritual took three nights and four days. There was no service in a funeral home. Sharon says her husband hated funeral homes. "He wanted to be at home and have all the relatives and friends come." The funeral took place on warm autumn days. Sharon remembers it well. "If every funeral could be nice, this was one of the nicest."

When Marv was alive, he and Sharon leased an old cabin on a spit of land with the Bad River Sloughs on one side and Lake Superior on the other. They typically moved out there when school was over and stayed until after ricing. "It wasn't anything fancy. Just a little square shack. We did it up really nice."

From the trailhead where they parked their vehicles, it was three miles to the cabin, accessible by snowmobile in the winter and either four-wheeler or boat in the summer. No running water, a woodstove to cook and heat. Two big gardens and five-gallon buckets from the river to water them. The cabin was furnished with double bunks to accommodate eight adults. The kids usually slept outdoors. The family had a protective Doberman, "a sweetheart," that kept the bears away.

"I've always had a thing with water," Sharon says. "When I go out there, I feel at peace." It transcends ownership. "It's not mine. I'm invading. The lake is all the spirits, and I'm trespassing." Whether she takes fish or deer, water or rice, she puts tobacco down for thanks. "You take anything, you put tobacco down. We're taking from that Earth. My grandmother taught me that. I grew up knowing that you don't take things. You have to give something back, and I taught my kids that, too."

The Ojibwe consider four plants sacred: tobacco, sweetgrass, sage, and cedar. All of them "bring your prayers to the Creator." Tobacco is the most powerful. Before tobacco arrived in the area, the Ojibwe used *kinnikinnick,* a mixture of dried plants and barks that they smoked. "My husband knew how to make it. He was going to show me, but he passed away."

Sharon's husband encouraged her to go to Wisconsin Indianhead Technical College in Ashland, where she received an associate's degree in business administration. She graduated in 1991, twenty years after finishing high school. Since then, she has worked for the Great Lakes Indian Fish and Wildlife Commission at Odanah, where she is helping with a project to gather the Ojibwe names for 177 north woods songbirds.

Sharon likes to dance at powwows. "I have powwows in my blood. When it's in your blood, it's in your blood. When you hear those drums, you just gotta go. It's like the heartbeat of the Earth."

She's been dancing since she was eighteen around the United States and Canada. "I feel exhilarated. I feel real proud going out there." She explains there are three kinds of dances: traditional dancing, shawl dancing, and jingle dancing. "Traditional dancers do a much milder step, a quieter step. It's been passed on for hundreds of years—that's why it's called traditional dancing. They've got what you call 'cut a rug'—and that's when you're standing in one place and going with the beat of the drums. The younger girls are shawl dancers. It's called shawl dancing because they do the fancier step. They dance like that and they have fringe all over the shawl because they're like butterflies, and they're trying to attract the younger guys, where your traditional dancers are usually your older generation. You don't move as well." And the jingle dancers? "They do the dancing for healing—not for oneself, but for someone else—and it's kind of a mixture of the other two." Jingle dancers sound like their name, and these days they buy bells to go with their regalia. Years ago they used empty snuff cans.

Sharon broke both legs in a four-wheeling accident and was confined to a wheelchair for four years. Wanting to dance gave her resolve. "My goal was to dance again, and I worked real hard to do that, and sure enough, I got back out there."

The accident occurred in 1997, a year after her husband died. She and her youngest son, Sam, were four-wheeling. He was going too fast, lost control, and pitched over the machine. Sharon went to brake hard but accidentally hit the throttle—she flew through the air, too. When she hit the ground, she knew her legs were broken. "I kept calling Sam's name. I thought he broke his neck. I pleaded with the Creator not to take him also." Sam was fine. "It took me months to get over the sight of my baby flying over the four-wheeler. I would wake up startled at the memory for months. I wished I would've hit my head so I didn't remember that vision."

Sharon tells me that the keeping of Indian traditions skipped a generation in her family. Her grandparents and great-uncles and great-aunts were punished for speaking Ojibwe instead of English and for clinging to native ways. "They had it the hardest," Sharon says. Therefore, they didn't impart the traditions to their sons and daughters, Sharon's parents' generation. "I wasn't brought up real traditionlike." But now some of her generation—not all—are returning to traditional ways, learning their language, for instance. Her grandmother was fluent in Ojibwe. Her mother isn't. "I probably know more than my mom."

She was close to her grandmother on her mother's side. The woman was always "quiet and vague" about her upbringing. When Sharon got older, she realized that her grandmother was simply hiding unpleasantness. The result, she says, is that stories, language, and herbal medicine have been lost. "It's just too bad. It was the way of the times." But some, like Sharon, sought out old ways of doing and thinking.

She feels she is a small part of a big movement. "They say in the prophecies that women are the ones who are going to keep the traditions and bring them back. There are so many beautiful, beautiful Native American women that are being strong. We're going to retain this culture. We're the life force. If I can take one young person and have them listen to me. One! That's one more that's going to pass it on. That's the way I look at it. You can't change everybody, but if you can get one more person to walk that red road . . ."

Sharon is a warm and welcoming person. "My husband always told me, he said, 'I don't care if it's your enemy, if they come to your house, you feed them and you treat them with respect.' Oh, yeah." So on my first visit, she serves up venison steaks, oatmeal, pancakes, maple syrup, breakfast casserole (potatoes, sausage, eggs, and cheese), wild rice, and walleye. "Help yourself," she says. "You're only a guest here for the first five minutes."

Her son Andy and his wife join us with their baby. Andy, who is in his thirties, has a vascular problem in his legs that flares up with severe infection, pain, and fever. He was in the army for five years and taught desert and mountain warfare. He loved it but couldn't continue because of his legs; he received a medical discharge in 2003. He is in pain all the time. "I'm used to it," he shrugs. Sharon describes him as "strong-minded and energetic." He runs five days a week when he is not bed-bound. She says he never whines. Broad-shouldered, he has brawn to go with his grit. He hasn't riced since he joined the service. "It's been years, but I haven't forgotten anything." Some parts of the sloughs, he says, are untouched. "You can get lost in there. You gotta watch the tree lines." They fill flower sacks and pillowcases with a hundred pounds of rice. "Work all day, morning to dark." He's a maintenance director at a nursing home and plans to go to college.

Later, when leaving, I tell him, "Good luck with school."

"Luck's got nothing to do with it," he answers.

"Our people have done things in circles," Sharon says on another visit. She's talking about both the redemptive and the vicious. Alcoholism has been an affliction among Indians ever since they started trading beaver pelts for beads and liquor. "I took a real hard look at all of this," Sharon says, "and I thought this circle has to be broken. And that's when I started my path. I wasn't an alcoholic. I've never been an alcoholic because I chose not to be one. I chose to fight that. I have a glass of wine, a beer, but I know enough to say one's enough. And I thought, 'If I'm going to break this circle, I'm going to have to be an example to my children.'"

She largely succeeded, but one son took to drinking to excess. "He rarely does it anymore, but when he was young, he did. It was a lot of peer pressure from other kids. He was in that circle. But I tried to break that circle." The wayward son these days is alright. "I'm real thankful," Sharon says.

She is a tolerant woman. "I believe everybody is entitled to their own religion. The way they worship is fine as long as it works for them. I grew up Catholic. I choose not to be Catholic. I was a very strict Catholic, and I didn't find as much comfort as I do now putting my tobacco out every morning, praying whenever I want to. I find more comfort in that, more inner peace, a lot of strength."

She believes that the environmentalists in the larger culture are on the right track. "They are looking at the people of color and realizing maybe they know something. There are many, many non-Indian people like that. Then you have the other bunch . . ." She continues, "In our prophecies, it is said that some day the white man will turn to the native for help. They will look to us for survival, as they realize how much in harmony we really are."

Sharon bustles about the kitchen cooking while we talk. "Oh, my goodness, do you want some coffee? Here I am just gabbing and gabbing."

Her four boys grew up well fed. "Everything was homemade. My husband could bake bread better than me. Ten loaves lasted two days."

She lives along U.S. 2, on Birch Hill. She says there's a spot three miles from her house where there used to be blackberries the size of shooters. "We've lost our blackberry patch to houses." She worries that the rice fields will also be destroyed. More cabins being built, motorboats speeding by, gas and oil from boats and snowmobiles—"The rice fields suffer. I'm really afraid for the sloughs."

Sharon typically harvests about 120 pounds of rice each year. It takes three days to a week, and her boys help out. There are two places to rice: the Bad River Sloughs and the Cacagon Sloughs. She prefers the former. "The rice is smaller but it has more flavor." Much like berry pickers, ricers have a favorite spot.

She describes this enduring family tradition: they enter the rice beds in a canoe, one person paddling and one armed with two round cedar sticks, half the length of a pool cue. You bend the tall rice over the canoe with one stick and sweep the rice off with the other, called a knocking stick. The rice drops right into the canoe. "When it's ripe, it should sound like rain falling," Sharon says. "Some of it drops back into the water, which is fine because it reseeds for the next year. Get as much as you can. Some people rice every single day. We usually just get enough for us and to give to family that can't get out there. You always make enough for your family." She says that some people plan vacations around ricing.

Her crew takes the rice home and lays it on canvas or tarps to dry. They put grass in a tub and burn it—"like seasoning a cast-iron pan"—then take the grass out, put the rice in, two quarts at a time, and stir it with a wooden paddle over the fire. It's called "scorching." "At first it's limber. It gets to the stage where it's like spaghetti, hard spaghetti. You gotta be careful or it'll burn. It'll pop, like Rice Krispies. It usually takes, depending on the fire, thirty minutes, forty minutes, to scorch rice." Scorching loosens the hulls, causing them to fall off. Some ricers have thrashers that blow the hulls off. For some, Sharon says, "It's nice to have these modern things." She prefers to scorch. A long time ago, ricers used to 'dance the rice'—like people stomping on grapes—instead of scorching it. The dancers had to weigh between 160 and 180 pounds. "Too big and it breaks the rice, too light and you can't dance the hulls off."

The ripe rice that she harvests is green. Elsewhere in Wisconsin and Minnesota it's black or brown. "Ours is the best because Lake Superior is here and it's cleaner water. But everybody says theirs is the best."

Sharon also tans deer hide with the deer brains. Sometimes she uses pig brains. "It's a long, hard, smelly process, but I love it." The brains soften the hide, which she soaks in water before scraping the hair off with a dull knife. "There's a tiny membrane of skin underneath that you have to get off. Then you stretch it out like you see in the movies." She says a deer's brain is about the size of her fist and it takes five or six for to tan one hide. "If you put the word out, some of the hunters around here will bring you their heads." She busts open the deer's heads with a screwdriver, takes out the brains, and then mashes and boils them until they look like oatmeal. After cooling them down, she rubs the brains into the rawhide and then soaks the hide in a mixture of brains and water. "It's a lot of stinky, stinky work. You can tell it's ready because you twist that hide all over and you should be able to squeeze water through it. It should bubble like water through a cloth. Then it's ready. Roll it up and twist it, on a tree with a stick. Twist it to drain the water out. It takes two people but could be done with one. You start pulling the hide, two people pull." Little streaks of white appear. "You start to see the buckskin come out." She takes up to six hours to squeeze it. "You get blisters." Then she stretches the hide on a frame and works it with a dull tool. It becomes clothlike. "That's what brains does. It starts to rot. It's a fermentation process. Cover the hide in brain water, and the fibers break apart." Then she colors it. She makes a small fire to produce what she calls "smudge smoke." She says, "You have to be in control of that fire" so it doesn't burn the hide. She hangs the hide over the smoke; it turns color, depending on the kind of firewood. Pine and any kind of punky wood make it golden brown. Alder makes it gray-black.

Some of these traditions are dying. "You know, the young people nowadays don't put the time in. They don't want to work hard. We keep doing what we're doing because somebody might want to learn."

When Sharon talks about her culture, her genial conversation turns to a simmering anger. Indians, she says, have been treated badly.

She has treated me well. When I get up to leave, I thank her for her time. She says simply, "Anything to get the word out that we're not going to take it anymore."

Another time I visit Sharon, on a chilly June day, she serves fry bread, Indian tacos, and a message about selfish people. "They take and take and take and never put back. The Earth is hurting. She is crying out, but nobody is listening." Her message: "Look what you're doing, people. Wake up." Sharon's Indian name is Healing Sky Woman. She is a healer not of people but of "our Mother Earth." She says, "It bothers me deeply that there are so many things happening with the Earth, and nobody is listening. She is hurting and no one feels it. That's why we are having all these natural disasters. So many people are taking from her and not putting anything back."

On this day, she is proud of her youngest son because he has just won a school award for an essay about Indian ways. "Yes," Sharon says proudly, "somebody listened to me." The lad, she says, wants to study journalism and help save the world. She tells him, "Don't get your hopes up. If you can help one family, you're doing good."

As well as people, Lake Superior needs help, Sharon says. "I love that lake. There's this pull, this sense of home. Look in people's eyes when they are looking at the lake—it's love."

Sharon, who is red beyond skin deep, wonders about the lake, and the forest, and the land—indeed, about the Earth: "How much can she take?" Then she pauses a moment and says, sounding lonely, "I think about stuff like that."

14
"The Blood of Our Earth"
Baraga, Michigan

It was on the shores of Lake Superior, in 1968, that Jim St. Arnold, an Ojibwe who had wandered a lot in his youth, experienced an epiphany and discovered a haven. Eighteen, he was visiting his grandparents in Baraga, which sits on the north side of the head of Keweenaw Bay, near where he was born. "I got up and was going to go out for a walk in the woods. It was October—I remember this—and my grandfather told me to take a rifle in case I saw something. So I took the rifle he gave me. Went walking in the woods. Picture an October morning, a little bit crisp. All the leaves had just peaked, so they're all still colory. The sun was coming up. There was a light mist over everything. And I looked out. All I could see was trees and the lake, and I knew I was home. And it's been my home ever since. It's like I found where I belong."

Part Ojibwe, part Norwegian, and part French, Jim is a member of the Keweenaw Bay Indian Community headquartered in Baraga, but he works on the Bad River Reservation in northern Wisconsin. He routinely returns to his home. One occasion is the annual Keweenaw Bay Powwow in late July, which is where I meet him for the first time. The event takes place in a little woodlot a mile from Baraga. At the center of the woodlot is a small clearing, about the size of a baseball diamond, which is surrounded by a campground, now filled with powwow participants.

Here to meet a man I know only by name, I walk up to the first stranger I come upon. "I'm looking for a guy named Jim St. Arnold."

"That's me," he says.

He leads me to his campsite, where he and his wife, Judy, have parked their small camper. Jim's raven hair is beginning to gray. His facial hair is distinctive—nothing on either the upper lip or the chin, just two thin trails of whiskers that go straight from the corners of his mouth to either side of his chin, and a little tuft centered beneath his lower lip. He has a receding hairline, and when he frowns, his forehead looks like a small-ribbed washboard. He wears jeans and a black hooded sweatshirt bearing an image of a dream catcher and the words "Native Pride." He wears his hair in a pompadour, and two long braids droop down his chest. Pine trees tower over ferns, blueberry bushes, and us as we sit in lounge chairs and talk. Jim has a ready smile and projects an aura of repose.

He was born in L'Anse, just across the bay from Baraga. He bounced around Montana, Wyoming, and Wisconsin in his youth, and he served four years in the Marines, from 1968 to 1972. After the service, he returned to the Keweenaw Bay Reservation, where he became a member of the Keweenaw Bay Tribal Council in 1979, and was elected chair in 1981. He left the council in 1986 because he moved off the reservation, residency being one of the prerequisites for membership. In 1988, he moved to Ironwood, Michigan, and went to work at Odanah, Wisconsin, headquarters of the Great Lakes Indian Fish and Wildlife Commission, which comprises eleven Ojibwe tribes. Formed in 1980, the commission represents six Ojibwe tribes in Wisconsin, three in Michigan, and two in Minnesota. Four reservations border Lake Superior; the rest are inland.

Jim says the Keweenaw Bay Indian Community's powwow is the most popular in the Great Lakes area, with a thousand or more people attending and hundreds dancing, and it has a reputation as the friendliest. The powwow attracts the young and the old alike. "The two most important age groups of our people are children and elders," Jim says. "The children are our future and will take care of us and our land. Elders teach us what we need to know to go through our life. The worst act people can do is mistreat children and elders."

As we visit in the warm late morning, Judy is about, as are a nephew and a niece, Bernie and Heather, and their two small girls: Isabelle and Caitlin. As Judy moves about the campsite, she touches Jim's arm lightly whenever she passes. They met at a powwow in Sault Ste. Marie in 1996. She admired the turtles on his traditional clothes, and he took them off and gave them to her. It is an Ojibwe tradition, he says: if somebody notices or admires a possession, you give it to them. "We're taught," he says, "that we don't possess, that we are only caretakers of possessions. We are encouraged to pass those items along. I lost some turtles, but I gained a wife."

Bernie and Heather are from Milwaukee. Bernie is Jim's nephew by blood; his wife, Heather, is part German and part Irish. She grew up in the Christian tradition, but she has adopted Ojibwe life. "It makes sense to me," she says. While we visit, she braids Caitlin's hair into a ponytail, to which she adds strands of white leather. Braids seem to be common. I ask Heather why.

Overhearing, Judy explains, "It's tradition for women to have their hair up and out of our faces—and it's cooler—we are a very practical people."

Jim and Judy go into their camper to dress for the powwow. There is much bustle all around. "It's the chaos before the Grand Entry," Jim tells me. The Grand Entry is the dance that opens the day's ceremonies; he and Judy, dancers both, will lead it.

We all walk to the clearing. In the center is an open-air structure perhaps twenty feet square, its roof covered with fresh boughs of cedar. One of three groups of drummers and chanters sits beneath the protection. Dancers, according to tradition, line up on the east side of the clearing. The moderator notes that this is the twenty-sixth powwow on the shores of Keweenaw Bay and that the location of the festivities is sacred ground and, therefore, all should stand. The chanting and dancing begin. Drums set the pace. Women, men, and children move in a circle that coils around itself. The dress is resplendent; the chanting is plaintive. Dust rises in the air like incense. Dancers carry many flags, including those of the United States and Canada, and there is a marked military emphasis—the black-and-white MIA-POW flag, the flags of the 101st and the 82nd Airborne divisions and of the American Legion—as well as tribal banners.

Some dancers wear bells that jingle-jangle-jingle. Some wear a "trail"—a three-foot sunburst of eagle feathers centered on the dancer's waistline at the back. Brown and white, they suggest a drab peacock's tail. One man sports a top hat. Another wears a bear head and cape. One woman with a long rope of black hair wears just a plain, tan leather dress with fringe cascading from shoulder to ankle; she has one feather in her hair and carries a green cloth and a small fan of six feathers. Some men have a roach—porcupine hair that sits atop their heads like a Mohawk haircut. Mostly their hair is roan, although some of it is dyed red, blue, or yellow.

Some dancers just walk. Some do a two-step. The children bounce and twirl tirelessly. Jim and Judy, "head dancers," lead every song. The first dance, with 249 participants, takes forty-five minutes, though subsequent dances are shorter. After a round or two, Jim and Judy take a break; Jim, flushed, sips bottled water.

The dancing will go on until five o'clock, when there will be a break for dinner, followed by more ceremony. I watch the dancing and listen to the drumming and chanting for three hours. Then, tired simply from watching, I go from the powwow to the Ojibwe Casino about a mile away. I feel sheepish about this until I talk to a casino worker, a native, who notices the powwow button pinned to my shirt.

"You went to the powwow," she observes.

"Yes."

"Did you have an Indian taco?"

"No. Fry bread."

"I love that Indian taco. It's the only reason I go—get my Indian taco once a year."

The next day I return to the powwow and talk with Jim again before that day's Grand Entry. A powwow is simply "a gathering—social and spiritual," Jim says. Besides the main festivities, he says, "small ceremonies are going on all over, naming ceremonies." He explains. "We're taught that everyone has a name that the Creator knows you by—that the spirits know you by." An elder or spiritual person helps you find your name. Naming ceremonies aren't just for the young. They also are for the old who have been disconnected from the heritage because they "grew up when it wasn't very good to be Indian," but who have found their way back to traditional beliefs. The names can be evocative. I have read about one: Woman of the Sound Which the Stars Make Rushing through the Sky. Jim's Ojibwe name is Nigaanigiizhik, which means Future. An elder from Minnesota gave it to him thirty years ago. He lives up to the name, concerned as he is about "where I want my people to be, and where they go in the future." He sees it as part of his duty to protect resources like Lake Superior. "I want my grandchildren to enjoy the same things that I do—to breathe the air and drink the water."

I ask Jim about the military emphasis in the celebrations. The Ojibwe have a strong warrior tradition, he explains. As an indicator, he notes that there was never any rift in the Ojibwe community, as there was in the general culture, about the stature of Vietnam veterans. "Among our people," Jim says, "veterans are very much honored." The previous evening, he tells me, there was a ceremony to honor vets. The eagle means many things to the Ojibwe; for one, it symbolizes "the warrior spirit." Jim says that sometimes an eagle feather falls to the ground during a dance. "A dropped eagle feather represents a fallen warrior and only veterans are allowed to pick that up."

When Jim goes into his camper to dress for the Grand Entry, I sit with Heather. She instructs Isabelle, who is putting down tobacco in appreciation for some blueberries she picked, "Never take more than you need. You don't need to take six bushels if it's only for you." Heather likes Ojibwe thinking. "It fits," she says. She was raised a Christian, but couldn't abide some aspects of Christian doctrine—like "the idea that babies are born into the world in sin," or that "if you aren't a Christian, you're eternally damned." She says, "No way I could accept that." So at a very young age, "the questions began." Today, having adopted Ojibwe traditions, she is comfortable. She especially likes the idea of circular rather than linear thinking—"Everything continues around and around. Everything affects everything." It makes more sense to her than "beginning to end."

She also accepts the idea that humankind is, or should be, in consonance with nature. "As two-leggeds, we're no more important than four-leggeds," she says. "There's not that hierarchy. You have to respect each other—whether plants or animals—so that we're all in balance, and everyone is satisfied, and needs are met. The whole idea is everything in balance. Don't take more than you need." To her, the world is like an extended family. "Family is very important to us," she concludes. "It's who we are."

Jim, in Ojibwe garb, emerges from his camper. He says that some Ojibwe call native dress "regalia"—he just calls it his "dance outfit." A neighboring camper, overhearing us, chimes in, "I call it 'my stuff.'" What it is not, Jim emphasizes, is a costume. "A costume is something you wear to be something you're not." Regalia, he instructs, is a walking, talking collection of totems. Some of it is a gift and recalls people, some of it is for show, and some of it has spiritual meaning.

Instead of bells, he has deer toes that click. He has a dancing stick that represents "a coup stick," with which one touches an opponent, escaping without being touched in turn. The feat, Jim says, shows that one's "spirit and strength are superior." "Counting coup" is sensible warfare, he says. His dancing stick, about eighteen inches long, is made of sumac and has fur and feathers on it, an eagle talon, a braid of horse hair, and a braid of sweetgrass.

Jim has a snapping-turtle shell for a shield. "The turtle is one of my helper spirits," he explains. It represents patience and endurance and evokes the proverbial Atlas. "During the Great Flood," Jim says, "the Earth was put on the back of a turtle" until the waters receded.

Eagle symbols are recurrent in Ojibwe dress. Jim has a whistle made out of eagle bone, an eagle beak carved out of a buffalo horn, and a fan made of eagle feathers. Besides symbolizing the warrior, the eagle, he believes, carries his prayers to the Creator. Eagle totems are so popular that Ojibwe apply to the U.S. Fish and Wildlife Service for eagle parts. Jim says there's a two-year waiting list.

He wears a vest made up of pencil-size elk bones; it was once armor. He has wolf claws, symbolic of his status as head veteran dancer. He has a knife made from a buffalo rib—a tradition carried down from the time of the Indian wars, when Indians on fort reservations weren't allowed to have metal knives. Beneath it all he wears buckskin pants and a red, white, and blue shirt, with stars and stripes, recalling his pride in his service in the Marines.

I remark that everything he wears evokes nature.

"Yes, the natural," Jim says. It's a world where "nothing is more important than anything else because we all rely on each other to exist and to live." He gestures to include the trees and the nearby bay. "All this is family, too," he says. "The trees are our grandfathers, and the water—the lake—is important to us."

All in all, "no one is dressed alike," Jim says. The regalia "is personal to us," and each person's elements depict "your own inner strength." Wayward people who transform their lives might be "gifted" with an eagle feather as a symbol of character. "You don't get an eagle feather just for being Indian," Jim says. "You've helped someone. You've done something on your own to show your own spiritual strength."

We leave the campsite and walk to the clearing for this day's singing and dancing and drumming. In between dances, I have snatches of conversations with Jim. Some people feel shy about dancing, he says, but "the only wrong way to dance is to not dance." He calls dancing "a celebration of life." The dance is also for "elders who can't dance" and for "elders who have walked on," by which he means died. He says the rhythmic drums are a heartbeat. "You can feel it. They match each other."

I ask Jim if he speaks the Ojibwe language.

"A little. I'm still learning," he answers. "When I hear people, I can understand the gist."

I ask him what a particular chant is about.

He sums it up: "Everybody has a good time and goes home safely." Chanting, he explains, is "words and vocables," the latter being sounds to replace words that have been lost over time. "Tradition is lost but coming back," he says. "There are people out there who have kept those things."

I remark that the drummers and chanters are all male. Jim explains that the tradition is not a matter of excluding women. Indeed, he notes, there are many matriarchal societies among natives. He says of a woman: "Her spiritual strength is so strong that she doesn't have to do things"—like chanting and singing—"to gain that strength, like I do. A woman is stronger than a man. A woman gives life, a powerful thing." The concept of women as property came from Europeans, not from Indian culture, he notes.

The poet sees eternity in the fingernail of an infant. The Ojibwe see all of life in a drop of water. In the Ojibwe world, water in the womb and in Lake Superior meet not in allegory, but in reality: one provides life itself, the other sustenance for both body and spirit. Women, then, according to Ojibwe tradition, are revered for giving life and for being caretakers of the lake. "As a man, I can see the link," Jim says. Indian women have walked around Lake

Superior to call attention to the lake and its vitality because, Jim says, "Lake Superior, water, is the blood of our Earth."

An acquaintance has told me that Jim is "a storyteller," and I relay that comment.

"Am I a storyteller?" he asks Judy.

"You've been telling stories ever since I met you," she jests.

Jim is often asked to speak at schools and gatherings. "I don't lecture," he says. "I tell stories. I'm proud of who I am. I'm proud of our people. I'm proud of my culture. That's all I do. Share stories I've heard from the elders—why things are."

Jim is soft-spoken and thoughtful, pausing often when he talks. He is a man of purpose. "What I do is going to be felt," he avows.

A grant writer and program writer, he drums up projects—and funding—that advance native culture. He worked, for instance, on a project to gather and catalog the names of plants that have nonmedicinal uses. There are, Jim informs me, more than two hundred plants and plant parts that were used by traditional Ojibwe: white cedar spigots to collect sap from maple trees; elderberry juice mixed with deer tallow for lipstick; wild bergamot, called horse mint, used as a rinse and hair conditioner; sweet fern leaves to keep hair black; chokecherries for wine; ferns and moss for packing material; honeysuckle nectar for juice; goldenrod stems for pipes; angelica stems for whistles; nettle stems for twine; cattail flowers for torches. The smoke of burning fleabane flowers attracts buck deer. Birch bark was used for containers, canoes, and caskets. "Take the bark off red osier dogwood and use the sap to rub on skin; it is not a repellent, but it deadens the skin and when an insect bites, it doesn't bother you." The inner bark of basswood is quite pliable. "One elder talked about how they remember their father making rabbit snares out of it. So I began to talk to different elders and asked them, 'Well, what did you guys use?' And they all kind of laughed and said, 'Number two picture wire.'" The men told Jim, "The guy at the hardware store could always tell when we were going out poaching rabbit." Jim says that the nonmedicinal plant project was the "most memorable" endeavor he's undertaken.

Prior to moving to Odanah and this kind of undertaking, when he was active in the Keweenaw Bay Indian Community in Baraga, Jim found that Indian politics are like politics everywhere: "Somebody has something that somebody else wants—power." Before getting involved in governmental affairs, Jim followed in his father's wake and worked as a commercial fisherman for three years. Fishing was "a decent second income" to support an expensive hobby and freelance business: photography and printmaking. He had a sixteen-foot boat and fifteen hundred feet of net that he set every evening and retrieved every

Jim St. Arnold: *What I do is going to be felt.*

morning, pulling it in by hand. He was what he calls "a small-boat fisherman." He stuck pretty much to Keweenaw Bay, where an east wind often funnels down the bay and roils the waters. "That lake can be meaner than hell," he says.

"Scary?"

"I've had times when I was on the lake and thought I wasn't going to get off. Yes. I got caught a couple of times. And I started singing my songs and putting my tobacco out to those spirits, hoping I wouldn't go under. I decided if they wanted me that bad, I suppose I was going, but hopefully they would decide that I was more important someplace else later on." In an odd way, he says, even the rough waters connected one with nature and could be "peaceful and settling."

Not everyone feels that way. A Navajo friend visited him one time in Baraga. She didn't like the area. "I can't see anything," she told Jim. He didn't understand that. Then he visited her in the Southwest and didn't like her country. "You can see for days out there, and I didn't care much for the openness. I like the lake. I like the woods." Both features describe the Ojibwe. "Archeologists and anthropologists and all those other *ologists* call Ojibwe people woodland Indians. In some way, they're right, but in another way we're also a water people, because a lot of our major foods come from the water: wild rice and fish. And the waters were our highway."

Such thoughts are the backdrop of Ojibwe belief. "Among our teachings," Jim continues, "we're taught that all life has a spirit."

"Even a rock?"

"Rock is seen as a grandfather spirit."

All life is equal, he says. "When I talk about people, I talk about the winged people—the birds, the owls, the eagles, and so forth. The four-legged people—the bears and the wolves and the moose and such. The people that crawl upon the Earth—the snakes and reptiles. The little people—the flies and insects and such. The water people—the fish and stuff." Lake Superior also has "merpeople," he says—mermaids and mermen.

"Is the lake a spirit?"

"I don't know so much that water is a spirit. That water is a collection of spirits. Do you know what jambalaya is?" Singling out water as a spirit, he says, "would be like picking out one spice in jambalaya."

Jim sees spirits overhead and underfoot. Spirits, he says, can be as plain as day or as invisible as the wind. "One of the most awesomest sights I've ever seen in my life, is one time I was driving between Baraga and L'Anse. It was in the spring and the ice was breaking up, and there was a hole in the ice about, oh, I'd say about twenty-five feet around. All of a sudden I seen this eagle coming down, and I watched him hit that hole in the ice and take off with a big ol' lake trout in his talons. That is the most beautiful sight I have ever seen. And that's part of that spirit of that lake. That's part of the interaction between those spirits around here. Man counts, the spirit of man, but all those spirits are there also, and they're interacting with each other, too. Whether the spirits be in the air, on the water, in the water, under the water, along the shoreline—you can watch them interact." In Jim's world, spirits help people ("They're watching over you"), and people help spirits (people bury the dead to face Lake Superior—because the lake spirits can be a comfort and a guide for those entering the afterlife).

I ask Jim, "Do you see ghosts?"

"Oh, yah," he answers.

One time he was tending a sweat lodge; he was working outside as "a fire helper," providing wood to keep the fire stoked. "This woman came out and this white bear came out behind her and stood over her. I looked at this guy with me, standing next to me, helping with the fire, and he says, 'Do you see that?' I say, 'Yah.' He says, 'That bear is there.' I says, 'Yah.' And we talked to some other people and we were the only two that saw it."

"I've never experienced anything like that," I tell him.

"You've probably just been too blind to see. No offense."

Part of the way to see spirits, he says, is to "acknowledge them," and part of the way to acknowledge them is to "accept the possibility of them."

"It takes a lot of faith?" I ask.

"It takes acceptance." He uses the word frequently.

It takes imagination, too. In Ojibwe teachings, Lake Superior is a remnant of a great flood, but the features of the lake are the result of a fight between Menaboujou, the trickster spirit who is part human, and Ahmik, the great beaver, "not a small creature." The geography of the lake was formed as the two titans battled. The combatants threw rocks at each other, which became Isle Royale and the Apostle Islands. Ahmik used his tail to dig up clods of dirt to throw at Menaboujou, which formed small inland lakes bordering the big lake. To get at Ahmik, Menaboujou built a mud path into the lake, which became the Keweenaw Peninsula.

"What were they fighting about?" I ask.

"Menaboujou was hungry."

Fact or fable? I ask.

"Those stories are one way of reminding you that there are other possibilities than just the scientific way of looking at things."

For Jim, Lake Superior is a palpable entity. He likes to go to the shoreline and gaze at the expanse. "I go by the lake as much as possible," he says. When he does, he chants softly.

"You eat seven bushels of dirt before you die," my old aunt says. That number crops up repeatedly in Ojibwe culture. There are seven meats on a turtle. There are seven prophets. There are seven clans. Each clan is represented by an animal: bear, crane, marten, loon, fish, turtle, and wolf. Each clan has its own specialties and duties. Members of the Crane Clan, for instance, are speakers and orators. The Bear Clan is known for its herbalists and medicine gatherers. A clan's duties don't limit a person, Jim says. "The clan is a guide." He belongs to the Wolf Clan and is a "protector" of the culture. Sometimes he is called upon to find people's Indian names. And he is a speaker.

In that role—spreading the Indian word—Jim has traveled around North America. In one story that he particularly likes to tell, a young man is talking to his grandfather. "The young man is always angry. And his grandfather says, 'You know, I have two wolves inside me. One wolf is a battler—he's a warrior wolf. He's always fighting, always angry, always looking for things to conquer. The other wolf is a peaceful wolf. He's a loving wolf and a caring wolf that protects family and watches over them.' The grandfather continues, 'Those two wolves are always fighting for control.' The young man turns to the grandfather and says, 'Well, which one wins?' His grandfather says, 'Whichever one I want to.'"

When Jim tells these stories, his message is simple. "I'm just a person, and this is how I think, this is what I feel, this is what I was taught." He is not one to rail against white culture. He is not embittered about past injustice, nor does he seek to avenge it. He has heard Indian speakers disparage all of white culture. "We can't go back," he says. "You have to accept. I mean, I use my computer at home. My son plays on his PlayStation. I really appreciate plumbing and electricity."

He sees life, then, not as it was, but as it is and as it might be. "What I'm looking for is what I can do to make things better."

He never rehearses a talk. "I have no idea what I'm going to say. You allow those spirits to put those words in your heart and bring them out."

Jim's faith is one he chooses over Christianity. He says that both Protestant and Catholic churches have strongly influenced the Indian community. Near Baraga, there was a Catholic complex—a monastery, an Indian mission, and an orphanage. Many Indians became Christians, but these days there is a gulf between Indian traditions and Christian beliefs. Jim says that there's a strong push among some Ojibwe to bring native traditions and beliefs back—and there is an equally strong push among some Christian Indians not to bring them back.

The divide has spanned three generations. "There is a time in our history," Jim says, "where kids were forcibly taken from the communities, from the reservations, from their families, and put in boarding schools. There are elders that still live today that talk about being punished for speaking their own language, speaking Ojibwe." He knows a woman who describes how, as a child, she was made to kneel on marbles for speaking Ojibwe. He knows a man who was locked in a closet for the same reason. "And when you're raised like that," Jim says, "you don't want your kids to go through that, so you don't teach them the language, you don't teach them the culture. I suppose you could say it was a matter of survival not to be identified as Native American."

As a youth, baptized but not raised Catholic, Jim was always "looking." Early on, he cast his lot with native ways. "I was always proud of being Indian or Native American or whatever word you want to use." When he was twelve years old, his mother urged him to try Sunday school. That lasted about a month because he proved to be too spunky—he calls it being an "unruly pagan"—as he battled with the nuns about the nature of God and good. He didn't like a lot of their ideas. Instead, he sought out tribal elders and listened to them. Elders, he says, impart "great stories, fantastic knowledge."

After his service in the Marines, he reconnected with his grandparents in Upper Michigan and immersed himself in traditional stories, especially those of his grandmother on his mother's side. She was a "devout" Catholic, he says, but she knew all the Indian teachings. "Myself and a couple of cousins were very fortunate," he says. "We got to spend time with her before she walked on, and learned quite a bit." He still seeks out elders and finds the association comforting. "An elder," he explains, "can be a woman. An elder can be younger than you. An elder is someone who has knowledge and is willing to share it. What makes that person an elder is knowledge, not age. Some people are just old."

He yearns to be an elder himself some day. "I want to be a teacher." Traditional stories are the sinew of Ojibwe life. They are meant to guide people, not to set down a canon of belief. The tribal elders have instructed him to be flexible—any given belief, they tell him, doesn't make one way right or another way wrong: "It's just a different way of looking at things." Jim likes that approach. "It's more open to freedom of thought. We take a bit of teaching here, a bit of teaching there, and make our story. You're encouraged to take what fits you."

If it is a spiritual world with elbow room, it is not a world where anything goes. Jim believes that common to all people, whether they realize it or not, is a sense of responsibility. Choose your teachings and live up to them, he advises. "The Creator gives you life. What you do with it is your responsibility." There are no scapegoats for failure. "If you do good, good will come back to you. If you do bad, bad will come back to you. You have no one to blame but yourself for what happens"—whether you wind up "a miserable old man or teaching the grandkids.

"It's a sense of responsibility that I thought was good," he continues. A lack of it leads to "abuse of family, people, and the Earth." But if one embraces it, "It's a way of life. It's an everyday thing. It's a way of looking at everything around you."

Not acknowledging spirits, he explains, "puts you above everything else" and therefore you don't recognize the need to protect everything else. "You need to respect all those spirits," he avows. "When you go out and cut down a tree, you put a gift of tobacco down, as a way of thanking that spirit in that tree for providing for you. If you go out and kill a deer, you put a gift of tobacco down, as a way of thanking that spirit of that deer for providing for you." Nature accommodates humankind, he says. "The moose allows himself to be hunted, and the fish allows himself to be caught."

Jim takes his message to whoever will listen—especially those in the general culture who work with natural resources. "I want to strengthen their own belief in their job." He encourages an ethic of moderation. "Nothing to excess." Whether it's blueberries or burbot, he says, "If you take everything, the next time you need something it's not going to be there."

His thinking, not his logic, is circular. Life is a circle, he maintains. "Everything relies on everything else. It's all tied together. If you remove one thing, you're putting everything else in harm. If you start taking things out of that circle, eventually you're not going to have a circle anymore. You're going to have a line. And one thing a line has that a circle doesn't, a line has a beginning, and, most important, it has an end. If you put an end to that circle, what's going to happen to us?" In this fragile world, Jim says, women, with their power to give life, might be the exception. "If that circle would have a beginning, woman is the beginning."

"Life is a test to see how much you can take," my old aunt says. Jim describes it as a quest for balance. "You can't have sunshine all the time without rain, you can't have day without night, because you can't really appreciate one thing without the other."

According to Jim, the Creator gives life, man disrupts it with selfishness and excess, and the journey back to the Creator and to unity is the human condition. Man's charge is to protect other life, but it is human nature to forget this duty. "As human beings, we look the other way when something is affecting the other spirits around us—whether it be ducks or wolves. That's one of the worst things about us."

Besides protecting other life, he maintains, humans must learn from it. "Those beavers can teach you how to make a home. A wolf can teach you how to raise a family. A bear can teach you where to find berries and how to catch fish. The weather, a thunderstorm, a rainstorm, can teach you the importance of water in keeping the Earth clean. A human being can teach you how to be brave and how to be humble. A child can teach you love and respect. Everything around you can teach you something."

"Someone," I suggest, "might say it's all superstition."

"It gets to free choice. You choose to blind yourself to all the possibilities that are out there. I choose to accept all the possibilities that are out there. There are so many different things out there, so much of what's good, so much beauty. If you look at it, you can't help but be awestruck by it, and if you close yourself off to those things by calling it superstition and scientific facts, you know, you're closing yourself off to another possibility, and why would you want to do that?"

Jim is practical about Indians and their livelihood. He points out that in the late 1980s, a study showed that tribes were twenty-five years behind the rest of the country economically. Unemployment rates were as high as 70 percent. The average educational attainment was tenth grade. Enter gaming. Casinos, Jim says, have given tribes an economic boost, have allowed them to catch up to the rest of the nation, and have fueled other ventures within Indian communities. Gambling didn't come about merely by happenstance. "What a lot of people don't understand," Jim says, "is that Native Americans were strong gamblers. People would win or lose all their possessions on the way a rock was hidden." He's talking about a betting game played with four moccasins and four stones—three alike and one different—in what was essentially an Indian shell game featuring sleight of hand, with people betting on which moccasin the odd-shaped rock was in. Traditionally, Jim says, "Most of our games were gambling games. There is a long history of gambling." Slot machines, then, have revived a culture grounded in nature and spiritualism.

Both the loss of that culture and its resurgence were foretold in Indian prophecies, Jim says. Those prophecies charge today's Indians with educating the general culture in the way that Jim does with his speaking. One message: protect Lake Superior. It's everyone's responsibility, Jim says. "A lot of people don't realize it's hurting. You'll have one person saying, 'Well, my little bit isn't going to hurt.' But when you have a hundred thousand or a half million people saying, 'My little bit isn't going to hurt,' it adds up. People need to look beyond themselves. They look at themselves as just one, but they're not. They're all of it."

Nature is not there to be ours for the taking, he says. "Some of those trees change beautiful colors—they don't need us to do that, but we need those trees. Those frogs you hear singing in the spring, they sing some beautiful songs—they don't need us to sing those songs, but we need those frogs. Those bald eagles you see soaring around overhead sometimes—awesome birds, awesome spirits. Those eagles don't need us, but we need those eagles. Because when we have destroyed everything, when that last tree falls, when that last bird is seen flying from bush to bush, when that last frog, that last fish, is taken out of the water, whether by hook and line, gill net or spear, or is taken out because it's washed up onshore because it can't survive in that water that's poisoned, when we have destroyed everything we need to survive, we will have destroyed ourselves." And that, he says, "will be the end of life as we know it.

"We talk among our people that we don't own the things people use. They belong a little bit to those who have walked on, some to those who are living today, but most of all to those generations yet to come. Our elders teach us, when we protect things, we need to protect them for seven generations."

Meanwhile, Jim is collecting Ojibwe names—in northern Wisconsin, northern Michigan, and northern Minnesota—for plants, animals, fish, birds, insects, reptiles, and places. One of his favorite words, *ode'min,* is what the Ojibwe call the strawberry—"the heart berry."

15

A Small Place by a Waterfall

North of Eagle River, Michigan

It is a warm day in early October. Autumn has been mild, and the colors that will burn across the forest are late—there is just a blush of the splendor to come. I am at a place called Jacob's Creek, where a small building called the Jam Pot is tucked into the trees, beneath the bewhiskered hills that spill down to the lake. The Jam Pot is a store owned by the Society of St. John, a small monastery located on the Keweenaw Peninsula between the two lakeside towns of Eagle River and Eagle Harbor, Michigan. When I enter the building on this day, Father Basil is bustling about. He readies the cash box, straightens up, and cleans the showcases filled with bakery items and the shelves laden with jars of jams. The Jam Pot will open at nine o'clock. At eight fifteen, a couple enters.

"You're only an hour early," Father Basil remarks.

"We saw light," the man replies.

Basil and his partner, Father Nicholas, began their trade in jam and bakery, along with their monastery, in 1983. "Hand to mouth," Basil recalls of the early years. He means finances, not food. He and Nicholas attracted no other followers for ten years, so for awhile, the north country proved cold and lonely. They eked by on work and charity, wondering whether it would always be just the two of them. Basil, who has lively eyes, doesn't dwell on the hardships. "Life is full of its dark moments," he says. "So of course we were discouraged." Now there are five: Ambrose came in 1993, Ephrem in 1995, Sergius in 2001.

The monks open the Jam Pot in May and close in late October after the color season, when the walk-in traffic ceases. But then the mail-order business gears up and goes strong until the holidays. They send jam and bakery goods all over the United States and Europe. Some people spend more for shipping than for the fare. One man recently bought and sent an assortment of cookies and muffins to his son in London. The cost of the goodies was $48, the cost of the shipping $75.

Basil is in charge of the store, Ambrose of the kitchen. Their fare is extensive. More than two hundred jars of preserves are lined up in rows on shelves, poised for the palate: two dozen different jellies and butters. Basil says it's been a "bad year" for strawberries, a "not good" year for pin cherries and chokecherries, an "okay" season for bilberries, and a "fine year" for blueberries.

Besides preserves, they make half a dozen kinds of fruitcakes, all of which are wrapped in cheesecloth that has been soaked in brandy, whisky, or rum. They also make six kinds of cookies, seven kinds of muffins, and truffles, using very good Swiss chocolate. "Truffles are as troublesome as the devil," Basil says, "but they're popular and fetch a nice price and don't take up much room." Basil says the shelf life of cookies and muffins is about a week. The shelf life of truffles is about a month. Fruitcake lasts "forever." All in all, there is little waste. "We seldom have to feed anything to the bear."

While he waits for customers, Basil keeps busy, stocking the display cabinet, putting lemon butter frosting on some muffins, and cleaning. "Dusty, dusty, dusty," he chants.

One customer takes Basil's picture while he stands behind the display case. His glasses have a toehold on the tip of his nose; his scraggly beard, heavy with silver, cascades down to his belly. The air is redolent of fresh bakery goods.

"I can't capture the smell," laments the picture taker.

"If you could," Basil says, "that would be a marvelous thing." He bags another order. "Enjoy it all," he tells the buyer. "Enjoy the beautiful day, too."

On a typical day Basil arises at three thirty in the morning and retires at nine thirty at night, "with luck." During the season the Jam Pot is open, the monks' only scheduled meal is dinner. Breakfast and lunch, says Basil, "are catch-as-catch-can."

I leave him to his work and visit the kitchen, where Ambrose is juggling many duties. He has dark, probing eyes and calls himself "a man of few words"—so few that he describes one of the hired workers in the summer as "a pathological talker." Ambrose says that the hired workers at the Jam Pot often are amazed at how "intense" the work in the kitchen is. At one point on this day, his duties include taking chocolate-chip muffins out of the oven; putting pumpkin muffins in; cooking apricots and steaming apples; cutting, washing, and juicing carrots; slicing and portioning dough; and making a raspberry puree that will become seedless jam. By midafternoon, he's been going nonstop. "You get weary. Persevere, persevere. Keep going. Keep praying."

"Is it a hard life?" I ask.

"Everybody is going in the same direction. Everybody is committed. You have scrapes like any family. You get over it. You heal. You go along."

Ambrose has help in the form of Terry Glenn, Nicholas's nephew and a friend of the monks. He lives in Chicago but is visiting after a backpacking trip on Isle Royale. The monks tease Glenn—"We've got room for you." Glenn tells me, "My lifestyle won't accommodate it. I enjoy being out here, but I'm kind of a city person. I'd have to have lots of toys—my bike, snowboard, and golfing."

Ambrose, who is from Ohio, puts paper liners in the muffin tins. They are stacked together like nesting coffee filters, and he is deft and quick with them. "You'd make a good poker dealer," Terry Glenn teases back.

Back in the store, Basil is waiting on a couple choosing fruitcake. The wife asks her husband: "Which do you want, the Jamaican or the traditional?" She ends up choosing the traditional. "This is what my mother used to make."

Basil says, "This won't be as good as hers, but hopefully it'll measure up."

"Isn't it something," the woman remarks. "We come in here and we remember our moms."

The couple leaves. Basil puts fresh cookies into plastic bags. Then he shows me a letter from Tarpon Springs, Florida.

> Dear Brothers,
>
> I've enclosed a check for $18.00. Please put a sugarless trio of jams aside for me. I'll be up there at Bete Grise from 8/23–9/14, and I'll stop in and pick them up. Also, as a diabetic who eats a lot of lamb and turkey—would it be possible to make me a special order of sugar-free cranberry jam and apple mint jam? (I realize jelly wouldn't be possible without sugar to jell it.) If there's any way you could do these—I'd buy six of each from you to take home with me.

Basil awaits quitting time. "We have had a busy day," he says. "Unexpectedly so. I'll sleep well tonight."

Later, when it's quiet: "Maybe the day has died away."

An old man comes in looking for bilberry jam. He tells Basil, "They say it's good for night vision."

"I've heard that," Basil says, filling the order.

When the man leaves, I follow him out to the parking lot to ask him about night vision.

"I'm not the only one who's heard that story," he says. "The RAF pilots in England in World War II had this jam with their tea before taking off for night flights. They claimed it helped their vision."

I go back inside to witness a rush of customers. One man orders one of each of the six cookies on sale. "The best way to decide," Basil says. Two young girls play patty-cake. A biker couple enters. A stutterer. Somebody buys $42 worth of cookies. "I hope you brought the camel train to carry this out," Basil says. People's T-shirts tout Bar Harbor, New Zealand, and the Mall of America. The bunch leaves.

There is a lull. Then another patron enters and remarks on the aroma, which I can almost taste. Basil says, "There's a mixture of fragrances." The place empties once again.

Basil comments, "People out of the monastery don't realize how busy monks are. They think we just sit around all day and dream up new meal prayers. They think we stand around all day levitating."

In the bakery, Ambrose and his help are mopping the floor, washing mixers and tins and dishes, and putting eggs in the cooler. Basil straightens up the front and tends to the cash box. He expects a last-minute rush, but it doesn't materialize. He's worn out. But, he says of the business, "It's an honest living."

A living the monks must make, for their way of life is based on the rule of St. Benedict, who charged his followers to do two things: work and pray. When Basil closes the Jam Pot, he and Ambrose retreat to the monastery for prayer and dinner. I retreat to the library and a book on Christian monasticism to learn about this way of life.

The word *monk* comes from the Greek word *monos,* which means *one,* or *one alone.* Originally, the term meant simply somebody living by himself, which the first monks did. In the early 300s, monasticism became cenobitic, a word that comes from the Greek for *common life* and refers to monks or nuns living and working together in a community. The term *monos,* then, came to mean *single-minded,* focused on one thing: God.

For hundreds of years the popular notion of monks was one of hair shirts and fasting. Enter Benedict in the 500s. He tempered ascetic excesses—what one writer calls "imbalance"—and insisted on literacy and scholarship—particularly, copying and preserving the classical texts of Western civilization. Under Benedict's rule, monasticism became practical: simple rules, simple meals, adequate rest, instruction, work for sustenance and social good, prayer alone and together, study, communal recreation, and hospitality for travelers. Benedictine monasteries in the West became wealthy and influential in matters of both church and state. Such was Benedict's influence that he came to be called "the father of Western Civilization."

FATHER BASIL: *It's an honest living.*

Basil is one of Benedict's children, and to learn of his sojourn, I visit with him again. On a calm but chilly November day when the sky and the lake are a clear blue, I knock on the door, and Father Basil invites me inside.

"How are you?" I ask.

"I'm just a dumb monk with white knuckles from hanging on," he answers.

He is earnest and witty and, as the saying goes, "courteous beyond duty." We talk in what the monks call the music room, which is outfitted with a grand piano, a harp, and a dozen chairs as well as a telescope on a stand by a big window looking over the lake. The telescope was a recent gift. "We will use it," Basil says—to watch the ore boats, the stars, and the northern lights. They don't often see the northern lights. "They usually come out late at night, around midnight, and all good monks should be in bed by then."

Basil wears dark religious garb. A wide black belt cinches a simple wrap-around brown-black tunic with buttons, symbolizing his readiness to gird for spiritual combat. His hood he calls the monk's "helmet," bestowed when the monk makes the full commitment to monastic life. The biblike cloth draped over his shoulders and down to mid-chest and mid-back is symbolic of "carrying around the lamb on your shoulders," but the little round dark skullcap he wears, Basil admits, "doesn't have any particular significance. It's not given as part of the habit. It's just to cover up the bald spot." If his hair is thin, his beard is thick—another tradition, he says, of no particular import.

A native of the Upper Peninsula, Basil is one of three children in an Italian family. His father was a lumberjack who led a life of "hard work, long hours, hard work." Basil studied history at the University of Michigan, where he met Nicholas, who studied music, although they knew each other only in passing then. Their association really began after college in Detroit, where Basil managed a restaurant and Nicholas, a black man from Ypsilanti, directed an orchestra and set up a community arts center to bring the elderly and the young together through music. The two ended up working together at Detroit's Orchestra Hall, which had seen better days and was being rescued from demolition by a handful of stalwart preservationists.

Basil had always been interested in construction projects and old buildings, so much so that his father thought he would become an architect. He began donating his time to the restoration project. "I heard that they were looking for some volunteer labor to shovel out the dead pigeons and fallen plaster, and so I thought this would be a good opportunity to put idle time to use and get into a building project." They worked "madly" to get the place ready for Nicholas's performances. Eventually, Basil's volunteer job turned into a full-time position with pay. He organized the labor, liaised between management and the musicians, handled the paperwork, pulled together loose ends. "I haven't been there now in almost twenty years. I understand they've finally put it all back together and it's a glorious place again."

In the meantime, Basil and Nicholas were becoming friends, and Basil learned that Nicholas approached music with reverence. "It was kind of a religious experience for him, and there was a lot of distress, on his part particularly, that people weren't sharing this spiritual feeling. They'd get all excited about the music, and then once the concert was over, the audience went home, beat their wives and kicked their kids and yelled at the dog, the orchestra players continued to bicker about money, and life went on." Basil says that the music "just was not having the kind of spiritual impact" that Nicholas wanted it to have. "There was a real frustration."

The two commiserated, and Basil, based on his knowledge of history, offered an observation that would prove to be portentous. "I brought up the fact that real changes, spiritual changes, in society—at least in the Western situation—have always, or almost always, come through monastic endeavors." Especially, he pointed out, when western Europe was in collapse. "So we started thinking, if we wanted to have any kind of impact on society, the best thing to do is to pull away from it and begin a monastic existence."

They tossed the idea around for a year. A priest friend chastised them for their indecision, prodding them to just take a leap of faith. "That was the foot in the behind," Basil recalls. It booted them six hundred miles north.

For they knew they had to get out of Detroit. "From our experience of living in the city and working in the city—and also from our knowledge of history—we decided that monks are best away from the urban environment." He describes the city as an assault on the senses. There's never true darkness, he notes, and the only quiet time is a couple of hours "somewhere between the closing of the bars and the early shift." An urban environment "is not conducive to prayer," he says. Also, he and Nicholas both believe that American life in general and urban culture in particular are morally adrift, poised to fall apart. This is a summary of their thinking: "Moral decline often presages cultural collapse. Urban areas will inevitably suffer more from the chaos than remote areas. In that vein, monks have always had a pessimistic outlook on the condition of general society. We always see ourselves as exiles in the world. Monks are survivors."

Right from the start, though, they ruled out finding refuge in, say, the Caribbean. "Monasteries in easy places simply don't make it. The life is too tough. So people just drift away from it and go eat the bananas and drink the coconuts and forget it. So we needed a hard place, but still a possible place." Monks, he notes, historically have sought wilderness. So they trekked to the shores of Lake Superior. Neither Nicholas nor Basil had ever been to the Keweenaw, but Basil, who grew up a 150 miles to the south, had always heard that the area was beautiful. They arrived in the winter of 1981. "We loved it," Basil recalls. "We loved the snow. It was so gorgeous. It wasn't a thaw. It was pretty cold. But it was sunny." He has written about that day. "The snow, brilliant with its pristine whiteness, lay heavily on everything. It weighed down the branches of the pines and spruces, festooned the naked limbs of the maples and oaks, and turned the twiggy birches into lace." From the outset, then, they were struck with "the rightness of this place."

They started looking for property. Nicholas, returning from a solo reconnoitering, described "a small place by a waterfall." What he'd seen was what would become the Jam Pot, a few hundred feet northeast of Jacob's Creek. The visit they made there together was daunting. "We went down to the beach. I remember it was a very, very cold, blustery day. We got chilled to the bone standing down there in late October. We scrambled up the steps that had been cut into the bank. Father Nicholas fell and almost broke his arm. And our feeling was, 'Well, let's get out of here.'"

The small four-room house on the shore where they would have to live wasn't winterized. Basil has two vivid recollections about the place: dead flies everywhere and, in the parlor, a woodstove, about which Basil said to Nicholas, "My grandfather heated a six-room house with one just like this. We can make it here."

Not long after they relocated, Basil's father paid his first visit to his son's new home. Basil remembers the day. Observing the location, his father said, "What the hell are you going to eat here this winter, kid? Snowballs?"

"Well, Dad, I hope it isn't snowballs. Might be polenta."

His father snorted. "Well, I ate lots of polenta in my life."

They went into the house. When they entered the kitchen, Basil's father right away spotted the cookstove. "Well, Ma had one just like that," he said.

They moved into the parlor, where there was the woodstove. Basil said to his father, "And Grandpa had one like that!"

His father said, "Yeah . . . Yeah . . . You'll be alright here."

I ask Basil now, "What's polenta?"

"Italian poor folks' food." He explains that it's "cornmeal mush," cooked until stiff, then spiced with cheese, butter, bacon—"You can do all kinds of things to it, but basically it still comes down to eating cornmeal."

As it worked out, Basil and Nicholas didn't need to resort to polenta. There were thin times financially, but they always had ample nourishment. "We never went hungry," Basil says. "There was no money, but there was always food. The local people are generous."

They have expanded on their original purchase of three acres. Now, through gifts and purchases, they own six hundred acres. Their land lies right in the middle of Great Sand Bay, a long sweep of shoreline that looks like a scythe. Basil says that Trappist monks tend to build their monasteries in valleys, surrounded by hills, while Benedictine monks tend to build their monasteries on mountaintops. Lake Superior is Basil's mountaintop. "The long view is important," he says, gesturing at the view outside the bay window. "It's been a very good presence to be here."

He has written about that, too. "Even the great Lake, its bays choked with ice, was chilled into silence." If winter offers solitude and hardship, the ensuing seasons reaffirm their choice to settle on the Keweenaw. Each season, Basil writes, "has its own beauty and offers its particular delights. Be it in crashing waves or silent winter nights, in pounding storms or gentle breezes, in narrow, rocky gorges, or in broad upland expanses, God's light pervades this land. He is manifest in the blizzard's fury and in the gentle rain. The blossoms and wild flowers speak of His love, and the berries proclaim His providential care. In the ever-different sunsets we catch glimpses of his glory." In Basil's eyes, the broad sweep of forest and lake is balanced by "the less apparent wonders, the small marvels . . . be they budding arbutus or the stalks of wild asparagus." The whole of it, Basil says, constitutes "intimations of divine beauty."

The lake, he adds, "is a real dominant presence on this little portion of the Earth. She's been a great comfort over the years. Yes, yes—as far as the never-ending awe, the beauty of it."

"How about the fury?"

They have seen the lake leap its bounds, but overall, it's a big but benign body of water. "We like to remember it in its curious aspects. But over the years, yeah, sure, there are storms, but by and large, it's like this"—Basil gestures out the window where the water is just a little ruffled and looks like hammered zinc.

"Is nature a spirit?" I ask.

"We don't have an animistic religion. We don't believe spirits inhabit stones and streams and things like that. But we do tend to see the universe as kind of a key entity."

"But you wouldn't see the lake as a spirit?"

"Not as a spirit itself, no. But certainly a manifestation of God's glory, and, how shall I put it, properly approached, it's a means to holiness. It's certainly been very good being next to it."

"Talk about that."

"It's hard to put your finger on it. Certainly there are the very beautiful aspects—the sunsets we've seen over the years. Or sometimes the lake will take on a particular color. It's just incredible. I remember once it turned bloodred. It was early evening. The sun was going down. And it must have been just the right conditions where the light reflected, and the whole lake, for the period of about the three or four minutes that it lasted, was just this red color. I'd never seen it before—or since. It's one of those things. I've seen it purple a number of times. A lot of times steel blue." The lake specifically, and indeed nature in general, resounds, Basil says. "I'm sure the whole thing is like one big hymn." Accordingly, on the monks' Web site, they quote from their prayer books: "Cold and chill, bless the Lord . . . Frost and chill, bless the Lord . . . Ice and snow, bless the Lord."

Basil has told me that Father Nicholas was walking through a windowed hallway between the living quarters and the chapel one night when he saw an owl, wings outstretched, "right up against the glass for some seconds." A few days later, Father Nicholas learned that a cousin had died on that day. "Spooky," says Basil now, "especially when natives consider owls a sign of death." "I think animals can be used in that way," he adds. "I don't think necessarily every encounter you have with an animal is a sign of something, but they can be."

He remembers reading years ago about an old man who had grown up around animals. "When the man was a child, everybody in the community had constant relationships with animals, with other sentient beings, with other forms of life—whether a pet dog or workhorse. As a result, people close to animals were closer to one another. They had a much better sense of their place in the universe than they do now when they just deal with machinery—things of their own creation. The animal is a creature created by God, not something made by people. That gives animals a certain independence from people, who have to win the animal's love and affection in order to get it to work or obey. In contrast, a machine is a product of ingenuity and technology, something people totally control, but which imparts no lessons."

It is Basil's nature—he believes it's his duty—to be his own worst critic. Typically, then, he came away from that story with self-effacing knowledge. "Now, I grew up largely without animals," he says, "so that spoke to me, and it told me something about myself—how I was lacking. How, had I grown up to have the horse or the donkey to move things around from one place to another, I probably would be a better human being because of it."

"It's not a big leap from there to the peaceable kingdom," I suggest.

"Where everybody gets along," Basil responds. "That's true. Everybody should get along. That's always been the Christian ideal."

He and his companions are trying to achieve that and to fit into a place, to blend into the landscape. "This is indeed a difficult place," Basil writes, "and life here is often something of a penance." But the "sheer beauty of this land" convinced them to stay. "We came looking for Purgatory. We found Paradise." This land of peace and quiet stirred them to dream. "It seemed the perfect place for the silent life of monks, and on every hill and crag we could envision towers and cloister walls rising above the serene whiteness." At the start, though, they had but one small, cold cabin—and a wing and a prayer.

The Society of St. John is a nonprofit religious corporation set up to hold the group's property. The Jam Pot, of course, is their business. The monks chose the name because of their main product and because, from the outset, they were in a jam for space. Poorrock Abbey is their registered trademark and the label on their fare; *poorrock* is a decidedly regional term that describes the gray boulders piled high throughout the land, leftovers from the copper mining, that look like talus slopes without the mountains to go with them. The Holy Transfiguration Skete is the name of the monastery. A *skete* refers to a small monastic community. The *Magnificat* is the name of their newsletter and is another vehicle to connect with the general culture, what they call "the world."

The Society of St. John is affiliated with the Ukrainian Greek Catholic Church; their patriarch is in Kiev; their bishop is in Chicago. The Ukrainian Church belongs to the Byzantine rite (2 percent of all Catholics), as opposed to the Latin rite (98 percent). Each outfit bows to the pope, but each has some of its own traditions and disciplines. When Basil and Nicholas first set up their monastery, they immediately sought canonical recognition from the Latin, or Western, church—a status that they believed would help secure both donations and vocations. They couldn't get that recognition because the Western church sanctioned only those religious communities with at least five members, and there were just the two of them. They thought at the time, "Well, okay, we've got to grow," and they went about their business.

Into this situation stepped their priest friend, who suggested that the monks look to the Byzantine rite for canonical recognition. Basil says, "It's the same faith, it's the same religion, but there are different ways of looking at a lot of things." One example of divergent thinking is the matter of married clergy. In the Western rite, priests take a vow of celibacy. In the Eastern rite, there is a different rubric: a married man can become a priest, but a priest cannot marry. The decision binds for life and has to be made before ordination. Another difference between East and West is music. The Eastern music is "more approachable," Basil says, "more earthy." In contrast, the Western tradition of Gregorian chant is "more austere and rarefied." "It seems like only angels can sing this stuff."

The subtle differences in the thinking and theology engross him.

The West: God is almighty. The East: God is merciful.

The West: Human nature is damnable. The East: Human nature is perfectible.

The West: Monasticism is authoritative and juridical. The East: Monasticism is more informal and intimate.

The West: Pray for "blessed repose." The East: Pray for "eternal memory."

The West: Founded "on a promise." The East: "Less promise, more grace."

Basil says that, all in all, Eastern thinking constitutes for him "a more complimentary way to look at God—the lover of mankind." He describes the differences as "almost like speaking a different language. It's a different way of looking at things." He adds that neither church is better than the other. They both "do what they're supposed to do." What about a mix? "No," he says, "you don't do that anymore than you would speak English with French grammar." He says some Western priests adopt parts of the Eastern rite. He disapproves. "You have to stick with a rite. Exhaust the possibilities in that rite rather than look somewhere else to gussy it up somehow." Nevertheless, he views the two traditions as a blessing. "That's what makes the world go round. People do things differently. I tell them at the Jam Pot, 'If people liked just one thing, I would have one thing on the counters.' And that would be a dull life."

All told, the two theologies are simply different manifestations of the same truth, Basil says. "There's a little different view," but "practically, the lives are not really different. The Holy Father says, 'The church has to breathe with both lungs.' Both of the traditions are necessary for a full understanding of the faith."

When Basil and Nicholas's priest friend exhorted them to visit the Ukrainian Catholic bishop of Chicago, they initially waffled, just as they had when they started the whole enterprise, but they eventually did. After pleasantries, the bishop asked, "So you'd like to come under my protection?" That question hit Basil over the head. He says, "I noticed right away that he used the word 'protection,' not 'jurisdiction'—'under my protection!' And we said, 'Yes.' He opened up his arms and said, 'Well, I welcome you.'"

Basil and Nicholas, then, found their niche both on a big lake and in a long procession of monks that stretches from the time of the apostles. When the two of them first struck out on their new lives, Basil and Nicholas called themselves "brothers" and kept their baptismal names. When they switched to the Eastern tradition, they became priests and took on new names: "You're leaving the world behind, so a name change is a symbol of that."

Their worship includes a regimen that the Catholic Church calls the office—prayers and readings at prescribed hours of the day and night. There are seven canonical hours in the office. The Jacob's Creek monks observe three when the Jam Pot is open and four during the winter, which Basil describes as a more "restful" time for them all. It takes about an hour or more to complete each segment of the office.

Another facet of their worship is their vows. These monks take four: poverty, obedience, stability, and chastity.

Poverty: Basil says, "Voluntary poverty for me has not been a big problem. I'm not attached to things." While the monastery itself is well off, should he leave, he'd have nothing.

Obedience: Nicholas is the authority of the monastery, although Basil always gives his opinion. "If I can't convince him, then I bow to his will—for better or for worse. It hasn't been for the worse. We're still here."

Stability: There is no place for wanderlust in this life. The only place monks roam is the spiritual landscape. Basil quotes an early monk, "Peace is like a plant. The more often you transplant it, the less likely it is to grow. Stay put!"

I don't ask Basil about his vow of chastity. It's a delicate and personal matter. But I do ask him, "What's the hardest vow to follow?"

Basil replies without pause. "Obedience. I think anybody who's been in religious life for awhile will tell you that. Because you always—this is hubris, or your pride—you always have this feeling that you know better. And in some cases you do!"

Contrary to some monastic traditions, these monks do not take a vow of silence, but they value quietude. "One of the main things a monk does is, he listens. He listens to God. And the more distractions, you know, the less likely you're going to hear something. Noise is difficult to shut out. You can close your eyes to something, but you can't stop your ears from hearing. So it's very important that all in the community do as much as they can to maintain a silence so as not to disturb the others." Even praying aloud is discouraged. "Benedict is very stern about that," Basil explains. "You shouldn't talk even about good things." Talking, Basil says, projects the self; silence makes one receptive. Their location on Lake Superior is especially conducive to silence in the winter when land and lake are hushed and white with snow and ice. "At times the silence is deafening. It's such a profound silence here. Sometimes there is no background noise—just dead quiet in the winter. Now, in the summer months, you've always got the lake like we're hearing it now. But when the lake is frozen, you get those still winter days and it is just so quiet. Unbelievable. It's really beautiful."

I ask Basil—hesitantly, because I know nothing about the practice—if he meditates. Meditation, he says, can be slippery stuff. "There can be a long, dry period. A lot of mystics go through a phase that St. John of the Cross described as 'the dark night of the soul,' where you feel like you're going nowhere and doing nothing. I'm not a mystic. We do meditation. I find it difficult to do real long periods of it. I'm not the type who will go into chapel and plan to be there five minutes and find myself coming out two hours later and saying, 'What happened?'" Basil says that after prayer services, the monks routinely sit in silence for a few minutes. He calls it an effort to achieve "emptiness, openness." Those are times when "God can actually touch you."

"What's your attitude about people out in the world?" I ask.

"We can't be judgmental. Withdraw from a bad situation and pray for it."

"So you don't look down on the world?"

"Heavens, no."

"Does each person have a fatal flaw?"

"Most of us have many."

"What trips you up?"

"It's something I continually have to work on—a quick temper. That's why maybe standing behind the counter at the Jam Pot is very good discipline for me. Over the years I've had a very quick temper and I still fly off the handle, and the members of the community have learned to take it in stride—'Oh, well, there's Basil again.'"

"Does everybody have a redeeming quality?"

"I would hope so. You want to know mine?"

"Yes."

"Bullheadedness. I keep trying. I don't give up on things easily."

"A friend of mine says there's nothing worse than a reformed zealot."

"I'm not cut out to be a firebrand of any sort. I really always try to follow the counsel of the elders. You read the Rule of St. Benedict, his greatest quality is moderation and discretion. Very stable, very stable. It's day-to-day stuff. It's everyday living."

"Your routine is not menial?"

"There is no such thing as menial work. It's noble and ennobling." It's also constant, he says. "Work never goes away. It just waits for you."

"One thing you'll never do is retire."

"A monk never retires."

"Is it a hard life?"

"I don't think so. I don't find the life terribly, terribly burdensome or difficult. I get short sleep. Monks traditionally have survived on little sleep. That's one of the things. Over the years, people have come and said, usually young men who are contemplating briefly monastic life, 'Oh, it's so hard, so hard.' But I feel like saying to them, 'Look, it can't be that hard. I'm doing it and who am I?' No, it's not that hard. People want to give up quickly."

"Are there rewards for sticking with it?" I ask.

"God sends consolations. He doesn't want you to lose heart."

"Like what?"

"Principally in the worship services. I won't say I went into ecstasy or anything. My feet stayed on the ground. But you get these kind of elated feelings from time to time."

For diversion in good weather, the monks go for walks or ride bicycles. They like to stroll along the beach looking for agates. "There is a certain amount of physical recreation. There should be a lot more." He allows that both he and Nicholas are "carrying" a lot more poundage than they should although, in their loose-fitting habits, they don't appear to be, as the jester says, "prosperously rounded." Indeed, they fast a lot. Basil figures they're essentially vegetarians 50 percent of the time.

Overall, that regimen is meant to put little in the belly but iron in the soul. "It's a discipline. It's to detach yourself from the things of this world. Food is probably the most intimate commodity that we have with the world. It's the thing that sustains us but also gives us an immense amount of pleasure. I don't think I know anyone who doesn't like to eat, even though maybe the choices are limited. So cutting back on that is a good discipline. I think it also turns out to be healthful, done in moderation. If it's spaced out over the course of the year where you have certain periods when you do this, I think it can be a physical as well as a spiritual cleansing." Such disciplines, Basil says, are the bedrock of devotion.

I note, "Yehudi Menuhin said, 'Freedom through discipline.'"

"Very definitely. The person who is not disciplined is certainly not free. They're constrained from doing a lot of things simply because they don't have the discipline to devote themselves."

"Can you help other people out spiritually by what you're doing?"

"I believe so. Yes. I believe we can help them through our prayer. I try not to make the prayer too specific. God knows their needs. I don't have to come with a shopping list."

"I read that Dostoyevsky said that a true monk is nothing other than what everyone ought to be."

"That's the Eastern outlook—that the monk is a paradigm of Christian life, that all he is doing is living the gospel in the most complete fashion possible."

"Have you suffered?" I ask.

"Aside from anxiety and some rather cold nights, I don't think we suffered."

He worries about the church, the edifice, that is. "It's not going to be easy sailing." The church cost nearly $1.5 million—"too much. Too much. It's a big, expensive undertaking." The monks embarked on it because they have benefited from largesse—the coin of the realm here being both commerce and charity. Compared to their beginnings, they're doing well. Their income is in six figures. However, Basil adds, "Financial struggles are never over. They just change over time. It seems the more you make, the more you are able to grow, the more is demanded of you. Growth always brings new responsibilities and expenses."

Beyond early travails and Spartan times, the experience has had other rocky stretches. There are two kinds of monastic endeavor, the *vita activa* or the *vita passiva*—that is, being active in society or withdrawing from it. When the monks first arrived on the scene, local priests expected them to help out in the parishes; there was ill will when they didn't. As well, some resented the financial support the monks received. And more recently, there have been squabbles with the county over land use and taxation. In the face of it all, Basil remains resolute. "Monastic life was never meant to be easy, and sometimes conflict with the world is inevitable." So, he writes, "the Struggle continues."

"Did you ever dream you'd get this far?" I ask Basil.

"No," he says. "It kind of blows my mind away." His surprise is tempered with disappointment. "As far as buildings and things go, we've always felt that what we needed would be provided, somewhere, somehow." Getting vocations, on the contrary, has proven to be a more difficult task and has taken a lot longer than they ever anticipated.

The next morning, I make my way to services in the chapel, which is about twenty-four by forty-eight feet and has vaulted ceilings with skylights. There is no stained glass, which, Basil tells me, is a Roman, not a Byzantine, tradition. A magnificent, ten-foot-high partition of turned wood, much of it figured, separates the chapel proper from the sanctuary. There are two half doors, like saloon doors, in the middle of the partition. These are called the "royal doors." Only clergy can pass through this entrance, which is meant to separate the world of God from the world of man. Scores of icons hang on the walls.

At the end of Matins, morning prayers, the monks sit quietly as the rising sun casts through the windows and skylights and flickers on the walls, the partition, and the royal doors. I hear soughing outside; I can't tell whether it's wind or waves.

After breakfast, I roam around. The grandest part of the place now is the new monastery, which sports the onion domes, octagons instead of true circles, common to the Eastern churches. The cedar-clad structure arises majestically out of the rock and trees. The monastery has a deck, snuggling into a copse of white birch, facing the lake, less than one hundred feet from the shoreline. The lake is gray and the sky is gray, and it's impossible to tell where one ends and the other begins.

I walk to the front of the monastery. Nicholas, who has gentle eyes, is watering more than a hundred pots of flowers. He likes his chore. "It smells so good," he says. He envisions the entrance to the monastery to be a rose garden. "That'll take awhile yet. There are so many things to be done."

At this entrance to the monastery, there are two wooden monks, three feet tall, welcoming visitors. Inside, in the vestibule, there are icons, a picture of a solitary miner in a shaft with a single, halfhearted light on his hard hat. There are also driftwood, a picture of Great Sand Bay in the winter, a portrait of Rosa Parks, who was Nicholas's friend from his Detroit days, a bird's-eye maple cross, a bowl with scenes from the American Revolution, and a cartoon monk.

Besides the chapel and recital room, there is an office, a kitchen, a refectory, a library on the second floor, a dormitory on the third floor, and bathing facilities. Parts of the complex are cloistered. Off of the vestibule, there is a small parlor that long ago used to be the chapel. I poke around. On a desk in the office, there is a small piece of wood with the inscription, "No one listens to the cry of the poor or the sound of a wooden bell." I wander to the Jam Pot. Only one customer is there.

Vespers, the evening part of the office, begins at five thirty. There are ten guests, including two babies. The monks sing and pray for "a painless, unashamed, peaceful end of our lives." They lament that Christ was "hung on the wood of infamy," but give thanks for "the curse wiped out."

The service lasts seventy minutes. Afterward, the monks visit with the guests in a little reception room off the chapel. Nicholas holds one of the babies. "All personality," he tells the mother. One guest asks Basil how the Jam Pot is doing. "Summertime, it's all wild cards," he answers. Ambrose tells another visitor, "There are strange and interesting people around Lake Superior. We're God-blessed to be a part of them." After the guests leave, we retire to the refectory for dinner.

Later, it's back to the chapel for Compline, or night prayer, which lasts forty-five minutes. It is the final service before going to bed. The monks pray for "no pain, no sorrow, no sighing." They repeat "Lord have mercy" forty times. They invoke protection "from the gloomy sleep of sin . . . and the commotions of mind and body."

The next morning, Sunday, the monks celebrate Mass. They pray for wisdom—"the eyes of the heart." Nicholas is ill and his homily lasts only three minutes.

After Mass, the monks serve a sumptuous breakfast. There are visitors at the table. One, who has been out on the lake, reports that it is warmer than it should be at this time of year—forty-six degrees at the surface when it is usually thirty-eight. "A cold lake," he says, "makes less snow. So they say. Everybody is always trying to second-guess the weather." Basil tells one visitor about matters in general, "We're doing real good. Growing big, aren't we?"

After his social duties are finished, Basil and I meet in the cozy study for a chat. There are crosses everywhere, even on the fireplace screen. A cross that Basil has had to bear is skin cancer, and he has to wear a wide-brimmed hat for protection from the sun. "I tell people, 'I'm a vampire—stay out of the sun or I turn to dust.'"

But the sun shines gently on this monastic endeavor, which has gone from a toehold to a bulwark. "The business is not a sign that you've lost your way?" I ask.

"It could be, you know," Basil muses. "There's a fine line. The business can easily consume you. The whole purpose is to support the monastery. That requires money, but you have to keep it in control. If the business takes over, you don't have a monastery, you just have a business. You have to have wisdom in handling any material wealth that may come to the community—be prudent." He adds that there should be some enterprise. "Even monasteries that have bundles salted away, they're still running the farm, they're making coffins, they're doing things. It's very important to the monastic endeavor."

I ask Basil's opinion of the New Christy Minstrels' lyrics: "The peaceful road is a hard road to climb."

"I don't necessarily think it is," Basil answers. "It's liberating."

"From what?"

"From all these entanglements out there. You see people out in the world who are bound up in so many different things they don't know which way they're going—caught in some huge spider's web."

Basil claims that he is just a lowly sinner.

I protest, "You work, you pray, you sing—you don't have time to sin."

"Oh, yeah," he says. "Somehow you always find time for that, I'm afraid. Sin is as much a matter of attitude as it is physical activity. So, yeah, it's very easy to sin. You sin in your mind and your heart." Sin, Basil believes, makes people "self-centered" and "ossified."

"What's the worst sin?"

"Despair. 'I'm so wretched that even God can't save me.' All sin has certain elements of that denial, that defiance."

I tell him, "A Lutheran minister I know said the worst sin is the failure to mature."

"Sounds more like a psychologist than a minister," Basil replies.

I tell Basil that I saw the pope when he visited Chicago years ago. "He said the world will experience greater and greater polarization."

"You see it," Basil agrees. "I don't know how it's going to end. Gets to be too bad and you end up with civil war or a totalitarian government that quashes down on everything to keep the peace. You don't want that, either."

Basil explains the meaning of the inscription I read on the piece of wood in the office. "One of the psalms says the Lord hears the cry of the poor. God listens anyway, even if the rest of us don't."

Basil sees the monks' work—"riding the tourist trade in the Keweenaw"—as part of a natural cycle. "Our life follows a similar rhythm that agricultural life would follow. We begin work in the early spring, as they do with the sowing and tilling and what not, and we labor through the summer and, actually, we begin to reap the harvest finally in the fall when we're selling off the inventory. So, yeah, it's very much like an agricultural, natural life. And then in the winter we kind of go into dormancy, into hibernation. The farmer in the winter months will spend a lot of time with his feet by the fire. They live off what they've done, what they've produced." So, too, the monks, Basil says. It's a way of life that makes him thoroughly content. "I'd rather be nowhere else in the world."

The essence of these men is prayer and hard work. At Jacob's Creek, there is not a breath of idleness. The Benedictine Rule, Basil says, ensures that "you will always work." "Hard work," he maintains, "is better than the other problem—sit around and do nothing." He adds, "Make hay while the sun shines. It doesn't shine terribly long up here."